SALES MANAGEMENT THAT WORKS

FRANK V. CESPEDES

SALES MANAGEMENT THAT WORKS

HOW TO SELL IN A WORLD THAT NEVER STOPS CHANGING

HARVARD BUSINESS REVIEW PRESS

Boston, Massachusetts

Library of Congress Cataloging-in-Publication Data

Names: Cespedes, Frank V., 1950- author.
Title: Sales management that works : how to sell in a world that never stops changing / Frank Cespedes.
Description: Boston, MA : Harvard Business Review Press, [2021] | Includes index.
Identifiers: LCCN 2020036313 (print) | LCCN 2020036314 (ebook) | ISBN 9781633698765 (hardcover) | ISBN 9781633698772 (ebook)
Subjects: LCSH: Sales management. | Sales personnel.
Classification: LCC HF5438.4 .C427 2021 (print) | LCC HF5438.4 (ebook) | DDC 658.8/1—dc23
LC record available at https://lccn.loc.gov/2020036313
LC ebook record available at https://lccn.loc.gov/2020036314

ISBN: 978-1-63369-876-5
eISBN: 978-1-63369-877-2

Again for Bonnie and for Elizabeth and Helen and their families, and now Marcus, who will make his changes

CONTENTS

SALES
MANAGEMENT
THAT
WORKS

INTRODUCTION

NEW SALES REALITIES

Selling is changing, but much current conventional wisdom about the impact on sales of e-commerce, big data, AI, and other megatrends is misleading and not supported by empirical data. If you as a manager fail to separate fact from hype, you will make decisions based on bad assumptions and, in a competitive market, eventually fall victim to those who *can* understand cause-and-effect links between buying and selling.

Look at how most newspapers reacted for years to digital competitors: try to mimic the online firm, but with a much higher cost structure and while giving away their own content online. This was a literal enactment of the joke about selling below cost but hoping to make it up in volume. Or look at how many retailers responded with self-fulfilling-prophecy actions to e-commerce competitors: cutting head count in stores, not investing in training sales associates, and often being oblivious to online/in-person interactions and the impact on sales and sources of advantage.

Consider The Home Depot when Robert Nardelli became CEO in 2000. In a business built on in-store personnel who provided advice to shoppers, Nardelli made cuts in those areas.

By 2006, Home Depot saw its fourth consecutive year of declining foot traffic, its market value had declined by 55 percent, and it was last among major US retailers in the annual University of Michigan Customer Satisfaction Index, eleven points behind its main competitor, Lowes. As a board member commented—after the fact—"The most experienced store employees, the real experts on plumbing or electricity, had been let go and replaced with less experienced and cheaper part-time store workers. New stores . . . were not generating good returns, leading to further staff cuts."[1] When new CEO Frank Blake took over, he made rejuvenating the point-of-sale experience a priority and that rejuvenated sales and the stock price.

You cannot manage a profitable response to market changes unless you understand changing buying behavior and the corresponding impacts on business-development tasks. Admittedly, this is not a simple TED-Talk-and-a-listicle activity, especially when you're operating in an industry rife with myths, unexamined assumptions, and fads. If you're an executive in most markets today, remember that (as they say in the movies) "you chose this life!" Selling involves a complex combination of factors: a coherent strategy, relevant hiring practices and incentives, and ongoing performance management that motivates the right behaviors in the face of many changes outside the control of your company. You can deny the complexity, but it's still there.

And that's the purpose of this book: to help you separate signal from the noise and clarify key choices and actions. This book can help salespeople respond to changes at buyers and help sales managers improve productivity and results. It can help investors get more from the sizable investments they already make in sales efforts. It can help those in the C-suite navigate the thicket of claims made about emerging technologies and better use those tools in customer acquisition and retention. And it can help all interested readers understand why, in modern economies, improving selling activities is not only a financial and growth issue but, in fact, a key social responsibility of business leaders.

What Is Changing and Why It Matters

It's easy to say things are changing, because change is perennial in business. Fogies, beware. But managers must move beyond platitudes and develop an accurate view of their current situation and how it might evolve. How sales is changing—and not changing—may surprise you. Let's look at some truths and misconceptions about that core business activity and the implications.

From Funnels to Streams

For over a half century, buying has typically been framed in terms of a hierarchy-of-effects model: moving a prospect from awareness to interest to desire to action.[2] The AIDA formula and its many variants are the basis (often, the unconscious basis) for sales activities and organization in most firms. It's fundamentally an inside-out process, and customer relationship management (CRM) systems are there to provide data about progression (or not) through that company's funnel—the "pipeline" metrics that dominate talk about sales in books, blogs, training seminars, and coaching initiatives.

But research (and probably some reflection on your own experience) indicates a different buying reality. Rather than moving sequentially through a funnel, buyers now work through parallel activity streams to make a purchase decision. Let's label those activity streams as explore, evaluate, engage, experience (see the sidebar for more detail on each).[3]

BUYING IS A PROCESS OF PARALLEL STREAMS, NOT A LINEAR FUNNEL

Explore. Here, buyers identify a need or opportunity and begin looking for ways to address it, usually via interactions with potential vendors and (as in the consumer auto market) self-directed information search on the internet. Activating a need can be instigated by internal triggers (e.g., a system breaks, a car or other machine wears out, a process fails, a new initiative is born). External triggers include regulatory mandates (e.g., the impact of the Affordable Care Act on health-care insurance purchasing), new technologies or markets, or perhaps advertising and sales promotion.

Evaluate. Buyers take a closer look at options uncovered while defining the need or opportunity, again leaning heavily on self-directed search, peer interactions, and sales representatives from potential vendors. This activity is not primarily about determining the specific product or service they will buy, but about determining the best approach and pathway (e.g., build versus buy, own versus lease, etc.). Buyers are comparing multiple options, identifying the solution type, and winnowing the options to a short list.

Consider buying a car. Consumers now do lots of online research. US auto buyers on average spend about 13 hours online researching car models prior to purchase, and about 3.5 hours at dealerships.[4] Yet most cars are still bought at dealerships (e.g., less than 1 percent of the 40 million used cars sold in the United States in 2018 were online sales and less than 5 percent of new cars). But because auto shoppers can access prices, product reviews, and other information online,

Engage. Buyers initiate further contact with providers to get help in moving toward a purchase decision. Depending on the market and product category, this might involve downloading a white paper or other form of content marketing, sending out a formal request for proposal (RFP) in many B2B markets, or (as they say in the ad business) initiating a "bake-off" between competing vendors. But in the twenty-first century, "engage" activities don't necessarily start and stop with the sales rep. Buyers interact with others in the selling organization. Indeed, another impact of websites, blogs, chatbots, and social media has been to make the seller's organization more visible to buyers. They value interactions with people in product and/or service, and they expect the rep to orchestrate that interaction purposefully.

Experience. A formal buying decision is made and buyers use the product, perhaps in pilots or proof-of-concept trials for new technologies, and develop perceptions about its value. As services become a bigger part of economies and as software becomes more embedded in products, more of that value is what marketers call "experiential value" that only becomes apparent in actual postsale usage. This has important implications for pricing, sales metrics, and other aspects of selling.

their buying behavior is changing.[5] For example, more than 50 percent will leave the dealership if a test drive is required to get the list price of the vehicle. Nearly 40 percent will not patronize a dealer whose website doesn't list vehicle prices, and about 40 percent will leave the dealership if prices aren't posted on the vehicles.

In the auto industry and others, information sources have changed customer expectations about the role of the salesperson as a walking, talking purveyor of a sliding scale of prices. Even when done with good intentions, many traditional sales practices unwittingly increase customer dissatisfaction. Moreover, buyers generally use online tools as a complement to, not a substitute for, sales conversations, and they are discriminating in using these tools. Car buyers, for instance, use third-party websites for model comparisons and reviews, car manufacturer sites for detailed model information and videos, and dealer websites to look for specific vehicles and information about local inventory.

Buying is now a continuous and dynamic process, not a linear funnel. Understanding where customers are, how they navigate between streams in your market, and how to interact with them appropriately in a given stream is now central to effective selling. For the most part, it is still the sales force that must do this. The research results in figure 1-1 echo what car-shopping studies indicate, but now with respondents across industry sectors in North America, Europe, and China.[6]

One reason the sales force remains so important is that most products and services are parts of a wider usage system at the buyer. This means integrating the product with driving, household, or other activities in B2C markets. In B2B markets, buyers must typically justify a purchase decision to others in their organization that are also competing for their share of a limited budget. Some of that combination of economics, solution integration, risk management, and organizational politics can be handled online, but most buying journeys still rely on knowledgeable sales help. Hence, this research also found that, across all buying streams, buyers emphasized the importance of product demonstrations, sales presentations based on their situation, and salespeople who can do that while bringing knowledge from their work with other companies. Among the least-valued interactions, by contrast, are cold calls in response to registering for webinars or online events.

FIGURE 1-1

The most influential B2B marketing activities

On average, business buyers say direct interactions with providers influence their purchasing decisions more than anything else.

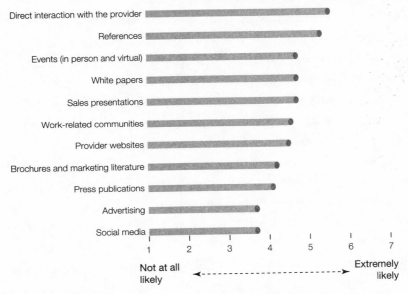

Average likelihood of influencing a purchasing decision

Direct interaction with the provider
References
Events (in person and virtual)
White papers
Sales presentations
Work-related communities
Provider websites
Brochures and marketing literature
Press publications
Advertising
Social media

1   2   3   4   5   6   7

Not at all   Extremely
likely   ← - → likely

Source: Frank V. Cespedes and Tiffani Bova, "What Salespeople Need to Know About the New B2B Landscape," HBR.org, August 5, 2015.

In other words, solution selling and account management skills still matter. But *how* this is done by effective salespeople—that is, the sales tasks—is changing. For example, in figure 1-1, customer references are a close second in terms of influence. But the nature of references has changed. In the past, the seller would cite a few satisfied customers (whose satisfaction, by the way, might be more a function of a price discount than product satisfaction). Now, through the web, customers can connect with each other and get unedited versions of others' experience through review sites such as PowerReviews and access to people at other companies who share purchase and usage experiences through community sites such as SAP Developer Network and Marketo Marketing Nation.

Also affecting sales tasks are activities like content marketing and lead generation by email and other means. Traditionally, these activities were part of marketing's domain, not sales. But these lines are blurring, putting pressure on companies to rethink sales models, metrics, and the relationship between marketing and sales—two functions that are more interdependent but different in their procedures, perspectives, and mindsets. More generally, it's important to recognize that buying streams mean prospects now touch your brand and company at many different points (online, offline, marketing collateral, and so on), and each touch impacts sales tasks.

Finally, if you consider these streams and what buyers value in suppliers' behaviors, then a big disconnect emerges. Despite advances in technology over the past decades, most sales models are incapable of dealing with the reality that buying is so often continuous and dynamic—an ongoing motion picture, not a selfie or snapshot in a funnel. Going forward, many companies must reconfigure their selling, and despite what you often hear, no single tactic (e.g., a given selling methodology, "challenging" the customer, or big data analytics) will do this. Aligning buying and selling is a process, not a one-shot deal.

The Importance of Talent

As firms confront new buying processes, required sales competencies change. Figure 1-2, based on an extensive database of company sales profiles, indicates the altered nature of sales competencies at many firms. Competencies that were considered essential only a decade earlier were lower in priority by the second decade of the twenty-first century. Does this mean that developing leads, qualifying prospects, persistence, and adapting to different buyer motivations are no longer important in selling? No. The way to interpret this data is in keeping with the punchline to the old joke about two hunters pursued by an angry bear: "I don't have to outrun the bear; I just need to outrun you!" As one should expect in any activity where success is measured by *relative* advantage, the focus of productivity improvement in sales is shifting. Yesterday's distinctive sales strengths have become today's minimum skill requirements in more industries. This has implications for hiring, training, compensation, and performance evaluations.

These talent issues also affect what most salespeople must now do *within* their firms in order to sell externally. Consider two recent surveys: one with more than 3,100 sales professionals about trends affecting their role in their companies, and the other with over 7,000 consumers and business buyers about their expectations when dealing with companies and salespeople:[7]

- About three of four sales respondents (73 percent) rated collaborating across departments (e.g., sales, service, operations, marketing) as critical or very important to sales success.

- Conversely, 73 percent of consumers and 78 percent of business buyers say they are likely to switch if faced with inconsistent levels of service from their suppliers.

As customers move between streams and deal with multiple people at a selling organization, a prospect and order touch multiple functions in moving from initial contact through exploration, purchase, and postsale activities like billing, warranty, or field service. When asked who is responsible for the customer experience at their suppliers—sales? service? operations? marketing?—buyers legitimately respond, all of them. But at the seller, each function usually has different priorities. Billing is evaluated on receivables, service on case resolution, marketing on lead generation, and so on. This is one reason why

FIGURE 1-2

Salespeople require different competencies than in the past

Top competencies in the past	Percent appearance in job profiles			Top competencies today	Percent appearance in job profiles		
	Pre-2000	2000–2009	2010–2014		Pre-2000	2000–2009	2010–2014
Develops sales leads	30%	12	8	Prioritizes tasks through logical analysis	10%	15	17
Commits time and effort to ensure success	20	12	6	Embraces strategic vision/ implements corporate direction	0	8	13
Qualifies prospects with standard probes	45	9	7	Able to learn the business	0	2	10
Willing to deal with multiple tasks	20	7	3	Has a controlled work approach	5	3	8

Source: "The Best Ways to Hire Salespeople," HBR.org, November 2, 2015.

"customer focus" is a perennial slogan but not a behavioral reality at most firms.

Cross-functional coordination—and its evil twin, misalignment—is pervasive in selling efforts today. The same surveys found that while seven of ten salespeople say it's critical to have a single view of the customer across departments, fewer than one in five (17 percent) rate their companies as great at providing this capability. In this situation, salespeople must often become the de facto integrator, if only because it's typically the rep who made the sale who gets called when the buyer has a request or complaint and who must then get other functions to respond. Hence, this survey found what other research about sales indicates: on average, sales reps spend only about a third of their time (in this survey, 36 percent) actually connecting with clients or prospects (either online or in person) and about two-thirds of their time (64 percent) on nonselling activities such as service, internal meetings, and administrative tasks. This has implications for the development of reps, productivity, and the best use of talent in a given sales model.

Multichannel Management

Should we be online *or* in person, interacting via the web or through salespeople, in our sales efforts? Answer: yes. Customers are unbundling many traditional channel arrangements as they switch streams. So, avoid a false dichotomy; face the facts and the go-to-market implications for your business.

First, some facts. E-commerce has been here for over thirty years. Books.com was selling online while Jeff Bezos, founder of Amazon, was still working on Wall Street. The number of salespeople in 2019 listed by the Bureau of Labor Statistics is more than 11 percent of the country's labor force, an *increase* in sales employment in the United States during the twenty-first century.[8] Further, the BLS data almost certainly undercounts the reality because, in a predominantly service economy like the United States (and many other countries), business developers are often called associates, managing directors, or vice presidents, not placed in a "sales" category for labor-department reporting purposes. But selling is what they do. Meanwhile, after decades free from sales taxes, e-commerce comprised 11.4 percent of retail sales in 2019 in the United States.[9] No one really knows the comparable numbers in China, because many stores are state-owned and internet data is censored. Estimates are that e-commerce in China in 2019 was somewhere between 25 and 35 percent of total retail sales. Why more than in the United States? Retail infrastructure is still developing in China, and air pollution makes going to a mall less pleasant.

Yet, daily you find articles about the "death of the salesman" due to disruption by e-commerce, where "disruption" is synonymous with death, not Schumpeterian creative destruction. The enforced shutdown of stores during the pandemic accelerated these predictions, but let's look beyond the headlines.

Much of the excitement about e-commerce and digital marketing is tied to the notion of virality: you post something on social media, it goes viral, millions of people see it, and you have not spent much to do that. But as my colleague Sunil Gupta points out, that's not easy.[10] A study of messages on Twitter, Yahoo, and others found that more than 90 percent did not diffuse at all, about 4 percent were shared once, and less than 1 percent more than seven times. Other studies indicate that most internet communication is between people who live near each other and are driven by what researchers call "homophily"—the commonsense observation that birds of a feather (people with similar interests) indeed flock together. As Wharton professor David Bell explains, the way people use the internet is largely determined by where they live, the presence of stores nearby, their neighbors, and sales taxes.[11]

Moreover, interactions between online and offline channels have important implications for revenues and costs. Shoppers who pick up their online orders in a store spend more—about an additional 25 percent.[12] Meanwhile, about one-third of all clothing ordered online is returned versus 8 percent for items bought in a store (fitting rooms: customers who try on clothing in the store are almost seven times more likely to buy than those who search for items on the web, according to research firm Body Labs). Yet processing a return in the store costs retailers half of what it costs when an online order is shipped back to the distribution center (and, thanks to competition with Amazon, shipping is now often "free").[13]

In fact, the biggest retail trend before the virus was "clicks and bricks," even for once pure-play e-commerce firms like Birchbox, Bonobos, Warby Parker, Wayfair, and—yes indeed—Amazon, among others. Philip Krim is a cofounder and CEO of Casper Sleep, the online mattress firm started in 2014. In 2018, Casper opened its first permanent retail store, announced plans to open two hundred more over the next three years, and also sell through twelve hundred Target store locations. Krim explains well the new streams of buying behavior and consequent multichannel requirements: "Consumers today are often online and offline at the same time. Our customers are shopping with us on average for 2.5 weeks . . . coming back to the website and consuming information there multiple times. They're coming to stores multiple times [and] all of these different combinations of customer preferences is something that we want to solve."[14]

Shopping has always been a social as well as an economic transaction since the Greek Agora, Roman Forum, Grand Bazaar in Istanbul, Le Bon Marché in nineteenth-century Paris, malls in the twentieth century, and through decades of global internet use. Will the social distancing necessitated by the pandemic mean a big change in this historical pattern? Look at what was happening online before the deadly virus of 2020.

By 2019, usage on the major social media platforms had been flat over the previous four years in the United States. In fact, social media usage had *declined* among Americans less than thirty-five years old, and the only age group using Facebook more than in prior years was people fifty-five or older.[15] Online ads were clicked by only 0.06 percent of viewers, and an estimated 60 percent of those clicks were accidental.[16] As a marketing medium, online channels were cluttered, subject to diminishing returns, increasingly viewed with suspicion by consumers as media attention to foreign hackers raised awareness of cybersecurity issues, and distrusted by many advertisers because of measurement issues and fear of their ads being placed near objectionable content. Combined with the ability to block ads, the rapidly growing costs of acquiring customers online, the experience of "Zoombombing," and controls on consumer data imposed by EU regulators and others, it's unclear how much buying and selling will be done online in the future.[17] It's also unclear whether social distancing made people more eager to transact online or simply demonstrated the limitations of buying, selling, and managing virtually.

"Predictions are always risky, especially about the future." But it is now and likely to remain a multichannel world. Buying behavior should drive selling, as retail history itself shows. Department stores were a response to the commercialization of women's fashion in the late nineteenth century, so stores offered multiple brands and pioneered consumer credit via installment-payment plans. Malls responded to suburbanization in the twentieth century. There's always been "disruption": in any market, some figure it out and others do not. Check out thedepartmentstoremuseum.org for a tour of dozens of defunct retailers over the past century. Technologies affect business, but business is always more than bits and bytes.

Your Road Map

I've organized the book around core categories: people, processes, pricing, partners, and productivity. The categories overlap, and that's the point: effective selling is ultimately an organizational outcome where people and performance management practices fit your sales process, pricing approach, and choices about go-to-market partners. Andrew Carnegie was once asked, "Which element is most important for the success of a business: brains, capital, or labor?" His reply: "Which leg of a three-legged stool is most important?" It's the fit of people, process, and pricing and partners that drives sales productivity.

> **People.** Who you hire, how, and what you do in training and developing salespeople are more important and expensive than ever. In the aggregate, hiring in sales is

often more expensive than many capital expenditure (capex) decisions in companies, and firms already spend 20 percent *more* per capita on sales training than they do in other functions. Yet most current hiring practices exacerbate the difficulties, and the ROI from sales training is disappointing. Part I examines aspects of sales talent that should inform your hiring practices, how to get better, and actionable links between hiring and training.

Process. Other things affect sales outcomes in addition to the skills and smarts of a sales rep. Part II looks at choices in constructing and reconstructing a replicable process of sales efforts and the implications for customer selection, call patterns, conversion analytics, developing a deal profile, compensation, and using data to understand buying journeys and inform relevant sales activities.

Pricing. This is a moment of truth in business. Part III examines how pricing can build or destroy profits in a changing landscape, the importance of price testing in today's information-rich markets, and how to link pricing with your value proposition, sales model, and selling behaviors.

Partners. It's an omni-channel world where prospects and orders touch multiple points in the distribution channel for most products and services. Selling now also means working with channel partners that are influential during the buying journey and after the sale. The options have increased, and so has the managerial complexity. We'll examine key components in channel design, and I'll provide guidelines and diagnostics for realigning the role of channels in sales programs.

Productivity. Because of the central role of customer acquisition in a company, changes in selling requirements have wider organizational implications. But many C-suite leaders are out of touch with the activities of their customer-facing colleagues. The final chapter examines why, what leaders can do to close this gap, and the social impact of improving sales productivity in the United States and other economies.

There are few universals that apply across all sales contexts, and you should be wary of gurus who say there are. How you drive that fit will depend on your particular business context. But my advice is to start with people.

PART ONE

PEOPLE

HIRING

As usual in business, everything starts with people. But, compared to other business functions, hiring in sales presents unique challenges. Consider these hair-raising stats.

The average turnover in sales across industries ranges from 20 percent to 30 percent annually (higher in strong economic conditions when people have more options and lower when they don't), meaning that at most companies, the equivalent of the entire sales force must be hired and trained every three to five years. Depending upon the position, it takes, on average, from three to four months to hire a new salesperson. Once hired, ramping reps up to full productivity now takes, across industries, more than nine months.[1] That is more than a year without a fully productive seller. The result is that each hire is a bigger sunk cost for a longer time. If you hear a so-called expert opine about talent management while ignoring the magnitude of sales hiring, tell them to save it for Davos or a TED Talk, where no resources are allocated.

In contrast to cheap talk, hiring in sales is expensive. According to Glassdoor, the labor-market research firm, the national average salary for a sales development representative (SDR, a relatively junior position in inside-sales models) was over $41,000 by 2016 and nearly $50,000 in many metro areas. In the same year, the annual fully burdened cost (salary plus commission, travel and entertainment expenses, and attributed back-office support costs) for a senior enterprise sales rep was $370,000.[2]

Making a bad hire is even more costly. Estimates indicate that the replacement cost for a telesales employee ranges from $75,000 to $90,000, and in sectors like medical devices, capital equipment, and professional services, replacement expenses, counting both direct and opportunity costs, are $1 million or more. Even that may be conservative when you factor in a year without a fully productive rep and consider that, across US companies, the average annual quota was about $2 million per rep in 2018.[3]

Although hiring in sales is as or more expensive than many capex decisions in companies, it rarely gets the same attention. This chapter looks at aspects of sales talent that should inform hiring and selection, the problem with typical sales hiring practices, and how to get better at this crucial activity so you can improve selling effectiveness and drive more profitable growth.

The Challenges and Problems with Sales Hiring Practices

Unlike many other business functions, there is no easily identified resource pool or educational background for sales positions. If you are looking for an engineer, you can go to an engineering school and find people who have studied electrical engineering, chemical engineering, and so on. For an accountant or finance person, you can find people who majored in those subjects. The same goes for software developers. But of the over four thousand colleges and universities in the United States, very few have, at the time of this writing, sales programs or even a sales course.

Meanwhile, more than 50 percent of US college graduates, regardless of their majors, will work in sales at some point in their careers. (Remember: whether you call them sales reps or something else, business development is what many associates, partners, and vice presidents do daily.) The result is that most salespeople start with little preparation and must learn by doing on the job.

And, unlike GAAP principles in accounting, the mechanics of an NPV calculation in finance, engineering equations, and the laws of physics, selling jobs vary greatly depending on the product or service sold, the customers a salesperson is responsible for, the relative importance of product or technical knowledge, and the people contacted during sales calls. Selling effectiveness is *not* a generalized trait. It's a function of the sales tasks.

In dealing with these challenges, companies often make crucial mistakes in their hiring practices, especially their interviews. Let's take a look.

Hunters versus Farmers

Many organizations divide potential hires (and current reps) into "hunters" and "farmers," with attributes like those outlined in table 2-1. But sales roles are far more diverse and nuanced than that simple dichotomy.

Consider the difference between reps who sell direct to customers versus those who sell through distributors or other channel partners. Or those who work in highly automated inside-sales models focused on small and medium business (SMB) prospects versus those who make in-person calls to enterprise accounts. Or those who sell individual products versus those who sell a bundled package solution. Or consider those who sell multiyear software license agreements versus monthly software-as-a-service (SaaS) contracts. The hunter/

TABLE 2-1

Hiring in sales: Many view the world like this

	The hunter	vs.	The farmer
Motivation	Develop new clients, new opportunities		Nurture relationships
Sales approach	Shortest path to close; then move on to the next opportunity		Consultative sales approach, ongoing account management
Selling style	High energy, competitive, much activity		Interpersonal and follow-up skills
Sales impact	Immediate, account entry, short term		Longer-term repeat business, loyalty
Company context	Hunters thrive in early-stage businesses and emerging markets where the brand, product, or company is not well known		Ideally suited to a more mature market or organization with longer sales cycles and established brand and sales process

farmer dichotomy is of little use in setting and distinguishing hiring criteria between these roles. In fact, categories like hunters and farmers are, in my experience, often used by managers as post hoc rationalizations for their hiring choices, not ex ante hiring criteria.

Chasing Stars

There is no doubt that talent matters and that sales stars exist. But an overreliance on stars from outside organizations can have unintended consequences.

Differences in individual sales performance are very wide in most firms. The top 20 percent of salespeople often account for 50–60 percent of their company's revenues. As one study notes, if 20 percent of your salespeople are making 60 percent of revenue, that's a 3x multiplier; and since the remaining 80 percent bring in only 40 percent of revenue, that is a .5x multiplier, meaning that the top sellers are 6x more productive than their peers.[4]

Sales is like other creative occupations where the stardom phenomenon is well documented. In areas like software programming, the arts, sports, and others, the best are not just a bit better than the average. They are typically a lot better: the top 1 percent often outperform average performers in those fields by 125 percent or more. Performance profiles in those areas are (in statistics terminology) a "power distribution curve," not a normal-distribution bell curve.[5]

However, as my colleague Boris Groysberg has documented, stardom is not easily portable. Less than half of performance in the jobs he studied stemmed from individual capabilities, and the rest from firm-specific qualities and resources—for example, brand, technologies, training, team chemistry, and other factors.[6] This is especially true in sales because sales tasks are determined by a firm's business strategy and its choices about which customers to focus on. In turn, selling behaviors are affected by your control systems and culture as well as whom and how you hire.[7] Those are all firm-specific factors.

Hence, when you hire a star from another firm, that salesperson leaves all of that behind. Talk to the corporation that hires the star sales VP from a competitor and finds that she doesn't perform there the way she performed in the previous corporation. Or consider the many startups that bring in an experienced big-company rep and he flounders in the early-stage firm. Those people didn't suddenly get stupid or lose individual capabilities. In business, there's no such thing as performance in the abstract. There is only performance in a given context—here, not there—and much of selling depends upon the relationships, knowledge, and mutual trust that the rep establishes with others in the company.

Further, the effects of successful talent management seem to be cumulative: good people learn from each other. Again, this is especially true in sales, where modeling behavior is a key driver of how people develop. Average reps get better by watching how the best of their peers perform key tasks. They pick up important lessons about how to pitch, how to answer objections, how to deal with competitive comparisons, and other aspects of selling that product at that price in that market. This is one reason why ride-alongs, coaching, reviews, and best-practice dissemination are so important.

Sales is a performance art, salespeople exhibit a wide variance in performance outcomes, and those outcomes depend upon innate talent as well as the context in which that talent is found, nurtured, and deployed.

Unstructured Interviews

Decades of research consistently show that managers overrate their ability to predict someone's performance and fit for job tasks on the basis of interviews.[8] Depending upon the sample, correlations between interview predictions and job success vary from about .1 to .4—less than the .5 rate of flipping a coin. Some studies show a *negative* correlation between interview assessments and subsequent job performance: the firm would have been better off selecting at random.

There are systematic reasons for this gap, and it's important to know those reasons in order to improve hiring and, when using new techniques, not unwittingly perpetuate or even widen the gap.

First Impressions

Oscar Wilde said that "only shallow people do not judge by appearances." Well, Wilde would like sales hiring practices, because first impressions are rife in hiring decisions as in many other facets of human behavior. A first impression takes about thirty-five thousandths of a second and it's involuntary: as a highly social species, our brains are built to process facial recognition instantly, and we are quick to judge faces as trustworthy, threatening, or competent.[9] The problem is that we extrapolate first impressions to make judgments about people that have little to do with their performance of relevant tasks.

Michael Lewis has memorably described this process among professional sports evaluators in *Moneyball* and other books. The market for baseball players was rife with inefficiencies because scouts relied on surface characteristics that often had nothing to do with field performance. Fat players were undervalued, and handsome players overvalued. "A scout watching a player," writes Lewis, "tended to form a near-instant impression, around which all other data tended to organize itself . . . The human mind was just bad at seeing things it did not expect to see, and a bit too eager to see what it expected to see."[10] Hence, the repeated studies correlating height and CEOs, and the prevalence of confirmation bias in interviews: we tend to process answers to our questions in ways that confirm the first impression. Lewis quotes one general manager as saying, "Job interviews were magic shows."

Inconsistent Judgments

Judging a person's fit for a sales job is, in most circumstances, a complex task. It involves evaluating the relevance of past experience, education, personality, fit with the culture, and so on. But people are inconsistent in making summary judgments of complex information.

When asked to evaluate the same information twice, we frequently give different answers, and that's also true of experienced experts. Daniel Kahneman notes that radiologists who evaluate chest X-rays as "normal" or "abnormal" contradict themselves 20 percent of the time when they see the same picture on separate occasions, and he cites over forty studies that show similar and higher levels of inconsistency by auditors, pathologists, organizational managers in various areas, and other professionals. Kahneman concludes that "this level of inconsistency is typical, even when a case is reevaluated within a few minutes. Unreliable judgments cannot be predictors of anything."[11]

Personality Assessments

To be more consistent in making judgments, many companies now routinely use personality assessments in the hiring process. The problems here concern both the instruments and their users. Two of the most popular tools are the Myers-Briggs Type Indicator, which assigns you to one of sixteen personality types based on four axes (extroverted/introverted, sensing/intuitive, thinking/feeling, and judging/perceiving), and the DiSC profile, which allegedly measures traits like dominance, influence, steadiness, and conscientiousness. Neither instrument was intended for use as an employment screening tool, and there are major methodological and reliability issues with both.[12]

On the other side of the desk, the users of these tests are rarely trained in interpreting the results, which are susceptible to multiple, subjective interpretations. As many have pointed out, every answer on these assessments could apply to anyone to some extent, and the same person often responds differently to the same question at different times. We're then in "assessment theater": using the tools as camouflage for following first impressions and a judgment based on that morning's mood.

More generally, research has not identified personality traits that consistently correlate with selling performance. The same trait is positively or negatively correlated with results in different sales jobs, and in the same company at different times. In sales, talent comes in all shapes, sizes, and personalities.[13] Selling effectiveness is a function of the task(s) and the fit of the person with that role.

Behaviorally Useless Folk Wisdom

When you ask sales managers what they're looking for in candidates and read their remarks about their practices, you typically get lists like the following:[14]

- "The Things All Great Salespeople Do": the best salespeople "own everything . . . are resourceful . . . help others . . . move quickly"

- "4 Signs of an 'A' Player": sense of urgency, passion, keep it simple, show me the money

- "Ten Vital Sales Traits": proactive work ethic, emotional resilience, communication skill, listening, integrity, humility and gratitude, ambition and drive, efficiency, commitment to succeed, and activity and results tracking

These traits and tips are like the mission statements on company websites. They are nebulous and behaviorally useless for doing what any hiring process must do: say yes or no to an individual applicant for a given job. When you're speaking with someone at an interview, how do you unearth whether or not they have a "sense of urgency"? Well, that author says, "Look for answers around impatience and fourth-quarter comebacks. Aka: Eli Manning and the New York Giants." Really? (And besides, this Boston-based author believes a better answer would be Tom Brady and the New England Patriots!) Confusing this stuff with job skills and useful evaluations is dangerous and a waste of time and resources.

Also, note the overlapping themes in these lists. In a job interview, who would *not* want to come across as hardworking, resourceful, efficient, and so on? Remember that you're hiring the person, not the polished interview version of the person, but only about a third of US companies monitor whether their hiring practices lead to good employees or even track cost or time per hire.[15] Most managers only learn this lesson from experience, including me. I managed a services firm where people were 80 percent of expenses, and interpersonal skills were key internally with colleagues and externally with clients. For the first few years, I relied on interviews to try to uncover candidate capabilities until, in answer to my questions about his "people skills," one wise-guy candidate informed me that he "loved people; in fact, some of my best friends are people!"

On reflection, I deserved that response to my vacuous questions. Author Iris Bohnet, in examining gender bias in hiring, puts it well: "A high-level partner in one company I worked with told me that his organization could never use the word 'experiment.' Doing so, he said, would suggest managers didn't know what they were doing. That, I told him, is exactly the point! People think they know what they are doing—based on a mixture of intuition, best practice, tradition, and industry norms. But only evidence can tell."[16] In sales, the best evidence, the gold standard, is behaviors.

How to Get Better

In sales, people must work with others in their companies; they represent their company and its products to prospects; a poor hire not only is costly but can also do collateral damage to your brand while representing your firm; and in a high-performance organization, managers *should* feel personally accountable for their hiring decisions. To get better, your goal should be to supplement personal interviews in finding and selecting sales talent. To do that, follow these guidelines.

Clarify the Important Sales Tasks

Good hiring starts with knowing what you are hiring for in terms of key sales tasks. We'll look at this issue in more depth in the chapters on training and sales models. But here, notice that in addition to their behavioral limitations, another problem with the feel-good trait lists cited earlier is their assumption that a salesperson needs all of those qualities to be effective. However, it's often advisable to shrink the span of sales activities. This requires understanding the customer-conversion process and where the salesperson (versus marketing or a customer success team) has the most influence.

In many inside-sales models, for instance, activities like lead generation and qualification are the jobs of SDRs, and postsale activities like renewals are given to service or customer success personnel. This allows the firm to focus more precisely on recruiting for account executive (AE) roles where product demonstrations, pricing, and closing the sale with a multifunctional buying unit are the key tasks.

At InsideSales.com, cofounder Ken Krogue did that and increased sales productivity. The firm hired its first sales rep in 2004. At the time, the job was to generate leads by combing through Dun & Bradstreet lists of companies, contact fifty of those companies daily, and if the rep reached a relevant buyer, pitch InsideSale's products. By 2006, after testing inbound marketing initiatives, Krogue changed the division of labor. Rather than having one rep responsible for lead generation, scheduling meetings, running demos, closing deals, and managing upsells, Krogue split the job into smaller pieces. More experienced reps focused on closing, while newer reps developed their skills on the phone with a lower ask (e.g., scheduling a demo). Krogue eventually created a model where SDRs generate leads, business development reps (BDRs) schedule demos and do outbound calling, and AEs then focus on getting that prospect from demo to close. What was 50 calls per day per rep in 2004 became 150 calls per day per BDR by 2015 *and* more time available for crucial stages of the buying process for experienced AEs.[17]

Similarly, as we'll discuss in chapter 10, the structure of your go-to-market channel should affect sales hiring profiles. In selling to retail trade customers, for instance, there is typically a range of tasks that can be grouped into three categories:

1. **Volume-influencing activities:** selling new items, getting more shelf space for established items, selling point-of-sale materials or in-store displays, negotiating trade promotions, and so on

2. **In-store service activities:** shelf audits, handling damaged merchandise, ensuring product freshness, and handling queries from store managers are examples here

3. **Supply-chain management activities:** sales forecasting by account, establishing and managing delivery schedules, and coordination with your firm's operations people for that customer

Companies that use service merchandisers in their go-to-market activities have less need for salespeople who focus on the in-store service activities. Companies that use automated replenishment algorithms with their accounts have less need to hire and train salespeople in those supply-chain management activities. In turn, this opens up a wider labor pool for the needed sales talent.

Hire for the Task

Because sales tasks are determined by buying contexts, not the other way around, what you do and don't need in a sales hire differs greatly by industry.[18] In computers and electronics, channel management is a key go-to-market capability, but not in metals and mining. In the former, the products are often part of a package that customers buy at one-stop-shop intermediaries; in the latter sectors, direct bulk buys are the norm. Account management skills are important in chemicals where managing a portfolio of specialty and commodity products over time is a key sales task, but not so much in computers and electronics where channel partners often perform account management tasks.

Hire for the task, not the title. But many companies do precisely the opposite. "Middle skills" jobs—those that require more education than a high-school diploma but less than a four-year college degree—are the bulk of the labor market and traditionally the engine for moving into the middle class for most people. My colleague Joseph Fuller and his research partners found that degree inflation (the difference between the demand for a college degree in job postings and the educational background of employees actually performing those tasks) is a growing phenomenon, and sales occupations are the biggest category affected by degree inflation, followed by office managers, bookkeepers, and secretaries.[19]

What is going on here? Sometimes requiring more education is justified: many sales jobs do have more data-analysis requirements. But too often, it is unnecessary and hurts both companies and society. Many employers have simply defaulted to using college degrees as a blunt proxy for a candidate's range and depth of skills. As an HR manager notes, "Industries have gotten lazy . . . It's just easy to slap on a BA requirement on a job posting." Indeed, Fuller and colleagues found that, across industries, the percentage of respondents who believe their companies screen out qualified job applicants as a function of a college degree requirement was far greater than those who disagreed. They also found that degree inflation increases search time for employers, pushes up the costs of hires, and often increases turnover when hires are demotivated or are otherwise a poor fit.

Especially in sales, where on-the-job learning is a big driver of development, you should embrace a more expansive view of talent, with less weighting given to degrees and more to the tasks involved. Every sales job has implicit required behaviors. Take the time to clarify and make that explicit in your job postings and hiring pool.

When companies focus on the tasks, not titles, the relevant labor pool typically expands. Coding boot camps, for instance, are now an accepted source of software talent for many firms because after a few months of intensive, task-focused work, the participants have job-relevant skills without (and often despite) previous formal degrees. In 2017, 80 percent of coding boot camp graduates found a job, with an average salary of $70,698 (versus an average of $49,785 for all US college graduates), and there are now similar initiatives in Europe and Asia. And if you consider the direct and opportunity costs involved in sales hiring, how many other activities are worth as much in managers' time and attention?

Use Multiple Perspectives and Behavioral Assessments

In any job with high variability in individual performance, there's inevitably a cloning bias: hiring people whom you perceive as having similar characteristics as you. To prevent the cloning bias, get multiple opinions and perspectives. Some firms get product and service involved in interviewing sales candidates. Their input is illuminating because those people must deal with the orders that sales reps bring to their firms.

There are other benefits. Doing multiple assessments often motivates a need to make the interviews themselves more structured. People in your firm then discuss and communicate the tasks you're hiring for and the questions and activities likely to elicit relevant knowledge. Conversely, no one person—even your future boss—can usually represent what it's like to work in an organization. This approach also provides the interviewee with a better basis to judge fit. Then, with multiple interview evaluations, take a page from the wisdom-of-crowds research: make them independent judgments and average the scores for each candidate as input to the ultimate hiring decision maker.

Complement interviews with role plays, task assignments, and whenever possible, job trials and internship-type hiring scenarios. Selling is about behavior, not only attitude. The best predictor of future work performance is performance at that same job: job performance from one time period to the next correlates at a much higher rate than interviews.[20] So probationary periods are better predictors of actual performance. When consulting and other professional services firms recruit MBAs, they don't simply rely on interviews, grades, and previous work experience. They typically hire first-year students for paid summer internships. Those two to three months are, in effect, a job trial, and the hiring firm is in a better position to decide who gets a full-time offer. This is expensive but worth it when, as in these firms, people are typically more than 50 percent of cost of goods sold (COGS) and their capabilities *are* the product. Firms in other sectors can cost effectively use less-intensive variations on this approach. Technology is increasing options for behavioral assessments by more people in less time via game-like activities, video, and online media.

Be Clear about What You Mean by "Experience"

Previous selling experience is the most commonly cited criterion in sales hiring. Driving this view is a belief that there is a trade-off between hiring for experience and the time and money you don't need to spend on training. But as noted earlier, performance at another company—within or outside the same industry—is not easily portable. So much of sales success depends upon a firm's strategy, the customer segments, and sales tasks inherent in that strategy.

Further, experience in sales is inherently multidimensional. It may refer to experience with any (or any combination of) the following:

- **A customer group.** For example, a banker or broker hired by a software firm to call on financial-services prospects; or in the health-care industry, companies sell very different products, but many sell to hospitals.

- **A technology.** An engineer or field-service tech hired to sell the equipment.

- **A company.** In many B2B firms, service reps move to sales because internal coordination is a key sales task, and they "know the people and how to get things done here."

- **A geographical market or culture.** For instance, someone from that country or ethnic group who knows, and has credibility within, the norms of the customer's culture.

- **Selling.** A retail associate with point-of-sale experience or an inside-sales rep who has demonstrated successful work in that kind of transaction-intensive sales context.

The relevance of each type varies with *your* firm's sales tasks. Consider what kind(s) of prior experience is truly relevant and then require the people doing the hiring to clarify what they mean when they use that criterion.

Understand the Limits of Data

More firms are using algorithms in hiring and for "people analytics" more generally. Companies are using AI to analyze candidates' word choices, emotional traits, and other human qualities. Some now use a video-interview service called HireVue in which an AI program analyzes candidates' facial expressions and language patterns. (Hint: don't slouch or wave your arms, maintain eye contact with the camera, and use short declarative sentences.) A well-known example is Google, which has algorithms that allegedly analyze the responses an applicant provides about the qualities that Google emphasizes for that job.[21] To the extent that these tools provide data that supplements intuition, this is a boon. But people use technology and people hire people, so understand the limits and potential biases in using these tools, especially (but not only) for sales hiring.

These tools are generally based on machine-learning technology: companies feed computers large amounts of data to identify patterns, while hoping to improve pattern-recognition ability with more data and adjustments to the algorithms. It's essentially the logic and database behind the recommendations you get from Netflix or Amazon: if you bought this book or movie, you may be interested in these other books or movies. As with all software, it is only as good as the data provided and the venerable garbage in, garbage out (GIGO) syndrome. In hiring, a typical key data input is thousands of LinkedIn profiles. As with most big-data analytics, moreover, we are basically talking about correlations, and with any database large enough, you will get correlations that are statistically significant, but not necessarily meaningful and often just silly.[22]

Also, these systems can unwittingly perpetuate biases via "statistical discrimination"—beliefs about average differences in abilities or skills between groups. Here's an example. A study created online experiments with a hundred participants representing workers seeking jobs and eight hundred representing employers seeking to hire workers. The job applicants completed a series of sports and math quizzes (stereotypically easier for men to answer) where some questions were easy to answer and others, hard. Overall, men indeed performed slightly better than women, answering, on average, one additional question correctly. Employers then had to hire a candidate, choosing between one woman and one man, knowing each candidate's score results on the easy questions but not on the difficult questions, and employers were told they would be rewarded if their hire performed well on the hard quiz. When informed that men did better, on average, than women on the sports or math tests, employers were much less likely to hire a female, even when two individuals had identical easy-quiz scores.

That bias at the margin may not surprise corporate diversity managers. But here is where this study gets interesting and raises core questions about the inherent limits of data-driven people analytics. The researchers then took gender out of the hiring decision. Candidates were simply identified to potential employers as born in either an even or odd month. Unknown to the employers, however, the researchers labeled all female candidates as "odd month" and all men as "even month." Using the easy-quiz test results as their guide, the employers still chose the even-month (male) candidates much more often than the odd-month (female) candidates. In other words, employers weren't biased against women per se (they didn't know the genders associated with the months). Instead, they used information about average performance of the two groups to drive their decisions about individuals. As the researchers note, "Mere membership in a lower-performing group—even when this membership is outside of the control of the worker and based on an arbitrary characteristic—is sufficient for discrimination to follow."[23] Big-data correlations can easily exacerbate this tendency.

Assume Mistakes Will Happen

Sales hiring is difficult, because it's necessarily based on people judging other people's future performance in a changing market environment. Recognize that sales hiring probably has lots of room for improvement in your firm, and you can make it better by following the guidelines in this chapter.

Also recognize that mistakes are inevitable. As a summary of hiring research puts it, "There will always be false positives—people you hire whose performance is disappointing. And there will always be false negatives—people you reject who would have been great . . . perfect performance prediction is a fantasy."[24] Yes, but while mistakes are inevitable, the sunk-cost fallacy—continuing to throw good money after bad—is not.

Consider Amazon's policy of offering a voluntary severance package it calls "The Offer." Annually, each of its service and warehouse employees is offered up to $5,000 to quit. Amazon adopted this policy when it acquired Zappos, whose founder, Tony Hsieh, used it after estimating that bad hires cost Zappos more than $100 million as it grew. The policy helps to deal with inevitable mistakes—by the hirer or the person hired—and with the human reality that people change and their relationship to their work can change with marriage, divorce, sickness, the need to take care of an aging parent, or any of the other thousand natural shocks that flesh is heir to. Amazon believes "The Offer" helps it shed less-committed employees while improving retention among others.[25]

Placing Talent Where and When It Counts

As the old saying goes, "You hire your problems." Exit interviews at most firms show that a primary cause of poor performance and turnover is job fit. People, especially salespeople with a variable pay component, become frustrated when hired for tasks that are a poor fit with their skills and preferences. Conversely, across functions, research indicates that allocating talent among strategic priorities is the single biggest driver of the overall effectiveness of HR practices.[26] It's now generally taken for granted that the allocation of financial capital should skew to the priorities with the highest net present value potential. The same is true for human capital.

In most sales contexts, some activities exhibit high performance variance but have little strategic impact. Think about PowerPoint presentations. Some people are better than others at making slides, but how much impact do the slides have versus other sales tasks? Other activities may be important strategically but exhibit relatively little performance variability—because the tasks are standard, because the firm has learned to reduce the variability, or because the go-to-market model limits the extent of performance variance. Think about the difference between sales personnel at a bespoke boutique shop, where personalized service and advice are core tasks, versus retailers where low price and product assortment make selling less complex and variable. Or think about how some inside-sales models can standardize and automate lead generation and qualification versus situations where these activities vary across unique buying contexts and so require selling judgment that's not easily routinized.

You'll never have enough stars for all positions, and you should allocate the best sales talent to those areas that have both high impact and high variability. Depending upon the buying context, that may be prospecting, qualifying, channel management, or postsale account management. In activities with low impact or little variability, you don't need stars and should not overpay, either in money, time, or untapped market potential. In many firms, for instance, an untapped source of growth is reallocating sales territories so that more reps are placed in the areas or segments with the most potential.

Effective hiring doesn't stop with recruiting. It's about building *and* allocating talent, and this has a temporal dimension in any growing company or changing market. A common problem is hiring the right person at the wrong time. In many SaaS businesses, for instance, sales activities with high variance and impact early on are about initial customer acquisition in a land-and-expand approach. As the market develops, key activities tend to shift toward reducing churn, working with engineering on custom applications for higher-potential accounts, and upselling or cross-selling additional services. Allocation of sales talent should change accordingly.

Similarly, in startups, "selling" is typically about customer discovery as well as closing deals. The successful rep at an established company with a known brand and selling process is often a premature hire at a startup without a known brand and where getting early adopters requires ongoing interactions aimed at discovering product-market fit, not only the sales person's fit with your culture and values.

⊕ QUESTIONS TO ASK . . . AND ANSWER

I hope this chapter has increased your awareness of the growing importance and complexity of sales hiring in contemporary markets. But I want to avoid what many management writers do: leave a message that life is complex, and you should do good and avoid evil.

TABLE 2-2

A sales hiring diagnostic

In our company, how well do we . . .

Know and specify key sales tasks, by role and by segment, in our recruiting efforts?	1 2 3 4 5 6 7
Train sales hiring managers in interviewing skills and the use of assessments?	1 2 3 4 5 6 7
Complement interviews with role-plays, task assignments, or job trials?	1 2 3 4 5 6 7
Broaden our hiring pool by linking our understanding of tasks to criteria beyond education?	1 2 3 4 5 6 7
Systematically gather multiple perspectives in our sales recruitment and selection practices?	1 2 3 4 5 6 7
Clarify what we mean by "experience" in establishing our hiring pool and selection criteria?	1 2 3 4 5 6 7
Understand the limits of any hiring algorithms or automated screening activities in our hiring process?	1 2 3 4 5 6 7
Place the people we hire where they can have the most impact on our selling activities?	1 2 3 4 5 6 7

I'll therefore conclude each chapter with a diagnostic about that chapter's topic. The questions can help to disaggregate a big topic like hiring into managerial issues that can be examined empirically, generate dialogue, and spur continuous improvement in your firm. Use them the way pilots use a checklist as they prepare to take off or what doctors do when diagnosing a patient. The humble checklist helps to reduce mistakes and keep the most commonly recurring issues top-of-mind in busy, complicated situations.

The questions in table 2-2 can spur dialogue and help better align a company's hiring efforts with its goals. Rating an item as 1 means the respondent believes that we are terrible at the activity or simply neglect it, while a rating of 7 means the respondent believes we are as good as the top firms at that activity.

A few suggestions about how to use the diagnostics in this book. First, you can and should customize the questions to your business. Effective selling is context dependent, and the relevant context is usually determined by multiple factors. You may generate clicks on a blog post by reducing a complex issue to one variable with the biggest emotional impact, but that's a recipe for bad decision making in business.

Second, aggregate group opinions are often superior to expert judgments *if* the individual judgments are made free of social bias. Don't do what I have seen some well-meaning but headstrong "leaders" do: fill out this diagnostic, show it to their subordinates, and then run a discussion that asks people if they agree with their boss. Have people on your team complete the diagnostic individually, and then aggregate or average the scores for each item.

Third, you might then focus your team's dialogue on the following questions:

- Which item(s) received the highest score? Why? Can you cite an example? Note the importance of examples in business discussions: they help decision makers understand if the issue is a recurring one in the business model or an outlier that happens once in a few years.

- Which item(s) received the lowest score? Why? Can you cite an example? The diagnostics can help sales groups, and other functions they interact with, to surface agreed-upon areas where the firm can improve and the cross-functional efforts needed for improvement.

- So what, now what? What actions should we start, stop, or do differently to align the organization for profitable growth?

- Rules of engagement. What should sales expect from other functions? What should other functions expect from sales?

Finally, as you consider your answers to questions about hiring, keep in mind an implication of the changes, research, and guidelines discussed in this chapter: you must build and allocate a talent portfolio relevant to *your* business, and that doesn't happen without proactive attention to training and development.

TRAINING AND DEVELOPMENT

US companies spend at least $70 billion annually on training, with some estimates as high as $90 billion. The training market grew at a 13 percent CAGR in the second decade of the twenty-first century, and the US ranks near the top of global surveys in this area, with 66 percent of workers receiving training, according to the Organisation for Economic Co-operation and Development.[1] Companies spend an average of $1,459 per rep on sales training—almost 20 percent *more* than they spend per capita in other functions. Yet, when it comes to equipping sales teams with relevant knowledge and skills, the ROI of training is disappointing. Surveys report a steady decline in the share of sales reps achieving their quota.[2]

To deal with changing buying behavior and sales tasks, many companies must confront common problems with their current training practices, rethink the purpose and focus of their training and development initiatives, and because it is difficult to develop the attitudes and skills of people who are not a good fit for the job in the first place, get better at linking their sales hiring and training activities.

The Problems with Training Practices

Despite changes in buying, most companies still approach people development much as they did decades ago.

Onboarding is usually a one-off session where reps are expected to absorb a lot of information in a short time. Then, additional training is often limited to new product introductions or annual kickoff meetings to set quotas: reps are flown in, given marching orders, and "fired up" by a motivational speaker (often a football coach, military hero, or other figure with zero knowledge of the business) and a team-building exercise (more hot coals, anyone?). And even if the training messages are relevant, they're not delivered when reps can use the tools or supported with actionable coaching and reviews.

There is also an overreliance on classroom training. Research indicates that participants in traditional classroom-type training seminars (about 42 percent of sales training hours) forget more than 80 percent of the information taught within ninety days—talk about quarterly short-termism!

Moreover, training programs tend to focus on a particular selling methodology. Although methodologies can play an important role—encouraging consistency, disseminating best practices, and providing common metrics to monitor and evaluate—the same methodology is rarely relevant across different buying-selling situations. Meanwhile, training firms have an incentive to apply their method everywhere. If you don't evaluate the fit of a methodology with the required tasks in your business, your training initiatives can unwittingly perpetuate "competency traps":[3] your reps (as is often said about academics) "learn more and more about less and less" that's relevant to their job today, not yesterday, in that market.

Sales training should be a process, not an event. At any point in time, most salespeople have multiple accounts and must deal with a changing array of people and buying criteria. For example,

Andrew Sullivan (disguised name) is a cofounder of Faraway Ltd., a startup in England that produces innovative pushchairs (baby carriages, in American English). He is calling on different retailers, from mass merchandisers to high-end department stores, which have different business and merchandising strategies, and different consumer demographics in their stores.[4] Same product, different customers, and so different sales tasks.

During the course of a week or even a day, salespeople encounter these differences. A customer involved in rebuys may not need the information required for a new purchaser in the category. Within the same category, one buyer is primarily concerned with innovative product features, while another is most concerned with just-in-time delivery. The vendor of a new solution typically faces different tasks than the seller of the existing solution at that account. If all customers sound the same to you, then you should probably not try to make a living in sales.

Salespeople need training that is specific to their unique needs and tasks. Remember, as noted in chapter 2, that notions of the born salesperson—pleasing personality, great storyteller with an inventory of jokes, and so on—are misplaced stereotypes. Research finds no clear cause-and-effect links between personality characteristics and sales success. Andrew Sullivan is, again, a good example. He notes that, before founding Faraway, "I always associated sales with hustling: market traders, people selling dictionaries door-to-door. I believed sales was mainly about clever patter . . . I'm not a natural 'salesperson' but believe I have the drive to sell something that I believe in."

Most people start like Sullivan, without much experience or confidence in their selling abilities, but have the ability to learn to perform the required tasks. Hence, as wasteful as most current training expenditures are, the managerial instincts here are sound: in a competitive market, if you don't invest in people's knowledge and skill development, you will soon get what you don't pay for.

The Power of Adaptive Selling

Selling is not a science, reducible to ex ante rules and certain personalities. But while research debunks the born-salesperson myth, it does indicate that salespeople learn by doing as they accumulate a base of experiences across buying contexts. Then, successful salespeople organize these experiences into categories of selling situations and apply the appropriate tool(s) to the relevant situation.

This is called *adaptive selling*: the ability to alter behaviors according to the nature of the customer.[5] This ability has been measured, related to positive sales outcomes, and operationalized in terms of behaviors such as adapting the information the salesperson provides in a selling situation, how that information is provided during the selling process, and (in certain contexts) the solution the rep adapts to that situation.[6]

Learning theorists call this "active retrieval." When people must respond to changing circumstances, learning involves the ability to retrieve a relevant model or rubric, and this ability is reinforced or reorganized with each iteration.[7] In fact, there's evidence that this positive or negative feedback loop from the environment—"the school of hard knocks," in sales parlance—actually reshapes neural pathways over time.

Research also indicates that there are certain steps involved in crafting a learning process that accelerates active retrieval.

Acceptance

Anyone who has ever taught a college class or training seminar knows that you must motivate recipients to learn the relevant skills, and motivation is enhanced by a few factors.

People need clear expectations about what they will learn and why, so they understand the gap between their current capability level and the level associated with proficiency. This may seem obvious but consider how much sales training fails to meet this base condition. Many companies have competency lists, but few incorporate particular sales tasks. Once you get beyond disseminating information about a new product's features, for instance, many sales training initiatives have few measurable expectations beyond "get better" maxims. Andy Paul, author of a smart blog about sales, puts it well: "Sales training is primarily concerned with the 'how' of selling. Sales education is about the 'why.' Sales education provides a seller with the context to effectively put into use what s/he has learned in sales training. Sales training is incomplete without sales education."[8]

Another factor is the relationship between motivation and the expectation of success. Too easy, and people get bored; too hard, and they get frustrated and give up. Note that unclear expectations only increase the risks in both directions. Effective learning matches the content and goal to the current capability of the individual and the desired outcomes. In a given situation, does "get better" mean selling against a new competing product or a substitute, better price negotiation or closing skills, or improving customer selection at the top of the funnel? These are very different behavioral goals.

Application

People learn to handle unpredictable, changing environments through repeated practice. Adults learn best when they can apply new information or a skill and see the results. In the classroom or seminar, this dimension of learning typically involves what researchers call "spaced repetition"—for example, a series of quizzes aimed at measuring and reinforcing the application and consolidation of knowledge. In the field outside the class-room, application involves "deliberate practice"—identifying specific areas of improvement (versus holistic changes to one's personality or temperament) and then practicing those skills with feedback on performance.[9]

This is crucial in sales where learning involves behaviors, not only knowledge. Talking about selling is not the same as selling. Research indicates that to acquire a behavioral skill (versus a concept or new information), people must apply that behavior multiple times (from three to twenty times, according to different studies) before it becomes practiced enough to be comfortable and effective.[10] This means that on-the-job learning, and the performance management practices that support such learning (see chapter 4), are key. The problem is that in most busy sales forces, on-the-job learning is a euphemism for no real training at all. It's a random-walk process, not deliberate practice.

Feedback

The purpose of practice is to get feedback about what works. In sales, the ultimate feedback comes from the customer: you win or lose the sale. But that is an outcome, and the purpose of training investments is to increase the odds of sales success. Companies that get good ROI from learning initiatives link their training to ongoing activities between the manager and reps.

A core vehicle for this feedback and advice in most sales organizations is the account planning process. So much of identifying relevant adaptive selling behaviors only becomes apparent at the account level, where dealing with specific buying processes can be examined and discussed. Good managers make account planning more than a recitation of next year's bogey; it's also a discussion of what is and isn't working at that customer in terms of getting access to more senior decision makers, introducing a new product, cross-selling, or another goal.

Reflection

A final step in durable learning is reflection: What did I learn? Was the skill applied successfully or unsuccessfully? What else do I need to learn or do to build and apply the relevant skills?

An underutilized vehicle for reflection in sales organizations is win/loss reviews. In most firms, win/loss analyses focus on losses and a scenario where the rep attributes a loss to "too high a price" and the manager says the rep was "outsold." But wins are as important to understand as losses. Wins provide information about strengths to be reinforced in learning initiatives, how to increase motivation to learn a new skill, and the type of practice that is relevant. What the military calls an after-action review (AAR) is a simple, disciplined approach that helps to focus on going-forward learning, not just apportioning credit or blame.[11] In my experience, an AAR approach is relevant to, and usually an improvement on, established win/loss processes in most firms.

Similarly, learning research emphasizes the importance of narratives in promoting reflection and durable learning. As one group of researchers puts it, "Narrative provides not only meaning but also a mental framework for imbuing future experiences and information with meaning, in effect shaping new memories to fit constructs of the world and ourselves."[12] Think case studies, customer visits, and the specificity of well-conducted win/loss reviews as force multipliers for learning in sales.

This research, grounded in psychology, neuroscience, and practical pedagogy, indicates that learning is a learned behavior. Organizations can and should take advantage of this research about what works and get more from their training investments.

Getting the Most from Your Training Spending

To improve the ROI in sales training, you must identify the skills that matter in your business. There is no such thing as effective selling if it doesn't link with your business model, the profit or cash-flow engine in that model, and the sales tasks relevant to starting and maintaining that engine.

First, you must understand the externals. Value in any business is created or destroyed in the marketplace. Key externals include the industry you compete in, the market segments where you choose to play, and the decision-making and buying processes at the customers that you sell to and service. Those factors help to determine the important sales tasks— what your go-to-market initiatives must accomplish to deliver and extract value, and therefore what your salespeople and other customer-facing personnel (e.g., service) must be especially good at to implement *your* strategy effectively.

Then, you can develop and align skills and behaviors with required sales tasks. The following are useful distinctions to keep in mind in analyzing sales tasks, crafting training initiatives, and keeping learning relevant and up to date in your business.

Identify the Skills That Matter Most

The best way to identify the skills most relevant to your business is to consider how your segment focus, products, customers, and salespeople—even within your own firm—differ from others.

Differences within an Industry

The most common response I get when I ask managers where they compete is a broad vertical-market answer like "health care" or "financial services." This is too abstract for determining sales tasks and training emphases. Sellers of medical equipment, for instance, must be especially good at managing and closing complex deals that involve price negotiations and custom applications. Meanwhile, in biotech, salespeople must be knowledgeable about the latest research and results of clinical trials. A training initiative about "health care" that is indifferent to these differences will have limited impact.

Differences within a Product Category

Sales tasks differ significantly within the same category. Consider a SaaS service like file sharing or collaboration software. Since these services are typically not mission-critical for customers and are sold at relatively low monthly subscription prices, buyers can gather much presale information via an online search, allowing them to act more quickly and decisively when dealing with these vendors. Here, inside sales organizations—"dialing for dollars"—are paramount. Sellers can conduct online demos and provide prospects a proposal with a few clicks on the website. Key sales tasks involve activities such as upsells (getting the customer to purchase a premium version of the product) and cross-sells (getting initial customers to provide positive referrals to others in that organization).

A SaaS platform service such as CRM or marketing automation service (MAS), on the other hand, requires sophisticated integration to install annual or multiyear contracts. This is a complex initial sale with a longer selling cycle that is harder to do online or by phone. Selling often involves the vendor's engineers, and key tasks focus on renewals, increasing product applicability and price with new functionality sold to different decision makers, while minimizing customer churn.

Differences When Target Buyers Change

Using "product" as a training focus is dangerous. At one level, firms know this. It's common in sales training to distinguish *features* (data or information about the product: e.g., it has a certain performance capacity like miles-per-gallon) from *benefits* (the customer outcome that the product addresses: e.g., cost savings or trip capacity). But buying changes make this distinction more important and complex.

An example is when companies move from SMBs to enterprise customer segments. ScriptLogic sold diagnostic tools to system administrators in the IT departments of SMBs. It built a growing business with a land-and-expand selling approach and a "point, click, done" value proposition, where the administrator could expense the purchase on the company credit card.[13] But this approach was not effective in selling to enterprise accounts, and ScriptLogic was eventually acquired by Quest Software, which employed a very different sales approach in the enterprise segment.

InsideSales.com (now called XANT) grew rapidly in SMB segments, but selling the same products to enterprise customers meant a change in sales tasks. In the SMB segment, inside sales is often a stand-alone function with few or minimal cross-functional issues. Most enterprise customers already have, for good reasons, a different account-based sales model in place. The same software sold to SMB accounts on a straightforward ROI basis must be integrated into (not substituted for) the enterprise customer's go-to-market model. As one Inside-Sales executive notes, "We learned they wanted us to build a whole new function *in* their current business model."[14] In SMB accounts, the business owner is often the buyer and decision maker: point, click, done! But in enterprise accounts, the decision-making process is more dispersed, and a champion for InsideSales's product must argue for that investment versus other initiatives competing for their share of budgets that are set over one to two years and hard to reset for any one vendor.

These differences shift the basis of the seller's credibility: *from* knowledge of the software product and best practices in stand-alone, inside sales processes *to* knowledge of that enterprise customer's go-to-market model and how the software fits into extant customer-acquisition activities. This means a different way of demonstrating ROI, the ability to shepherd a project—not only a product—through the buying process, and salespeople trained in knowledge about postsale service issues at those customers. Notice that these are differences generated by buying criteria and usage, not core product features.

Differences in Salespeople and Selling Tasks within the Same Firm

This element is especially important when the salesperson *is* a part of the product being bought, as is often the case in professional services like legal services, consulting, and accounting, among others.

The buyers for corporate legal services, for example, vary greatly and typically call law firms after a legal-liability event like being sued, initiating litigation, going public, or raising additional funds. By and large, it is a derived-demand market where it's tough to create new demand—hence, the stereotype of the ambulance-chasing lawyer. Surveys indicate that general counsels at companies employ the following criteria (with various weights) in purchases of outside legal services: (a) Does the attorney have the *expertise* and *experience* for the legal issue we face? (b) Are they *committed* to me as a client? (c) Do I *like* and *trust* this attorney?[15] The "like/trust" or relationship criterion is typically the most difficult to predict and communicate. Yet it is vital because in most situations, the attorney(s) and client must work together closely and in stressful, high-stakes environments.

The managing partner of a leading law firm set out to develop a sales training program for the firm. He interviewed the firm's partners about their business-development practices. The most successful lawyer for corporate development business (IPOs, M&A work, etc.) described how he and others in that department cultivated relationships with financial institutions that resulted in referrals often years later and client engagements where orchestrating multiple legal services was key. By contrast, the most successful tax lawyer focused on referrals from other lawyers in the firm and often provided discount rates to be part of legal work where an area like corporate development was the client manager.

Meanwhile, the head of the firm's real estate department (environmental, permitting, and other legal services for property owners and developers) was a high-fee and high-profit island unto himself. He rarely received or provided referrals from others. Why? He said, "I have very strong relationships with my clients. So if I bring in another lawyer to help with a tax issue, the client still wants me involved to manage the whole thing. I don't like being in the position of having to answer questions in areas where I don't have complete expertise. In the end, it's better for me to avoid these situations since they'll really drain my time." You might say this is a missed cross-selling opportunity. Or you could say that this lawyer truly understands the buying and client-retention criteria in his business and is making the best use of his limited time. What you cannot say, however, is that sales tasks are the same across the firm.

The Sales Tasks Inherent in a Growth Strategy

There are few alternatives to growth for most companies. It's the rare firm whose goal involves getting smaller, and for employees, there is a strong correlation between their company's growth, promotion opportunities, and job satisfaction. A growth strategy must be intentional, clarifying where the growth will come from and what it requires in terms of business development. In recent years, growth has often been treated synonymously and narrowly with product innovation. But a simple matrix developed years ago by Igor Ansoff helps to clarify generic growth options for most firms (see figure 3-1).[16]

Ansoff's point was that growth scenarios generally involve selling the same products to current or new customers, or selling new products to current or new customers. The resulting quadrants have different implications for sales tasks and training emphases. In the upper-left quadrant, the company grows by expanding into new markets or segments with the same products. This was what ScriptLogic and InsideSales.com were doing, and those examples indicate the kinds of tasks

FIGURE 3-1

Generic options in growing a business

Issues: Why? How? Resources?

	Products/services	
	Same	New
Markets/customers — New	Expand into new markets	Explore new types of customers
Markets/customers — Same	Enhance the core	Expand into new products

and training initiatives relevant to that approach. In the lower-left quadrant, growth involves enhancing the core by leveraging what you do in current markets with current products. Here, important tasks typically involve cross-selling, initiatives to increase repeat purchases, ongoing account management skills, and training in price negotiations so that a "value-added bundle" is not just your sales rep's euphemism for a discount.

The right side of the matrix involves different requirements. In the upper-right quadrant, growth means selling new products to new customers. Here, customer discovery skills (see later) and issues discussed in chapters 5, 6, and 7 are important: expertise in customer selection, qualification, coordination between sales and product managers for applications development, and disseminating learning as the sales force gathers information about what works and what doesn't in these new areas. Finally, in the lower-right quadrant, growth means expanding share-of-wallet at current customers with new products or add-on services. This approach often means new buyers and buying processes at current accounts, the ability to leverage reps' existing account relationships in order to get positive access to those buyers, team-selling approaches, and perhaps a different compensation plan.

These are not mutually exclusive growth options, but the options have different implications for sales approach and behaviors. When a company does not pay attention to these differences, the sales force is basically being told to "go forth and multiply" without the relevant training and skills. That's a random bet, not strategy implementation.

Develop the Fundamentals

The next step in getting better training ROI is to focus on core skills and tools that prepare reps for the situations they'll encounter in customer interactions. Here I'll focus on three areas that require training in most sales forces: customer discovery interviews; structuring and conducting sales conversations; and closing a sale.

Customer Discovery Interviews

To sell a product or service usually means asking and answering certain questions. What problems does our product solve? Do prospects view those problems as important? Which potential customers? Who at that customer has that problem? How do they buy? Market research studies, focus groups, and user forums help to address these issues. But visits offer advantages over other techniques, including the ability to understand a usage context in depth at the customer, not at your lab, office, or website. At Intuit, founder Scott Cook supplemented other demand validation techniques with "follow-me-home" customer visits to observe otherwise inaccessible behaviors. Those visits are one of the firm's operating values: "Customers Define Quality."

Especially in B2B contexts, in changing markets, and for new-product initiatives, customer discovery interviews are often part of sales's responsibility. Training should provide reps with skills and guidelines for doing this. Figure 3-2 outlines a useful process for training reps for customer visits.[17]

Set Objectives and the Visit Team. A sure way to do poor visits is to impose too many agendas. Set realistic expectations about the knowledge that can be obtained through customer interviews. A rule of thumb is that effective visits tend to have two or three research objectives. Training should help reps to make these objectives explicit and, depending upon the objectives, who should perhaps participate in the visits besides sales. In general, the people at the seller who will use information from the visits should be there to get direct feedback

FIGURE 3-2

A process for customer visits and interviews

Step 1: Set objectives and the visit team
• Specify the kind of information you want to collect and identify who should participate

Step 2: Develop a discussion guide
• Organize the topics and questions into a sequence and set priorities

Step 3: Conduct the interviews
• Specify roles for team members

Step 4: Debrief and follow up
• Begin a process of analysis and next steps

---

and probe deeper. If the objective relates to product design, engineers should probably participate; if the objective relates to the buying process, then marketing as well as salespeople should be there.

Develop a Discussion Guide. A discussion guide is not a questionnaire. Rather, think of it as a going-in agenda with sequenced topics and conversation starters. It helps for pattern recognition, and patterns are important to guard against the tendency to equate "the market" with what a rep heard at the most recent visit. Because of inevitable time constraints, moreover, the guide can help to prioritize, during the interview, what topic(s) to drop because others are more important.

Conduct the Interviews. The interviews are the main event and require asking useful questions about priority topics. Asking questions is a subtle skill that usually comes with experience, but training can help reps to acquire that skill or at least avoid common mistakes. For example, new reps usually need to get beyond "what keeps you up at night" types of questions that rarely yield useful information. Conversely, many reps often ask leading questions ("Don't you think that X is the emerging standard?") that undercut the purpose of interviews: to get the customer's beliefs and perceptions, not confirm your own ideas. "What features would you like in this product?" may sound like a reasonable question, but it tends to produce open-ended wish lists.

Instead, focus questions on what prospects are trying to accomplish in a given context and the obstacles or opportunities they encounter in doing so. Cindy Alvarez, a consultant who has helped many firms to plan a program of visits, makes an important distinction: "Customer development isn't asking customers what they want; it's seeking to understand what they need, how they work, where their pain points and highest priorities are. Customers may not be able to articulate what they want, but they can't hide what they need."[18] In other words, the goal is to become familiar with the customer's task demands as a basis for *your* choices about product design, value proposition, target buyers, and pricing.

That last issue is especially important for sales training to clarify. "How much would you be willing to pay?" is *not* a good topic for customer visits. Reps may be speaking to *users* in the customer organization, not *deciders* with budgets and purchasing authority. Further, market research repeatedly uncovers big differences between what people *say* they are willing to pay and their actual purchase behavior. A continuing example is espoused willingness to pay for green products versus actual behavior in those categories. By focusing on tasks that users must complete, how current solutions are utilized by customers, and the underlying needs behind them, you can begin to make inferences about the potential value you provide. But you must ultimately test it in the marketplace, not in interviews, and we will discuss that in the chapters on pricing.

Debrief and Follow Up. A final and often overlooked step is to debrief while impressions are still fresh. A customer visit can yield many insights, but making sense of information does not occur automatically. Devote time to considering the implications for going-forward behaviors by salespeople and others. A debrief provides a forum to discuss how to do this in a way that increases organizational learning. It is also important to provide closure for salespeople. What will you start, stop, continue, or do differently as a result of the visits: About the product? About other aspects of your go-to-market approach? About whether or not you should do any more customer discovery visits?

Structuring and Conducting Sales Conversations

Customer discovery is about understanding what and to whom you are selling. Conversations with particular prospects are where sales do or don't happen. Training should help reps make the best use of the limited time they have in sales conversations. As outlined in figure 3-3, these interactions have multiple dimensions: context, content, and contact.

Context. This dimension, which is about setting the stage, is often overlooked. The result is that the prospect may expect a conversation about X, while the salesperson talks about Y. Or, even worse, the salesperson begins a call with an unfocused PowerPoint presentation about his company and its products. Selling varies by company, but across firms, setting context is

FIGURE 3-3

Structuring sales conversations: A road map

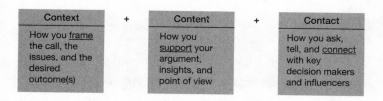

a core skill and should not be taken for granted. What starts well has a higher probability of ending well. A useful tool for establishing context is what David Mattson of Sandler Training calls the "up-front contract," which has the following elements:[19]

Purpose. Make sure that buyer and seller are on the same page about the purpose and desired outcomes of that call. The rep may be clear about this because they have thought about this call for days or weeks. But whatever else they are, buyers are not mind readers. Train reps in setting and articulating a purpose for each sales conversation, especially when there are new people at a given call.

Time. Confirm the time actually available for the call. Most sales calls are not like pitches or speeches at a conference, with preset times that stay set. Most buyers are time-constrained and subject to fires going on in their workplaces. Confirming the real time available up front signals your respect for the buyer's time and helps the seller to set priorities for discussion in that call.

Buyer's agenda. Ask the buyer what topics they want to hear about and any questions they have that you want to make sure are answered. As Mattson notes, "The prospect looks at their watch 15–20 minutes into the call and says, 'this is interesting, would you put this in writing and send it to us? We'll review it and get back to you.' That may sound like a good future, but it's really a stall." Clarifying the buyer's agenda up front helps a good seller to respond to those items throughout the time available.

Seller's agenda. Let the buyer know what you are going to ask. This allows the buyer to think about their

answers and not be surprised, and increases the likelihood of having a true conversation.

Outcome(s). Tell the buyer what you'd like to accomplish by the end of that call. It may be a purchase order,
another meeting, or a demo where others from that
customer are present. But if it is a call on a qualified
prospect, then the conversation should move toward
some commitment to constructive follow-up action and
next steps.

Content. This dimension requires a salesperson to think
through what she wants customers to know, beyond what
they already know, about the product, the seller, and the data,
referrals, or other information relevant to supporting her messages. As noted earlier, relevant content varies by new customer versus established customer, initial product sale versus
add-on services or cross-selling, and so on. Training should
educate reps about these differences in your target segments,
provide the appropriate collateral, and (via feedback from the
sales force) keep the organization up to date with what does
resonate with prospects and installed-base accounts.

Contact. This dimension refers to what a rep must learn to do
and to communicate, verbally and nonverbally, in their interactions throughout a sales conversation. It's core to the art
of selling, and contact skills depend on context. But virtually
every discussion of selling you have heard, and will hear, will
rightly stress the importance of active listening. This skill is
rarely innate and must be developed.

On average, people talk at about two hundred words per
minute but can process three hundred to five hundred words
per minute. As a result, listening easily becomes waiting to
talk and present prepackaged information. At a dinner party,

FIGURE 3-4

Some behavioral protocols for active listening

Dos	Don'ts
• Keep mouth shut, ears open	• Interrupt constantly
• Affirm nonverbally	• Tune out or shut down
• Acknowledge their issues	• Shift conversation to self
• Paraphrase/clarify your understanding of what you heard—explicitly, implicitly	• Present "the solution" before you clarify *their* perception(s) of "the problem"/opportunity
• Ask questions, and learn to use words like "and" (vs. "but"), "you/we" (vs. "I/they")	• Evaluate too fast or critique the idea (or the person)

this may be annoying. In sales, this is a missed opportunity to hear and respond to information about the buyer, the company, the competition, or changing usage needs. The hopes, quotas, and product biases that salespeople bring to the interaction can also make it harder to hear what a customer is saying, what questions are relevant to unpacking their needs or doubts, and response(s) required. Figure 3-4 outlines some simple but important dos and don'ts for active listening during sales calls.

Active listening earns a rep the right to be right and to be heard. In turn, training initiatives should develop salespeople's ability to understand and, in the give-and-take of sales conversations, execute the wisdom in the old aphorism, "Never miss a good opportunity to shut up."

Closing a Sale

In pop culture, Alec Baldwin's performance as a tyrannical sales manager in the film version of David Mamet's *Glengarry Glen Ross* popularized the phrase "always be closing." Closing is vital, and many business developers, confusing a good conversation with a successful sales call, fail to get the order. But in the film and many training initiatives, closing is treated as a seller-centric activity and asking for the order at the end of the call. Research about how people make purchase decisions indicates otherwise.[20]

Recall from chapter 1 how more buyers now work their way through parallel streams as they explore, evaluate, and engage with sellers via websites, white papers, social media, and user forums. As a result, the end of a sales call is typically the *worst* time to handle objections in an attempt to close the sale. Prospects have usually been contemplating their potential objections long before a climactic close and, when reluctant, will often cite a socially acceptable rationale such as price, which may not be the real barrier to buying. To deal with this reality, training needs to reflect what research indicates about closing: small incremental commitments lead to larger ones.

A decision to alter behavior is not simply made in response to a persuasive or good ROI message, but *throughout* a persuasive message. When a prospect makes a significant buying decision (versus an impulse purchase), that decision comprises a series of previous actions that prompt the final commitment to purchase. The positive decision may be revealed at the close of the sales conversation, but it must be cultivated throughout the conversation and customer journey.

This is a difference that makes a difference. Most sales training, like Baldwin's sales manager, treats closing as the time to increase the sense of urgency and push buyers "over the goal line." Reps are taught to listen for phrases such as "that makes sense" or "that's a valid point" or nonverbal signals such as head nods as markers for a propitious time to ask for the order. Often, however, this is the first time the seller has asked the prospect to make a substantial commitment and it is a bridge too far. This approach also confuses very different aspects of buyer decision making. Cues such as head nods or "good point" only mean the prospect comprehends the message. They are analogous to the conversational *si* in Spanish and other languages that means "I hear you," *not* "I agree with you."

Successful closing requires more than comprehension and agreement; it requires commitment to behavioral action, and incremental commitments are vital. As a general rule, the earlier a rep can identify objections and gather commitment to small tests or other actions, the more likely the sale will occur. An incremental approach allows reps to get more information sooner from prospects and better evaluate opportunities. Conversely, if a prospect has a doubt or objection before a closing discussion, the party unaware of this is the salesperson, and that's a big disadvantage. Effective closing is the consummation of previous commitments made by the prospect, not a high-pressure response to the seller.

Reps must be taught how to be appropriately proactive and intentional in framing and securing those incremental actions, and this has implications beyond training. For example, sellers at a firm that provides complex technical services to telecom companies were spending nine to twelve months of a twenty-four- to thirty-month selling cycle in proof-of-concept meetings with multiple groups at the customer—a big sunk cost if the sale was not closed. By instituting smaller, different requests earlier in the process, and by scheduling demos at various parts of their buyers' journeys, salespeople decreased the selling cycle by six to twelve months, increased close rates, and freed up more time for calling on other prospects.

New tools make it possible to treat incremental commitments as a measurable sales activity. Services from firms like DocSend, Showpad, and others allow reps to send materials to prospects and observe how they engage (or not) with the content. Does the prospect look at the price list? Do they forward the proposal or other documents to others in the buying unit?

Which collateral or trial offers do and do not generate action? This helps, much more than bland assent in a conversation, to pinpoint where incremental commitments can be best located. Do not treat closing as the last step in a sales call. Instead, train salespeople to always be closing throughout the call via incremental commitments.

Training When It Matters Most

Traditional classroom-type training has its place, but an effective training approach should increase your team's productivity, not take net time away from productive selling activities. Buying processes require more firms to provide just-in-time training when and where it matters most to reps, who benefit from additional training in time frames connected to actual buying processes.

Technologies can help companies provide training when it matters most by providing reps with timely access to information and in formats that increase comprehension. With traditional classroom training, reps typically remember little of the information a week later, but when video is added, retention of information increases more than sixfold. Here is an example of how one company incorporates just-in-time technology into sales training before, during, and after sales calls.

Pacific Life Insurance, which sells insurance, retirement products, and mutual funds to financial advisers via its field wholesaler sales force, now uses video coaching. Wholesalers record and share practice pitches with regional sales managers (RSMs), who provide feedback from their mobile devices when those reps need it. This allows Pacific Life to leverage a scarce resource—face time with advisers—and disseminate best practices faster and with more impact. Each wholesaler must articulate a positioning statement for a particular investment product via a five-minute video. RSMs then select the best videos and use them as examples of engaging sales presentations. This helps the wholesalers refine, rather than improvise, their presentations during sales conversations and increases the consistency of messages, while accelerating a continuous improvement dynamic in the sales organization.

Pacific Life also faces a common challenge in twenty-first-century sales management: how to effectively coach a geographically dispersed sales force while minimizing time out of the field for that feedback. Mobile video coaching has allowed its RSMs to coach wholesalers (who often work out of their homes at far distances from the RSM) without needing to be in the same time zone. It also enables these sales managers to identify potential weaknesses and improve wholesalers' skills, rather than having them practice these skills on advisers.

Good training is not reducible to a YouTube video or snappy TED talk, and managers who can't or won't do the coaching and other performance management practices discussed in the next chapter will be ineffective regardless of the technology they employ. But companies already spend a ton on sales training. The impact of that investment resides in how you spend that time and money, and technology can enable training when it matters most.

Linking Hiring and Training

Throughout this chapter, I have emphasized that because markets and sales tasks change, ongoing training is important. But it is difficult to train and develop someone who is a poor fit for the job in the first place. Hiring and training are linked in their impacts on performance. Yet these activities are often managed in separate silos that inhibit growth, for the company and the salesperson.

Hiring is typically done by the frontline sales manager, while training is handled by HR, learning and development, or a corporate training center, which, to amortize costs, adopts what accountants call a peanut-butter approach that "spreads" a uniform training curriculum across diverse markets, segments, and distinct sales tasks. Further, common practice increases training budgets when sales are good and cuts them when sales decline. This approach makes it hard to determine cause and effect, and inhibits scaling as a market develops and buying criteria change. Conversely, linking recruiting, hiring, and training processes can support growth and help to build a sales team for long-term success.

Splunk, a B2B software firm, is a case in point.[21] Founded in 2003, Splunk was among the first companies to target the big data space. It had no track record to point to when recruiting talent and, in fact, no recognized industry to point to. During its critical early years, there was a classic internal debate about allocating time and resources to recruitment and training versus R&D, trade shows, and other tasks competing for scarce cash. This situation necessitated a creative approach to recruiting, hiring, and training as Splunk scaled.

"For recruitment," says Bart Fanelli, Splunk's vice president of global field success, "we set our sights on talent from companies already operating at the level we wanted to operate at . . . If you're a $50 million company and your goal is to grow to $250 million, consider targeting hires from firms at that level." To do that, you must make recruitment and hiring an ongoing part of the sales management culture. Splunk adopted many of the principles explained in chapter 2 about hiring. It complemented an individual manager's assessment of a candidate with multiple interviews with diverse people (to offset the cloning bias); it established a structured interviewing and evaluation process (so comparisons could be made across common factors); and it emphasized behavioral criteria in skills assessments supported by simulations, onboarding programs, and other means (because gut feel does not scale).

Splunk developed profiles that specified desired skills and capabilities for each sales role, while establishing certain behavioral elements that, in management's view, were important across roles. For a field sales position, for example, Splunk specified skills that managers could look for and discuss in the applicant's work history during interviews—for example, forecast accuracy, messages and experience in relevant market segments, and other categories. Behavioral elements refer to on-the-job choices that people make. Do they interact with others without giving a sense of being entitled to special treatment? Do they work hard without being offensive or disruptive in a negative way with others? Fanelli notes, "We believe both types of screening criteria—skills applicable to the specific job and culturally compatible behaviors that we seek in all of our people—are equally important. We all own the culture and I don't believe that any company can make a habit of hiring brilliant jerks." Processes like this also help to develop the right mindset and expectations. There are only a finite number of great people available in any market, but effective and repeatable recruitment and training practices create a multiplier effect: a network of good hires generates referrals to more good hires.

As Splunk grew, these profiles were updated, refined, and became the focus of quarterly reviews with sales managers. After hiring, sales managers were also accountable for coaching and developing their people based on the elements in the profile. Many companies, as Fanelli puts it, "reduce their field of vision by following a hire-and-forget approach. Our assumption is that if we understand our business, if we get and keep the profiles right and if we execute the process consistently, we will succeed. The quarterly reviews help to prevent the common scenario where down the road management is sweeping up broken glass due to performance or interpersonal behaviors."

Any sales force is composed of people with different temperaments, capabilities, and learning styles. Effective training addresses that heterogeneity if you control what you can control. At Splunk, as Fanelli explains, "we kept a certain leader-to-contributor ratio in mind to make sure the first-line sales manager can train on the desired skills. We tracked this quarterly, looking at training and coaching with the same attention that we use to review the [sales] numbers because the effectiveness of our first-line leaders is the gateway to the performance we want to see in sales outcomes." This review cadence helped to drive training and coaching up the chain and make it an ongoing developmental tool. According to Fanelli, "The first-line review process connects quarterly to every manager in the field. The second-line review (a review of those who manage and review the first-line managers) focuses on a broader set of skills, happens annually, and goes into more depth than the quarterly process."

⊕ QUESTIONS TO ASK . . . AND ANSWER

Splunk uses a variety of good practices that helped it to scale in its market. But markets are different, strategies vary, and so should specific practices in hiring and training. It's not the customer's responsibility to make selling easy; it's the job of effective training to help align selling skills with actual buying behavior in your market. Evaluate your company's investment in training by answering the questions in table 3-1.

TABLE 3-1

A sales training diagnostic

In our company, how well do we . . .

Train for key sales tasks as reflected in buying processes at our target customers, by segment?	1 2 3 4 5 6 7
Know and use learning research in our training and development efforts?	1 2 3 4 5 6 7
Link training to our account planning process, win/loss analyses, and performance reviews?	1 2 3 4 5 6 7
Make sure we develop and maintain core interview, questioning, and listening skills in sales training?	1 2 3 4 5 6 7
Understand the impact of any changes in our product, target buyers, or growth initiatives for selling skills?	1 2 3 4 5 6 7
Use technology to provide training and coaching when it matters most to our salespeople?	1 2 3 4 5 6 7
Understand the limits of any selling methodology we use and monitor its relevance to changing objectives?	1 2 3 4 5 6 7
Reflect what we know about relevant training and development in our sales hiring criteria?	1 2 3 4 5 6 7

Developing people is complex, and therefore you may find in dialogue with colleagues that there are not clear, unambiguous answers or ratings to these questions in particular. But that doesn't mean that all answers, and responses in areas where you do find gaps, are equally good. Training and development require time and resources, not just a speech at an offsite seminar. Your company must be worthy of talent by making recruiting, hiring, and training a real priority in daily practice. As Aristotle said a long time ago, "Excellence is a habit." In addition to the right people and developmental initiatives, you also need repeatable performance management practices, which are the focus of the next chapter.

4

PERFORMANCE MANAGEMENT AND COACHING

The venerable maxim still applies: "People join companies, but they leave managers," because performance feedback and coaching are crucial for professional growth and development. Throughout my career, I've been struck by how many successful people, when asked about pivotal incidents in their careers, point to a manager who provided them with useful—even if initially unwanted—feedback. In turn, they come to realize that, as managers, they must demonstrate that they care about their people and are worthy of trust in assessing performance.

People's level of motivation is largely the result of how they are managed. Especially in sales, *how* you allocate and manage resources and people often has more impact than *how many* resources you allocate. The problem is that many performance management practices are flawed or misused. Most companies rely on ad hoc appraisal processes and don't make performance feedback relevant to the unique needs of their sales reps.

To get results, you need the capabilities that we'll cover in this chapter: the right tools and criteria for diagnosing performance, and managers who coach their people on an ongoing basis.

Problems with Performance Appraisals

Dissatisfaction with performance appraisals is ubiquitous across industries. They are routinely seen as time consuming, demotivating, inaccurate, biased, and unfair—like the quip authors make about literary critics: "no more than prejudice made plausible."

These perceptions are shared by managers and the people those managers appraise. A global survey by McKinsey indicates that most CEOs don't find the performance management process in their companies helpful in identifying top performers, while over half of their employees think their managers don't get the performance review right. A Gallup study is even more negative: just one in five employees surveyed agreed that their company's performance management practices motivated them.[1]

These attitudes create a self-reinforcing dynamic. Managers do cursory reviews that are really up or down compensation announcements, not helpful feedback. Employees then see the "appraisal" as nonexistent or unfair, and they approach the next annual review with that attitude. Managers (especially sales managers facing monthly or quarterly goals) then try to avoid the unpleasantness and potential disruption to sales cadence and do even more cursory, quickie, drive-by reviews . . . and so on in a downward spiral that promotes a culture of underperformance.

Another result is a recurrent tradition in business commentary: the annual articles by management pundits advocating the abandonment of appraisals and even feedback to employees about their performance. As the authors of an HBR article on the topic put it, "Telling people what we think of their performance doesn't help them thrive and excel, and telling people how we think they should improve actually *hinders* learning."[2] Well, no one ever suggested Socrates would have made a good sales manager. Maybe it's the examined life that is not worth living?

Indeed, some companies have done away with performance ratings altogether. But the reality, as two experienced consultants note, is that when "organizations scrapped the performance ratings, they found a need for a form of annual documented administrative evaluation to make employment decisions, such as promotions and raises. To address this need, these organizations often implemented 'ghost' ratings—a system of evaluation that is, ultimately, just another annual performance rating."[3] In other words, meet the new boss, same as the old boss.

Rethinking Performance Appraisals

Performance appraisals clearly need rethinking. A good place to begin is with some commonly held but erroneous assumptions.

Peter Cappelli and Martin Conyon examined seven years of appraisal data from a large US company. Contrary to conventional wisdom that everyone gets an above-average score, appraisal ratings varied a lot across individuals. There was a slight upward bias in appraisals, but there were more poor scores than excellent ratings. Managers can and do make distinctions. This research also found that managers reflect those distinctions in pay and promotion recommendations: the best performers got the best bonuses and were more likely to get promoted, while the worst were more likely to get fired.

When they looked at employees' actual performance outcomes, Cappelli and Conyon found little evidence that good performers in one year would be good performers the following year. Performance varied, meaning that ongoing appraisals are important, as are performance management practices that recognize this variability over time. The notion that there's an inherent consistency in A, B, and C players and that an individual's appraisal score and performance in a given year should be the basis for long-term outcomes—as, for instance, in some forced-ranking systems—has no support in this research. This study has the value of being an empirical study of actual use by managers of performance appraisals, not just attitudinal surveys of perceptions. As Cappelli emphasizes, "If you're sure that performance appraisals at your own company don't work, you ought to look at your own long-term data to make sure."[4] It may be that, for better or worse, your appraisal practices are working as intended.

Overt performance feedback is needed in contemporary organizations. As sales jobs—like many jobs in twenty-first-century organizations—become more intertwined with other functional activities, there are fewer natural and immediate sources of feedback about whether you are doing the right things as part of that interdependent chain of activities. Sales outcomes are a lagging indicator and, as we'll see later in discussing the uses of data in analyzing sales performance, outcomes are susceptible to multiple interpretations, only some of which are empirically true in your sales context. You want your people focused on the correct causal relationships and not just enacting the natural human tendency to ascribe credit for good outcomes to oneself and the causes of bad outcomes to someone or something else.

Also, notice what happens in the absence of feedback. Many people will assume that no news is good news. If managers are not clear about priorities, people in effect create their own priorities, spending time and effort in areas and activities that have an ad hoc, hit-and-miss relationship to performance. Many reps in most sales organizations have assumptions unsupported by the facts in their market: for example, prospects will buy only if I have the lowest price; it's impolite to ask a lot of questions, and so on. Moreover, the use of "ghost ratings" in place of appraisals raises ethical issues as well as inefficiencies. When budget constraints make cuts necessary, it's the poorly rated ghosts who feel mugged and legitimately aggrieved. Finally, if you do agree that people seek recognition and meaning as well as money in their jobs, absence of feedback inhibits that as well.

Contrary to blithe prescriptions to abolish appraisals, performance feedback—"telling people what we think of their performance [and] how we think they should improve"—is *more* important than ever. Rethinking performance appraisals should not mean getting rid of this essential managerial responsibility. Fewer touchpoints between managers and their people are not the answer. But to provide useful feedback, you first need to have, and know how to use, performance data.

Data Analysis and Performance Diagnoses

The purpose of appraisals and coaching is twofold: an accurate and actionable evaluation of performance, and then development of that person's skills in line with sales tasks.

Any appraisal ultimately relies on the data and metrics used. Most firms focus solely on sales volume, but that is a deceptive measure of profitability and value creation in many businesses. Top-line growth is good for firms with high returns on invested capital (ROIC), neutral for firms with returns equal to their cost of capital, and *bad* for firms with returns below their cost of capital. As I've discussed elsewhere, selling in negative

ROIC situations only accelerates the destruction of value in an enterprise, and this confusion about the dynamics of sales revenue and value is reflected in companies' financials and valuations.[5] Further, many managers rationalize this confusion with justifications that ignore opportunity costs, the differences between accounting profit and return on capital, and other factors that contribute to the sunk-cost fallacy: throwing good money after bad. Selling is then like the situation in the old antiwar folk song: "We were knee-deep in the Big Muddy, But the big fool said to push on."

Sales is undergoing a sustained data revolution. Among other things, sales managers now receive more scrutiny from other executives with access to that data. AI and big data groups of various kinds are, more often than not, reporting up through the finance function in firms. With that data, finance executives ask questions about their companies' big investments in sales, and sales managers must have answers that understand the difference between volume and value.

Similarly, sales operations groups that apply analytics to sales processes are the primary users of many new data tools and often staffed by people with finance backgrounds. By 2018 at Dunkin' Brands Group, forty people in a function called financial planning and analysis (FP&A) worked on projects involving customer acquisition and retention. The CFO (who ran FP&A before becoming CFO) notes that "we stick our hands in absolutely everything." At internet domain seller GoDaddy, a similar function focuses on analyzing performance metrics and reallocating marketing and sales spending. Sales ops is widely established as a dedicated function in the tech industry and others.[6] Meanwhile, the Association for Finance Professionals offers credentialing programs in FP&A, and thousands enroll annually.

The good news is that more data means more transparency. In many firms, sales has long been treated as a black box—essential for meeting quarterly revenue targets, but hermetically sealed off from other parts of the business. Many sales leaders like it that way, but those days are passing. The tools available for tracking conversion and other sales activities mean more continuous improvement opportunities, and the scrutiny generates more incentive to improve performance practices.

The bad news is how the tools are often used. Tools are only as good as their makers and users. Many sales leaders understand activities that drive the top line in their firms, but not financial aspects of selling beyond sales volume. Finance executives rightly demand value creation from sales leaders and not only top-line motion, but many in finance are inexperienced with how sales actually works. It's a dialogue that rarely happens. The resulting use of data often enacts the statistician's joke about the drunk under the lamppost. One night, you see an inebriated man searching for his car keys under the lone lamppost on a street. You want to help and ask, "Where did you drop your keys?" He says, "About two blocks back there." "Then why are you looking here?" "Because this is where the light is."

Consider how much commentary about sales, and performance reviews, essentially does this: focus on data factoids independent of context. Technologies now enable companies to measure almost anything, which leads many managers to try to measure everything. The resulting proliferation of metrics produces immaterial key performance indicators (KPIs) that dilute the focus of employees, and salespeople get lost in the day-to-day noise. HR studies regularly find companies emphasizing in their performance appraisals KPIs that account for less than 5–10 percent of outcomes in that job.[7]

Perhaps worse is the belief that the algorithm is the answer. This is often the overt or implied message, and it's no coincidence that AI and big data have for years risen steadily on

Gartner's "Hype Cycle for Emerging Technologies."[8] Software analytics are increasing in scope as well as accessibility via cloud computing. When you see a machine beat a chess grand-master, you may be tempted to echo Ken Jennings's comment after he was defeated on *Jeopardy!* by the IBM Watson pro-gram: "I for one welcome our new computer overlords." I per-sonally find most impressive an AI bot called Pluribus that, in Texas Hold'em games with star poker players, not only won but also *bluffed* better than the human players.[9]

But data, even self-correcting data as in some AI programs, is never the same as the answer to a management issue. Peter Drucker in an article aptly titled, "The Manager and the Moron," emphasized this: "The computer makes no decisions; it only carries out orders. It's a total moron, and therein lies its strength. It forces us to think, to set the criteria."[10] As Picasso allegedly said, "Computers are useless; they only provide answers." Billy Bean—the dean of data analytics in sports—makes the same point. There has always been lots of data in baseball, but do you have good questions to ask of the data? Bean notes that baseball statistics (like sales outcomes) "are accomplishments of men in combination with their circum-stances . . . I do not start with the numbers any more than a mechanic starts with a monkey wrench. I start with the game, with the things that I see there and the things that people say there. And I ask: is it true? Can you validate it? How does it fit with the rest of the machinery."[11]

Context matters in diagnosing and evaluating performance. Figure 4-1 provides an example. On the vertical axis is a sales-person's close rate, a measure of wins. Think of the horizontal line in the matrix as the average or median close rate in your sales force; those in the upper-left quadrant close at superior rates, and those in the lower-left quadrant at inferior rates. On the horizontal axis is how much is sold when a rep closes a sale: the amount of sales volume or, if you have a subscription

FIGURE 4-1

Data analysis: Hypotheses vs. answers

How much is the person? The market? Incentives?

Penetration: Sales or ARR per account

	Low	High
Close rate — High	Too few leads or demos? Not enough proposals? Pricing?	Good salesperson? Great leads? Market conditions?
Close rate — Low	Ineffective salesperson? Unmotivated salesperson? Unfocused salesperson: too many leads, calls, etc.?	Selective salesperson? Nature of the leads? A few windfall accounts?

sales model, the annual recurring revenue (ARR) per account. Those in the upper-right quadrant have high top-line or ARR numbers, and those in the upper-left quadrant perform poorly on those metrics.

Consider people in the upper-right quadrant: the data tells us they close at superior rates and sell a lot when they close. One possibility is that they are very good salespeople: the high-performing stars that, as we discussed in chapter 2, drive the 80:20 rule in many sales organizations. On the other hand, these may be reps who, in effect, have won the lottery in receiving leads that are more likely to close at high ARR, or they may be selling in especially favorable market conditions—for example, in a geographical or vertical segment where you currently have little competition or a better product. Conversely, those in the lower-left quadrant are poor performers on both of these metrics. They may be ineffective reps, either because they're a poor fit for our sales tasks or just inexperienced and still coming down the learning curve. Or they may be unmotivated salespeople because caps in the comp plan provide little incentive for them to do more than they already have done. Or they may be unfocused salespeople pursuing too many leads and making many calls on poorly qualified prospects that no one can close.

Now consider the upper-left quadrant: high close rates but low sales or ARR per account might be a function of the rep's prospecting, demo, and other activities. Or it may be tied to pricing: many subscription pricing models, for instance, generate these sales outcomes with low-entry prices. Finally, look at the lower-right quadrant: low close rates but high sales or ARR per account might, again, be the result of the salesperson's selective pursuit of opportunities, or the nature of the leads allocated to that rep, or simply a result of a few big windfall wins that quarter or that year.

The point here is not a version of "everything is relative" or that data and outcomes don't matter. The point is that outcome data is susceptible to multiple interpretations. The data provides hypotheses, not answers, and you won't know which interpretation is more behaviorally accurate just by looking at the data. In business, interpreting data is not only a search for approximate truth. It's also about actionable dialogue with the people who use and receive that data. To diagnose and improve performance, you must place the data in context in order to understand how much is the person, the market, incentive systems, or other factors that you can control, alter, or mitigate. Then, you must link that diagnosis to behaviors relevant to that salesperson, which is what good sales coaching does.

Sales Coaching

Most of us believe that we are above-average drivers, but we're not. The same is true with coaching.

A study gathered data from over 3,700 managers (across functions) who assessed their own coaching skills and then asked others to assess these managers as coaches. About one in four (24 percent) of the managers significantly overrated their coaching effectiveness. Not only were they not as skilled in this activity as they thought, they were way below average, reaching only the thirty-second percentile or in the bottom third.[12] Sales managers also overestimate the time they actually devote to coaching their people. Sandler Training finds that only 15 percent of sales managers spend as much as 25 percent of their time on coaching.[13]

One reason for this gap between self-perception and reality is that many sales managers believe coaching is about sitting down with a rep to examine sales results and discuss pending deals. It takes more than that.

Another reason is that few people are willing to admit they don't really know how to give developmental feedback that is focused on behaviors and actionable options versus "get better" exhortations. But this is a trainable managerial skill. In fact, after training, managers recognize this and decrease their initial assessment of themselves as coaches by almost 30 percent.[14]

What does effective coaching look like in sales? Any sales organization comprises people with different capabilities and approaches. A manager must adapt feedback to individuals and their behaviors in relation to important tasks in that sales model. Coaching is about clarifying the relevant behaviors and diagnosing whether the issue is motivation or ability. Some reps may work hard, but lack certain capabilities: Can training enhance those skills? Others demonstrate capability but seemingly lack motivation or effort: Are their abilities better utilized in a different role, or is there an incentive that increases smart effort in their current role? Let's consider an example and the implications.

Sales Coaching in Action

ZenRecruit (disguised name) sells recruiting software to SMBs that helps those firms attract prospective hires and organize the hiring process.[15] Its product has three categories of features: (a) candidate attract features that include the ability to publish and monitor social media messages with prospective hires; (b) candidate nurture features that enable companies to keep candidates "warm" until they enter the job market (e.g., a high-quality product manager might not be currently looking for a new opportunity, but the recruiter could add that person to a sequence of emails or blogs tailored toward maintaining the relationship); and (c) candidate hire features that organize hiring information into a single digital record and workflow across the relevant hiring and onboarding people at ZenRecruit's customers. Pricing is based on the number of applicant contacts the customer maintained on the software: $200 per month for 100 contacts to $2,000 per month for 100,000 or more contacts, with an average price of $750 per month per customer.

ZenRecruit used an inside-sales model. Most leads were generated by content marketing, search engine marketing, paid media, retargeting, and email marketing—all directing prospects to ZenRecruit's website. Visitors who clicked on the site were brought to a page explaining that a ZenRecruit rep would reach out and schedule a demo if they provided their name, company name, email, phone number, number of employees, and number of hires planned for the next twelve months. Leads that matched ZenRecruit's target customer profile were allocated in a round-robin fashion across the sales team. Then, the sales tasks were the following:

- **Contact.** When a rep received a qualified lead, the rep contacted the prospect and tried to schedule a time for a more in-depth conversation about their hiring needs and practices.

- **Discovery call.** Here, the rep asked questions about the recruiting process at that prospect company—for example, how the company attracts hires, results of current recruiting tactics, which roles they needed to fill, and so on.

- **Demo.** If, after the discovery call, the rep believed the prospect was a fit for ZenRecruit's product, the rep scheduled an online demo that typically took about an hour. In preparation, the rep was expected to tailor the demo to that prospect's industry and hiring needs. For example, if the demo was with a VP of engineering, the rep would personalize the product demo with social media communities where engineers congregated, case studies of other successful engineering recruiting processes with ZenRecruit, and a cadence of relevant email messages.

- **Trial.** If, after the demo, the prospect decided ZenRecruit's product was a fit for their company's hiring needs, there was typically a thirty-day free trial, either because the buyer requested a trial or the rep suggested it. The rep recommended actions the buyer should take during the trial and was expected to check in periodically throughout the thirty-day period.

- **Proposal.** After either the demo or trial, the rep sent a formal proposal, recapping the hiring challenges and opportunities at that buyer, how ZenRecruit's product could help, and pricing.

- **Follow-up and close.** After the prospect had an opportunity to review the proposal, the rep answered any questions about price, terms of use, and other issues. Price negotiations were common, but all discounts had to be approved by ZenRecruit's sales manager.

The average length of the selling cycle, from lead creation to close, was about five weeks at the time of the case study. As in most subscription sales models, ZenRecruit reps had both monthly and ARR targets; they had to generate $4,500 of new monthly recurring revenue in order to receive the full portion of their compensation, including variable pay tied to quota attainment. As in nearly all sales organizations, moreover, not every rep made quota, but the reasons differed.

In the case of one rep, the data indicates a problem with prospecting: the rep's contacts are significantly below the number for others in the sales force (see figure 4-2). A common cause of prospecting issues is the salesperson who spends too much time on unqualified opportunities. Coaching here can usefully focus on better customer-selection criteria. Other behaviors that often dilute prospecting are time management issues, especially in call-intensive inside-sales models. Coaching and follow-up should then focus on setting a cadence

FIGURE 4-2

Prospecting issues

Not enough contacts

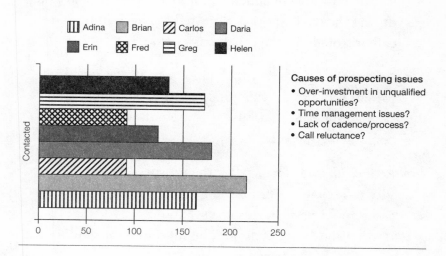

Causes of prospecting issues
- Over-investment in unqualified opportunities?
- Time management issues?
- Lack of cadence/process?
- Call reluctance?

of calls and perhaps metrics to monitor that cadence daily, weekly, or monthly. A surprising number of reps are reluctant to make cold calls, or in inside-sales models, they abandon contact attempts prematurely—for example, after three or four attempts when it typically takes six or more attempts to reach prospects who have indicated potential interest by going to the website and providing the requested information. Here, coaching needs to make clear the realities of customer contact in the market and confront a tough judgment: Is this rep a good fit for this sales model?

A second rep, by contrast, did not have an issue with prospecting. Indeed, contacts and the number of demos she conducted were significantly above the average number for the sales force. But she had a low conversion rate from contact and demo to interest and trial (see figure 4-3). Here, the issue is not effort, but questions about relevant skills. Is this rep building trust and credibility on the initial contact and during the demo? Coach-

FIGURE 4-3

Opportunity-creation issues

Many contacts and demos but low conversion from demo to trial

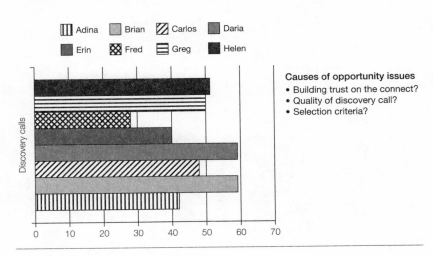

ing might involve having this rep listen to other reps who do have high conversion rates. Or the rep might not be conducting discovery calls in sufficient depth (the manager can listen and coach the rep on questioning techniques and product features to emphasize with prospects). In turn, contact and discovery-call deficiencies might result in poor selection criteria and a downward spiral in sales performance. This rep is perhaps making too many calls and conducting too many demos with poorly qualified or tepidly interested prospects, and as a result, the time spent on those one-hour demos leaves less time for good contact and in-depth discovery calls, and so on. Sales performance issues at any point in customer conversion are typically intertwined, and coaching is about breaking this Gordian knot with behaviorally appropriate advice geared to that individual.

A third rep had a common sales problem. This is the rep whose behaviors and numbers are exemplary at each stage of the selling cycle except the crucial one—closing the sale (see figure 4-4). Poor close rates often involve a failure to develop the right sense of purchase urgency; coaching for this rep should

FIGURE 4-4

Closing issues

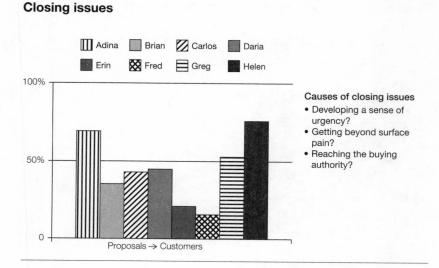

Causes of closing issues
- Developing a sense of urgency?
- Getting beyond surface pain?
- Reaching the buying authority?

focus on articulating the total value proposition and how various product features translate into customer ROI. Closing issues also often have their root causes earlier in the selling cycle; this rep might not have gotten beyond surface needs in their discovery calls and therefore in the proposals sent to prospects. Coaching can correct this and also help the rep conduct appropriate follow-up with prospects during the free-trial period. A third cause, on the other hand, might be a failure to reach the right buying authority. In other words, the rep might be doing all the right things but with the wrong person—someone who lacks a budget and actual purchase authority. Coaching here should focus on how to help this rep get the right people at prospects to attend demos and provide input for proposals.

With a round-robin method of allocating leads, it's unlikely that the variation in performance is due to some reps getting better leads. That may be true on any given day, but as in a baseball season, the good and bad luck is likely to even out. The performance issues differ by rep and in terms of sales tasks, raising distinct questions and improvement initiatives relevant to each rep. A one-size-fits-all approach, or a focus limited to outcomes, will not be effective and can be counterproductive. Overly general feedback increases feelings of defensiveness, rather than openness to behavior change, because it involves broad and unfocused judgments. Good coaching helps to clarify the differences inherent in any sales force and lets both manager and rep then concentrate on behaviors that *can* be improved.

Peer Coaching

Coaching is not only what managers do in diagnosing and supporting individual salespeople. Because much learning in sales jobs is through peer learning, it's about how to help people do that.

The impact of peer learning is consistently reflected in studies of sales organizations. Almost three of five (56 percent) reps say they go to "peers, my network" to improve their skills—a percentage much higher than any other source, including "my manager" (48 percent), training resources (43 percent), or blogs, news sites, and published materials (30 percent).[16] Another study finds that the most effective sales coaches are top-performing sales reps (26 percent), other experienced reps in that organization (22 percent), and the sales manager (24 percent), but not often professional coaches, trainers, or others from outside the organization (6 percent).[17] Managers must manage and coach, but firms must also augment that feedback with tools and practices that encourage peer coaching when and where reps need it. Here are examples of how some companies move peer coaching beyond slogans about teamwork and ad hoc encounters between reps.

Sharon Ruddock is chief learning officer for sales at SAP, which, over the past decade, has transitioned to a blended coaching approach of formal face-to-face coaching by managers and ongoing experiential learning supported by peer-created resources in the field. It's what Ruddock calls "a learning arc. With these methods at our disposal, the lines between formal and informal learning are blurring. [And] everything is data-driven so we can analyze a rep's performance and suggest coaching in specific areas." SAP's process is instructive, because it productively brings together a number of the topics we discussed in part I: hiring, training, performance diagnoses, and coaching.

It begins with hiring. SAP Academy is the company's onboarding program for recent college graduates. With over 12,500 applicants each year, the admissions rate is lower than at Harvard, Yale, or Stanford. The academy introduces reps to core sales concepts through classroom training and on-the-job exercises. But new reps also record and share videos of themselves delivering product pitches, view videos of pitches from experienced high-performing reps, and get video feedback from those reps about how to handle specific situations. As Ruddock notes, "People are more open to learning from peers who have 'been there, done that.' It's one of our most powerful learning tools. We've had over 100,000 views and 10,000 videos created by the 8,000 people in our sales force worldwide."

Once in the field, other tools improve coaching by managers and via peers. Comparing a rep's performance on digital learning assignments with that rep's deal history over time helps to indicate why and how the rep would benefit from coaching about objection handling or how to prepare for executive-level conversations. Managers can then do what performance feedback must provide to be effective: coach to specific topics and skill sets. Ruddock's team works with sales managers on their coaching skills, forecasting, and ability to diagnose performance and learning opportunities with their people. Managers must know their people and individual strengths and weaknesses. But by evaluating pipeline build, win rate, sales cycle time, and customer satisfaction data, Ruddock's team can indicate which coaching initiatives improve which metric. Sales managers who complete the program have increased their team's win rate by 28 percent and the average value of closed deals by 23 percent. "This changes the conversation about coaching," Ruddock says. "Now, when someone asks, 'Why learn?' we can point to our data."

Equally important, the learning and coaching by managers is reinforced with timely peer-created learning resources when reps need it. Videos via chatbots allow reps traveling to a prospect easy access to other reps' advice and behavioral examples. Ruddock notes that "reps can find what they need to have a real conversation about a customer's unique challenges and not just rely on a generic response," and she emphasizes that this just-in-time content has to be short, two to five minutes per video, tailored to a specific question, and tagged correctly using keywords so targeted answers can be located quickly. SAP's practices reflect what we discussed in chapter 3 about the reality of adult learning: the importance of periodic reinforcements and targeted, micro-learning lessons that are sharp, concise, focused on behaviors, and easy to access and revisit via flash drills and visual good-practice examples.

SAP isn't the only example. At Citizens Bank, the retail division's "Monday Morning Mission" meetings and Friday wrap-up calls are now accompanied by short videos that communicate a behavior or best practice and weekly action items with branch managers. Kimberly Dee, head of sales strategy and distribution, notes that "our meetings have gone from about 45 to 20 minutes, and we're getting more information across. Video is more engaging than the email recaps previously shared post-meeting and opens lines of communication: managers respond within the video platform with questions or clarifications easier and sooner." Moreover, not everyone learns the same way. Reps have different starting points depending upon their experience and customers, but the path of least resistance for many managers is a standardized approach pitched at the lowest common denominator. Some people are visual learners, some respond to audio narrative, and others need to see it in writing. Dee emphasizes that "by augmenting our content, we're able to connect the dots for many people in a way we couldn't before. Fifty-two percent of our employees are millennials. The days of having people in multi-day training classes are disappearing, because it's inefficient and it's not the way those people learn."

There are lessons about form, content, and performance management in these companies' practices. First, the "forgetting curve" is a challenge in coaching salespeople, who want information when they need it—for example, when heading to a meeting with a prospect and trying to home in on industry and role-specific pain points—not days, weeks, or months earlier or later in a training session or performance review. In business, the value of information and advice that's relevant but arrives too late to be used is less than zero, because time and resources were spent in finding and delivering the information.

In our personal lives, we routinely use tools to get information at the time of need. Waze, for example, doesn't only provide driving directions; it also provides real-time information from other drivers about current road conditions—access to collaborative knowledge. YouTube users view 5 billion videos daily, and emails with videos have four times the click-through rate of those without video. But the medium is significantly underutilized in sales coaching and training where, as these examples illustrate, it can provide access to just-in-time advice from peers and is easily refreshed when outdated. Further, the benefits go beyond sales. Once established, these practices help to unlock and disseminate knowledge that in most companies is trapped in inboxes or tedious PowerPoint presentations.

Second, SAP and Citizens operate in selling environments where consistent messaging is required, but so is adaptation to diverse customers and usage contexts. "Increased access to the sales community at SAP ensures that the best messaging is not only being used but used across the globe," says Ruddock. "Instead of star reps performing individually, the entire sales force can benefit from their insight and experience." These cross-cutting demands for adaptation with consistency, as another manager notes, reflect a growing need in organizations to "better connect the decision makers with those seeking a decision. What began as an initiative to improve sales training has helped to flatten our organization and increase agility."

Finally, there's a lesson here that goes beyond coaching. Companies struggle to increase organizational agility and collaboration for good reasons. Remember the changes in buying we examined in chapter 1: customers expect an organization to present them with a single, coherent face. For much of the past few decades, the message has been to break down silos via reorganization, cultural change, and superior leadership capabilities. But that is a rough, lengthy, uncertain road. Another route is to begin where value is created or destroyed in most firms—in the external market with customers—and in your performance management practices, use tools to increase collaboration by making your organization easier to navigate and your people better and more willing navigators.

⊕ QUESTIONS TO ASK . . . AND ANSWER

As this chapter explained, performance management includes how you communicate sales goals relevant to strategy, the metrics used to measure activities and results, and procedures for building capability and allocating talent. Metrics are part of but not synonymous with performance management, which is a systemic link between company goals, identifying the activities needed to achieve those goals, and ongoing attention to selling behaviors where it counts most: in interactions with customers. Evaluate your company's practices by answering the questions in table 4-1.

The topics discussed in part I of this book—hiring, training and development, performance management, and coaching—are within a manager's and company's direct influence, not in the less controllable external environment. That's why people are a good place to start improvement in an organization.

TABLE 4-1

A performance management diagnostic

In our company, how well do we . . .

Know how much time our frontline sales managers actually spend on performance appraisals of their people?	1 2 3 4 5 6 7
Make sure our frontline managers take seriously the performance appraisal process and provide feedback?	1 2 3 4 5 6 7
Approach performance appraisals not only as reviews of past performance but as developmental discussions?	1 2 3 4 5 6 7
Have data about sales activities at each stage of our selling cycle?	1 2 3 4 5 6 7
Understand the limits and uses of data in evaluating sales outcomes, putting that data in context?	1 2 3 4 5 6 7
Have in place metrics that track and align KPIs with what our managers emphasize in performance reviews?	1 2 3 4 5 6 7
Tailor our coaching to the individual's needs (e.g., prospecting and/or closing issues)?	1 2 3 4 5 6 7
Use technology to provide opportunities for peer coaching and advice when it matters most to our salespeople?	1 2 3 4 5 6 7

A frontline sales manager, for instance, can usually shape and use all of these levers of selling effectiveness. But even the best hiring, training, and coaching cannot long substitute for a flawed sales model, which is the focus of part II.

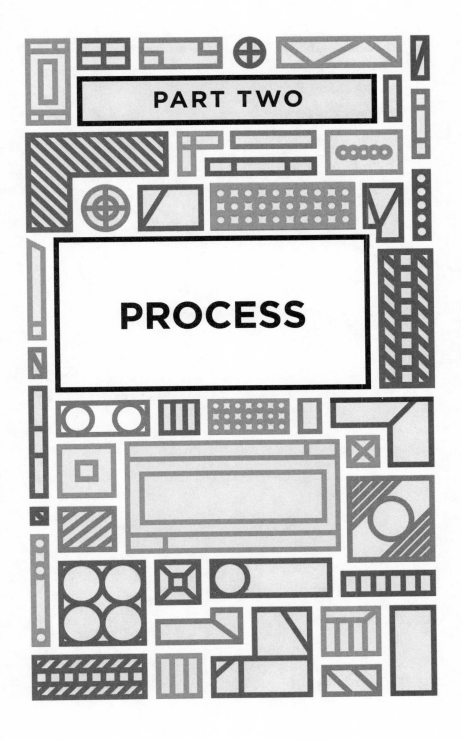

PART TWO

PROCESS

CONSTRUCTING AND CLARIFYING SALES MODELS

Every company has a sales model—a process of selling efforts, based on implicit or explicit choices. The issue is whether your sales model deals effectively with target customers as they buy today, not yesterday, and reflects correct strategic choices in a process that can be communicated and scaled.

This chapter discusses the failure of many sales models to respond to the current buying landscape, core components of a coherent sales model, and the value of clarifying these components for issues ranging from cash flow to pricing to metrics. The next chapter discusses required analytics in managing and reconstructing sales models. Together, the chapters can shed light on assumptions, priorities, and requirements inherent in your firm's sales processes.

Challenges and Problems with Sales Models

Most companies' sales models are the accumulation of years of reactive decisions, usually by different managers pursuing different goals. Market forces and buying changes increasingly expose the loose screws.

Like perishable goods in grocery stores, every sales model has a sell-by date; markets don't stand still, and neither should your go-to-market process. Consider what happens over the course of a product and market life cycle (see figure 5-1). Customers typically start as generalists in a new category and, through usage, become more sophisticated and discriminating. As standards evolve and more competitors enter and saturate segments, buyers have more choices and can take more for granted in quality or performance attributes across vendors. If firms fail to adjust, they lose their distinctiveness, competitive advantage, and the relevance of their sales models.

This dynamic has played out in countless categories over time, dislodging seemingly impregnable firms from market leadership positions. As of this writing, for example, we see

FIGURE 5-1

What tends to happen during the product/market life cycle

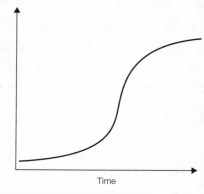

- Standardization of product/service design

- Saturation of individual account/market segments

- Sophistication of customers re usage, alternatives, etc.

Time

it unfolding in digital advertising, 3D printing, and numerous social media and app categories. Google makes almost all of its money from ads and once had a de facto monopoly on digital advertising. But Amazon, Facebook, and native ads in content feeds have begun the dynamic outlined in figure 5-1. The cachet and distinctiveness of Apple's iPhone are harder to maintain as the basic product design and functionality standardize. The smartphone industry has coalesced around design principles like all-screen and notched displays with cameras on the front and back. Hence, Apple's share of global smartphone shipments went from 16 percent in 2015 to 13 percent in 2019, but it uses phones to generate a growing services, accessories, and payments business.[1]

As this happens, what a company requires in its sales model also changes. Early in the cycle, for instance, market development objectives may make the sheer number of sales calls an important goal. Later, the nature of the call (e.g., applications development with a customer or merchandising assistance to a retail account) often assumes greater importance. At some point, tweaks will not suffice, and reconstructing the sales model—the focus of the next chapter—is necessary.

Second, buyers in many categories now begin their buying process online via websites, social media, Amazon, or other vehicles. Traditionally, in most companies, marketing is responsible for generating awareness via advertising in the initial stages of the buying journey and then a handoff to sales and service for later stages. However, prospects now pursue parallel streams in their search, consideration, and evaluation activities, often contacting multiple parties in the firm during that process. Meanwhile, new tools enable sales to perform many awareness activities previously handled by marketing. Prospects in the early awareness stage of buying, but not yet ready to transact, may be more receptive to content marketing than a sales call. Those in later stages and more ready to transact are more likely to respond to calls, demos, or (depending upon the product and sales model) search-engine marketing initiatives. The issue facing many firms is whether their current sales model allocates these responsibilities appropriately, targeting and aligning marketing and sales messages, and helping sales reps to know when and how to have a conversation with customers.

An example is affiliate marketing—that is, referrals from or sponsored posts with bloggers or content aggregators that focus on a category and may receive a commission for sales they help to generate. This is now a big expenditure in many consumer goods sales and marketing budgets as TV viewership declines and ad-blocking devices increase. Spending on affiliate marketing in the United States is growing faster than e-commerce sales.[2] An estimated 40 percent or more of Amazon's revenue comes from affiliates, and in some cosmetics, fashion, apparel, baby-care, and other categories, a majority of consumers are believed to select brands based on the recommendation of a trusted online publisher. In many sales models, however, much of that expenditure is wasted in targeting prospects at the wrong time. Similarly, humble email remains a cost-effective medium when it's used to deliver tailored messages at the right point in the buyer journey. But in many sales models, reps use emails indiscriminately and, in effect, train prospects to ignore their emails as spam.

Third, any sales model creates—for better or for worse—a feedback loop that affects selling and resource allocation in other aspects of the business. Think about core activities like forecasting and quota assignments. Most firms put their available data into a CRM system weekly or monthly and review the volume and value of leads in that pipeline. They then extrapolate future performance from that data snapshot: "Bob did $200,000 in sales last quarter, so let's budget Bob for $250,000 next quarter," and so on. But without clarifying the underlying sales model, the firm and its sales managers are often relying on deceptive metrics to forecast and allocate capacity. In a SaaS model, for example, you want to know, "What is Bob's ratio of monthly recurring revenue to sales qualified leads (SQL)?" and "What is Sally's ratio of contacts versus SQLs?" Answers to these questions will inform a key sales management decision: hire more people like Bob, or find out what Sally is doing right and disseminate that practice?

Fourth, an effective sales model should make the abstract—"profitable growth"—tangible and help sales managers to prioritize what they should be optimizing for in customer acquisition efforts at a point in time. Is it volume, margins, or (in many early-stage ventures) discovering product-market fit? All are important, but a focus on all means a focus on none and inevitable disconnects in aligning sales capacity with market opportunity.

All businesses face opportunity costs. Money and time allocated to accounts A and B are resources not available for accounts C, D, and so on. That reality drives the distinction between effectiveness (optimization by doing the right things) and efficiency (doing things right).

If we use an auto analogy, sales efficiency initiatives, like CRM and KPI dashboards, improve the engine's horsepower. Sales optimization decisions—like customer selection, aligning reps with the sales model and business strategy, and sales force deployment across opportunities—set the direction in which the car will travel. "If you don't know where you're going, any road will take you there." But if a car is going in the wrong direction, getting there faster is not the solution.

For instance, a common metric used in evaluating sales is the expense-to-revenue ratio or, its sibling, customer acquisition cost. These SE measures shed light on the relative cost efficiency of selling activities, but not (by themselves) on their cost effectiveness, which is a more complex relationship between selling costs, revenues and margins achieved at that cost level, and the types of customers acquired through that means of organizing sales resources. The relative importance of each type of metric depends on the sales model. In many subscription businesses using an inside-sales model (see discussion in the next chapter), SE measures indicate much of what you need to know about your sales productivity. But in other markets and sales models, SE measures may be a deceptive sidebar to the real story, lead you to cut selling costs and prices, and unwittingly accelerate a downward spiral in terms of both the quantity (sales volume) and quality (who buys at target accounts) of customers. Either way, the issue is knowing what data is important and how to use it in the relevant sales model.

Components of a Sales Model

The foundational elements and issues in a sales model are:

- **Customer selection and qualification criteria.** Who are core customers, given the scope of your business strategy? How can you identify and get access to the right people at those customers? How can you develop and communicate a relevant deal profile to sales and others in the firm?

- **Clarity about the buyers and the buying process at target customers.** Does the sales model align prospecting and selling activities with the relevant buyer personae and buying journey(s)? What, then, are relevant metrics for evaluating selling activities in that model?

- **The go-to-market economics.** What does the sales model mean in terms of customer acquisition costs, cost to serve different segments and accounts, the selling cycle and time to cash for the business, and customer education requirements?

The outputs of a sales model are the capabilities and call capacity of the sales force. By *capabilities*, I mean what the sales or other customer-contact people know or need to know to execute the business strategy, and the type of effort a company gets and requires from those people. By *call capacity*, I mean what old-school sales managers often referred to as "feet on the street"—the reach or number of customer contacts inherent in the model—but I also mean the amount of time spent selling versus servicing or on other activities inherent in the customer-conversion process.

The configuration of a sales model's components, and the behavioral outcomes, largely determines the role of the salesperson and, as a result, many aspects of hiring, training, compensation, and performance management. Here are two contrasting examples.

A Tale of Two Sales Models

Clef Company (disguised name) sells keys and machines for cutting key blanks to retail accounts through field sales reps.[3] The company increased sales by 67 percent in five years and doubled net income, while decreasing the size of its sales force and having sales force turnover rates of 50 to 65 percent each year. Why? Clef has a sales model linked to its strategy. It sells low-salience, low-priced products where volume and frequent cost-effective calls drive profitability, develop an annuity installed base in each store, and create an entry barrier in a mainly single-sourced retail category. Clef's sales model and performance practices focus on call frequency, account coverage, and point-of-sale tasks. Turnover in this model is not debilitating because "selling" here is largely inventory stocking and machine maintenance. Finding reps for these tasks is not difficult, and turnover keeps Clef's selling costs low while having some ancillary benefits in a lean organization with few promotion opportunities for reps. Like a number of firms, Clef provides an early-career opportunity for hires who then leave for other jobs.

By contrast, Promontory, Inc. sells promotional products—that is, the cups, caps, shirts, and other items that companies give to employees and customers at events.[4] Outsiders may be puzzled by the different and seemingly conflicting methods used by each Promontory salesperson to develop and retain business. Here (as in Clef), the products are simple but (in contrast to Clef) usage contexts, product customization, who buys at a given account, their particular evaluation criteria, and other requirements differ by customer. Each Promontory salesperson, in effect, segments the market by customer, and (again, in contrast to Clef) the sales rep and their usage ideas, design insights, and experience with other accounts is part of what the customer is "buying" in addition to caps or cups imprinted with their firm's logo. Like traditional ad agencies, consulting firms, and providers of custom capital equipment, Promontory's sales model—in this case, a model that integrates prospecting with design ideas and quick, custom service—supports and sustains diverse selling styles with consistent order fulfillment for its accounts.

Clarifying the sales model is important because interactions with customers affect core elements of enterprise value creation. So, if you are a CEO, CFO, or other C-level executive, make sure you understand the sales model in place at your company. Projects and capex initiatives in most firms are driven by revenue-seeking activities with customers. Hence, the customer selection criteria used in sales directly impact which projects the firm invests in. The orders that sales bring into the firm have a domino effect on asset and time allocation in product customization efforts, presale applications engineering, utilization in the factory, postsale service, and so on.

Those selling activities also drive financing needs, especially the working capital required for conducting and growing the business. According to a study by PricewaterhouseCoopers, public companies had $5.2 trillion in working capital on their books in 2017, about one-third of which (that's over $1.5 trillion) could be deployed more wisely, and CFOs hadn't made much progress in speeding up the cash-conversion cycle in the past decade—as the cash crunch generated by the pandemic in 2020 quickly and painfully demonstrated.[5] A question for your next board meeting is where to start climbing this mountain. Well, most often, the biggest driver of cash out and cash in is the selling cycle inherent in a sales model. Accounts payable accrue during selling, and accounts receivables are largely determined by what's sold, how fast, and at what price. Understanding a sales model is a key part of effective financial oversight as well as sales management. Let's start with customer selection criteria.

Customer Selection

Customer selection and qualification are at the heart of the crucial scope component of business strategy—decisions about where to play in a market, the kinds of opportunities relevant to your value proposition, and the process most relevant to getting and keeping those opportunities.[6] Scope is not determined by senior executives sitting in a room and discussing the market; that's brainstorming. In practice, scope is determined by the daily call patterns inherent in a firm's sales model: where that time, effort, and expenses are or are not allocated.

Every firm is always making it easier or harder for different types of customers to do business with it. Most executives
pay lip service to the truism that "you can't be all things to all
people," yet many companies fail to make this an explicit and
managed part of their sales models. Either directly in meetings
or implicitly in compensation plans, they basically tell their
sales forces to "go forth and multiply." Salespeople then sell to
anyone they can, often at discounted prices to make a volume
quota target. The firm then deals better and worse with different customer types, leading to a loss of brand positioning
and, over time, the nurturing of commodity competencies and
deals.

Customers differ not only in their preferences for products
and services, but also in the way they respond to marketing
and sales actions. Understanding customer heterogeneity is
crucial, and if you don't choose customers, competitors will
choose for you. It's better to be proactive in this aspect of
management because so much else in a sales model follows
from customer selection criteria, including cost-to-serve and
cash-conversion cycles as well as core product and growth
decisions.

For example, consider some economic basics: profit is the
difference between the price a customer pays and the seller's
total cost to serve the customer. Some customers require more
sales calls or geography makes them more or less expensive to
serve; some buy in operations-efficient order volumes, while
others buy with many just-in-time or custom orders that affect
setup time, delivery, and other elements of cost to serve. In
turn, these factors are drivers of the selling firm's return on
capital because many capital costs are embedded in cost-to-
serve differences. If you ignore these differences, you will then
chase price and volume, misallocate resources, and wind up
damaging profits and the business. Many sales models do this by
using obsolete criteria in their quota and territory assignments.

Those firms are ultimately at the mercy of companies that *do* select more rigorously.

Customer selection also affects time to cash. Especially in long-selling-cycle businesses with multiple RFPs and a buying process involving diverse decision makers and influencers, a sales model needs clarity about how to "separate the suspects from the prospects" earlier rather than later. If not, the number of false positives in prospecting will increase SG&A, prolong the cash-conversion cycle, drive up working capital and funding requirements, and (without deep pockets) sink the business.

Take TaKaDu, which sells software that detects problems in a water utility's infrastructure.[7] Amir Peleg, TaKaDu's founder, describes himself as "a high-tech plumber." Using a utility's data, his firm's software can identify, in real time, leaks or bursts in pipes; speed up proactive prevention and after-the-fact repairs; and lower water loss, service interruptions, and potential damage to homes, streets, and other parts of the community. Water loss is a big problem globally, and few utilities are against better management of that resource. But water-utility costs and incentives vary widely, depending upon their cost to transport and treat water and, when a leak occurs, whether the utility is penalized (as in Australia, the UK, and some other countries) or can simply pass on the costs to consumers.

TaKaDu initially pursued any sales lead as long as the utility collected data from sensors—a technical requirement for its software analytics. The result, as Peleg notes, was that "Many leads were coming in and we put in significant effort only to have prospects hesitate and decide not to buy. You can get quite far in the process and end up disappointed." Peleg found that 80 percent of customers with sensors were willing to discuss adoption, and of that 80 percent, about 25 percent expressed strong interest, and of that 25 percent, about one-fourth signed a contract with TaKaDu. This may sound promising, but do the math: .8 x .25 x .25 means that 5 percent of prospects (one of twenty) become paying customers, and the venture must absorb the deadweight loss of chasing the other nineteen. It was not until TaKaDu clarified its customer selection and qualification criteria more rigorously that it was able to scale profitably.

The same is true of other businesses because customer selection also affects what the sales force sells, or must sell, and the value proposition. Toast began by focusing on a seemingly simple issue for restaurants and diners: the need to split a check when dining with a group and the time and frustration of having to get the waiter's attention to settle the bill. Toast's mobile app let each diner see what each had ordered, split the check, and pay with a credit card as soon as they were ready to leave, without waiting for the server to make two more trips to the table. But that initial product did not sell with restaurants, which mainly relied on cash-register systems from the 1990s and where desired product features varied. Pizza restaurants wanted the ability to specify different toppings for each side of the pie; others wanted to capture diners' email addresses as part of loyalty programs; upscale restaurants wanted course and table numbers attached to each dish; casual dining places wanted to take orders when lines were long and then send a text to patrons when their table and orders were ready.

Toast's founders decided to build an order-taking and cash-register system using cloud-based technology. As cofounder Aman Narang recalls, "We had this light bulb moment [and] the customers sort of led us."[8] In turn, this affected pricing (average monthly subscription revenue of about $80 per month versus capex hardware pricing) and the value proposition articulated by Toast's sales reps. The pitch that resonates, Narang notes, is helping restaurants to turn over tables faster when they're busy, generate additional business through online ordering when they are less busy, and the fact that managers can access financial and inventory data from a laptop or phone, rather than showing up early or staying late at the restaurant to do that work, and so spend more time with their families.

Conversely, changing a target customer has many consequences. An example is Bunnings, a retail hardware chain with locations across Australia and New Zealand, where its target customer is a worker (usually male) involved in do-it-yourself building and repairs or working in a trade. For years, its ad slogan had been "lowest prices are just the beginning."[9] In 2016, Bunnings's holding company, Westfarmers, purchased a struggling UK chain, Homebase, with the goal of converting those stores to the successful Bunnings sales model. But Homebase's target customer, the home and garden enhancer, was generally a female professional in an above-average income household with children. This change affected most aspects of the relevant customer-acquisition model from product and brand to price and competition.

After acquiring Homebase, Westfarmers eliminated many bathroom and soft-furnishings products and installation services in favor of home-improvement products sold by Bunnings. To integrate the brands, it changed from the Homebase colors of soft green and white to Bunnings's dark red and green. As the product line, merchandising, and in-store experience changed, many traditional Homebase customers left. Meanwhile, Bunnings's ad slogan and low-price focus pushed the company into direct competition with larger hardware chains in the UK that were better able to compete on price in that market. Westfarmers spent a reported $990 million to acquire Homebase and, in two years, sold it to a PE firm for 1 euro (US $1.30 at the time) and 20 percent of proceeds from any subsequent sale of Homebase by the purchaser—a costly lesson in the importance of customer selection in constructing a relevant sales model.

This link between target customer and sales requirements is not unique to retailing or consumer businesses. Via his "crossing the chasm" framework, Geoffrey Moore has documented this link as tech firms seek to grow beyond early adopters to more mainstream customers in a market.[10] Early adopters like to test new products, even a so-called minimum viable product (MVP). With their aptitude for developing creative applications, they can supply the missing elements of an MVP. Identifying these customers is often key for a technologically innovative product. Mainstream customers, by contrast, require what Moore calls the "whole product," not an MVP or evolving set of features. They want a product that can work today in their organization or household with no or minimal disruptions to the established usage system. These buyers want references, but don't trust references from early-adopter enthusiasts, whom they perceive as often adopting new technology for its own sake, not for ROI. Instead, mainstream customers want other, more-relevant reference sites.

Some have quarreled with this framework's characterizations of customers at each stage. But Moore's basic point is correct: it's a process of technology *adoption*, and the pattern is determined by the changing buying behavior of customers. The product in the initial stage of many markets is more like a project, and the important sales tasks are not what the plug-and-play mainstream buyers require.

To construct a coherent and scalable sales model, therefore, you need to disaggregate the big issue of customer selection into a more manageable message that your sales team can use in prospecting and qualification of prospects across different segments at a point in time. In other words, you need to develop and communicate a strategic deal profile.

Developing a Deal Profile

Here are two real leads (names disguised).[11] The first is an email from an inside-sales rep to a sales engineer at a company that sells hardware and software to call centers:

> I have a warm lead for you! This came in through the Hotline. This account had in the recent past owned a large call center and sold it only to miss it and decided to open another one. There is no hardware in place at this time. He will start with thirty agents and four supervisors, growing to sixty agents in a short amount of time. The customer wants scripting, reporting, scheduled call backs, the ability to modify campaigns on the fly, recycle lists, and full monitoring.
>
> The proposal is due 6/11 and they expect to make final selection by 6/18. They want to be up and running by the end of July. He wants to speak with someone ASAP.

The second lead was sent by email to the general mailbox of a medical device company from the equipment department of a large California hospital:

> Dear sir or madam: Please quote on quantity 100 syringe pumps similar to New Era Model 1000 with capacity of 0.73ul/hour – 2100ml/hour. Quote must be received by 15 November to be considered.

Initially, one might assume the first lead is more promising: it suggests a funded project with time urgency and provides much technical information. The second looks like a boilerplate RFQ, and you might assume the decision will be made primarily on price. But the first lead indicates one week between receiving a "firm proposal" and a purchase decision: Is that realistic? If so, does it suggest this prospect already knows whom it is choosing and the technical detail here is evidence of another supplier having specified the deal to its specifications and competitive advantage? Is this prospect simply looking to generate more proposals and negotiating leverage with its preferred supplier? This prospect has been in and out of the core market of call centers, and whenever a prospect indicates future growth (e.g., doubling the number of agents from thirty to sixty "in a short amount of time"), how do you determine if that is real or a standard come-on to entice multiple bids? On the other hand, the second lead may be an invitation to an auction *or* it may be a chance to land an entry order and expand within a big account. Is it worth time and effort to understand how service, delivery, proven quality, and (if a company has them) positive referrals from other hospitals may be among the decision criteria "to be considered" by this customer?

These are all speculations, and unfortunately, that is what companies rely on in the absence of a deal profile as part of their sales models. In practice, then, sales capacity is typically allocated to chasing both leads, resulting in many false positives, higher selling costs, and negative second-order impacts on sales morale and nonsales engineering and other resources.

A deal profile provides guidelines and parameters that salespeople can use in prospecting and in conversations with prospects and that sales managers can use in practices ranging from territory and account assignments to incentive compensation.

Here's an example of how to do that.[12]

Alphatech

Alphatech sells software that allows businesses to deploy applications consistently across their desktops, laptops, and other devices. Since each business has a somewhat unique combination of hardware and software, Alphatech has grown by taking responsibility for integration and after-sales support. But as growth and revenues flattened, management began evaluating who were good customers.

Previously, Alphatech's sales reps considered any organization in which workers used laptops as a qualified prospect. As a result, selling efforts were fragmented and selling cycles were lengthy. When reps did close deals, they did so at highly discounted prices and often included unwieldy service requirements that affected asset allocations in other parts of the business. False positives and negative return-on-capital prospects littered the sales pipeline, and about 75 percent of profit came from just 25 percent of the deals—almost all of which were managed-services contracts versus one-off project installations.

With analysis, Alphatech identified regional hospitals as its target customers. These hospitals faced mandated digital-records requirements and usually lacked the scale and IT staff to do that on their own. Regional hospitals also represented a large enough market to support renewed growth. Further, these customers were accessible to sales while offering operational advantages for other functions: Alphatech could oversee integrations remotely via the internet.

At this point, Alphatech knew it wanted to sell to regional hospitals and felt it had the capabilities to do so. But it needed a deal profile—a set of guidelines and performance practices that would link the approach used by its salespeople with those target customers. The first component is figuring out how to *define success* for the selling company as well as the customer. Alphatech standardized its proposals to include managed service offerings as an option and changed its marketing collateral and lead-generation activities. It reorganized its sales force by segment within the broader regional hospital category and trained both its sales and service teams (which now accompanied reps to customer sites earlier in the sales cycle) on outcome-based selling. As a result, sales calls focused on defining success outcomes with the customer, such as time to deploy applications and system up-time guarantees.

These mutually agreed outcomes were key to the value proposition because many of the applications affected patient care, reimbursements, and health-care confidentiality requirements. Different stakeholders in hospitals had different perspectives on these issues. Hence, establishing up front a common language of value also helped customers to communicate in their organizations, which accelerated sales cycles and minimized further selling expenses when a customer and Alphatech could not agree on outcomes. This approach also improved access to more-senior decision makers. In the past, sales reps primarily dealt with IT system administrators. Now, they were conversing with CFOs and other executives, which better positioned Alphatech to expand services at accounts where it did land deals.

The deal profile also specified ways for reps to communicate ongoing value to customers. Alphatech was now implicitly selling a change process as well as hardware and software. Reps were therefore required to establish monthly conference calls with IT and others at their accounts, and periodic customer business reviews (CBRs) with these personnel and administrators after implementation. For customers, the calls were reviews of agreed-upon outcomes. They were also opportunities to talk about best practices with diverse hospital personnel and troubleshoot any service issues. For sales reps, CBRs provided opportunities to extend or expand a contract. Since a longer-term contract typically needed approval outside IT, it was in Alphatech's interest to keep senior executives at the account involved.

Pricing and compensation processes were a third component of the deal profile. In the past, Alphatech's pricing had been driven by competing proposals, often from competitors who provided less service. Compensated in terms of revenue bookings, the sales force was often closing initial deals at a loss in the hope that the value delivered would lead to higher prices. With the deal profile, Alphatech changed sales incentives from bookings to commission payments tied to margins, service mix, and duration of the subscription agreement. Further, sales reps could only offer discounts of 5–10 percent off book prices if the customer agreed to at least three months of initial service. This three-month period was beneficial to both parties. It lowered customers' risks of trial, while the network and service terms gave Alphatech access to better information about outcome drivers and change requirements at that account, as well as a price benchmark if and when expanding service became a reality with that customer.

With the deal profile in place, Alphatech's sales model generated improved results. The firm's profitability more than doubled in a year while return on invested capital increased almost 300 percent with fewer salespeople. Moreover, while the deal profile and its supporting performance management processes meant that Alphatech was saying no to prospects more often than in the past, customer churn decreased, while customer lifetime value and profitability increased. Not everything went without a hitch. Many salespeople left because they found the revised focus and selling behaviors alien to their skill sets and preferences. But a coherent sales model is about clarifying the links between customer selection and required selling behaviors. A deal profile is a basic building block in that process.

Clarity about the Buyers and Buying Process

Next, you need to deconstruct your sales model, by which I mean analyzing its components, understanding cause-and-effect activities in that model of customer acquisition, and making improvements. This involves clarifying the buyer persona(e) and buying journey, and then aligning sales efforts with buying via relevant metrics and customer-conversion analytics (discussed in the next chapter).

"Buyer persona" and "buying journey" are the current terms for time-honored good practice in sales and marketing: knowing who buys your product (persona) and how they buy (journey). Other nomenclature for essentially the same things include the decision-making unit, customer value chain, touchpoint analysis, and others. Whatever language you use, specifying the who and the how of buying are prerequisites for constructing and evaluating a sales model.

Buyer Persona

If a firm has a deal profile, then it has the rudiments of buyer personae: profiles of archetypal customers based on a synthesis of findings from data, customer interviews, and other research. Typical elements of personae include a memorable name or other identifier, relevant information about their role(s) and motivations in that product or service category, their perspectives on existing solutions in the category, and quotes or other comments that reflect their needs and buying criteria in their language.

For example, Oversight Systems sells an analytics platform that allows companies to monitor their data for errors, fraud, and operational inefficiencies. The firm focuses on applications for corporate purchase card transactions and travel-and-expense (T&E) spending. Companies spend billions annually on purchase card and T&E spending by their employees, and fraud occurs (an estimated one in five employees submits at least one questionable expense item annually). Monitoring this spending and reimbursement is typically the job of people in finance functions like audit and compliance or a T&E manager. In its sales model, Oversight uses the personae illustrated in figure 5-2: fictional buyer persona Ken (a corporate compliance or audit executive), persona Tina (a T&E manager), and Carla (a controller in the finance department).[13]

As these examples illustrate, personae typically include biographical details that make them *seem* like real people, while emphasizing their responsibilities, pain points, and how they tend to gather information about addressing those needs. Why do this? Well, markets and companies don't buy; only individual customers and people at those accounts do. It's one thing to say your target customer is a corporation that spends a lot on T&E. It's quite another to specify whether you are selling to the CEO, CFO, CMO, an auditor, or someone else. Buyer personae help to keep the sales force aware of these differences and turn "customer focus"—seeing the world as customers do—into a behavioral reality, not an empty abstraction, in prospecting, selling, and account-management activities.

Personae are also relevant to marketing messages and media, and the kinds of data and examples useful for communicating value. Persona Ken, for example, is concerned with reputational risks and cost-benefit calculations in ways that are not as prominent for Tina and Carla, who are involved in high-volume review and reimbursement transactions with employees. In most selling situations, some buyers are motivated by technical specifications, and others by ROI, time savings, or another issue. Similarly, there's evidence that tolerance for risk, and thus propensity to buy new products or from new vendors, varies by function—generally less risk tolerance among IT and accounting personnel versus marketing, for example.[14] Personae help sellers to create and test hypotheses about key buying criteria.

There are important spillover benefits as well. Personae help to spur dialogue among salespeople, between salespeople and sales managers, and between sales and marketing managers, about buyers and purchasing criteria by segment, how that might be changing, and the implications.

FIGURE 5-2

Examples of buyer personae

Buyer persona – Ken

"I need to catch reputation and financial risk issues before they become significant or before the government catches them."

Identifiers

- **Title:** Director of compliance, corporate compliance director, chief compliance officer, chief audit executive
- **Role:** Responsible for compliance, regulatory, and internal policies. Protect company from reputation and financial risk
- **Salary:** $131,000–$159,000
- **Company size:** Multinational, enterprise organizations

Demographics

- Male, 45–55, with master's degree in auditing, regulatory affairs, or accounting. 15–20 years experience
- Detail oriented, risk averse, skeptical, loyal, very responsible, honest to a fault
- Thrives in structured environments where roles are well defined
- Seeks logical outcomes, integrity, and honesty across the organization
- Personality type: ISTJ characteristics—integrity, practical logic, and tireless dedication to duty, enjoys responsibility

Responsibilities

- Establish companywide ethics and compliance program
- Conduct or direct the internal investigation of compliance issues
- Oversee and ensure that operations within the company adhere to all applicable rules, regulations, policies, and laws
- Assess product, compliance, or operational risks and develop risk management strategies
- Ensure company is protected from reputation and financial risk

Information sources

- Influencers: Advisers/consultants, associations, and peers
- Events: Association meetings, conferences (FCPA Conference), and continuing education
- Online: Blogs, vendor websites, association newsletters, compliance and accounting publications (FCPA blog, ACC newsletter)
- Assets: Research, white papers, slide decks, vendor websites, product reviews, webinars

Overarching pain points

- Complexity of multinational compliance policies
- Compliance itself is creating risk by diverting resources
- Fear of scandal and negative exposure
- Visibility into compliance risks and individuals (they actually need to boil the ocean)
- Balancing the need to self-report with the actual likelihood an incident will be discovered (prioritizing risk)

Immediate needs

- Addressing recent significant fraud
- Automating policy analysis and reporting
- Providing visibility to compliance processes
- Identifying unusual and habitual errors, excess, and misuse
- Prioritizing and mitigating risk
- Doing business in high-risk countries
- Enforcement of FCPA

Use cases

- Reputation management
- Automating transactional monitoring and visibility
- Compiling data for self-disclosing fraud issues

Use cases (cont.)

- Helping ensure compliance in internal audits and external investigations

Market drivers

- Increased legislation, regulation, and rules
- Heightened focus on holding individuals and corporations accountable
- Lack of public trust in big business
- Doing more business globally

Buying criteria

- Ease of use and implementation
- Proven prepackaged analytics
- ROI and time to value (compliance)
- Sufficiently robust

Common objections

- Status quo or competitive products "good enough"
- Staff too small to help implement and leverage features of solution
- Difficult learning curve and lack of time-savings in existing processes
- Focus elsewhere (a nice to have, not a need to have)

Purchase process

- Identifies problem
- Identifies potential solution
- Online research of vendor websites in detail
- Discusses with influencers (consultant/adviser, analysts)
- Requests demo
- Evaluates features based on immediate needs
- Takes decision to influencers
- 30- to 60- day trial/POC
- Finalizes decision with influencers, makes purchase (departmental sale)

Role in process

- Primary researcher, evaluator, and decision maker

(continued)

FIGURE 5-2 (*continued*)

Examples of buyer personae

Buyer persona – Tina

"I can save my company money by identifying trends in noncompliance T&E."

Identifiers

- **Title:** Travel and expense manager; director, T&E; T&E expense specialist; senior representative, T&E
- **Role:** Management of overall day-to-day corporate card and T&E program
- **Salary:** $50,000–$90,000
- **Company size:** Enterprise organizations with employee base of at least 5,000 (4,000 expense reports annually)

Demographics

- Female, Gen X, 30–50, with bachelor's degree in accounting, 5–10 years experience
- Collaborative, assertive, communicative, analytical, logical, compartmentalizes, risk averse, work-life balance important
- Thrives in a fast-paced and pressurized environment
- Seeks recognition, training, and career growth

Responsibilities

- Manages overall day-to-day corporate card T&E program
- Reviews, validates, processes, and audits expense claims to current T&E policy
- Ensures all T&E claims are processed timely and accurately
- Provides training and support to the accounts payable T&E team
- Liaises with legal, HR, and audit departments
- Conducts preferred-vendor rate audits

Information sources

- Influencers: Peers, CFOs, controllers, financial operations, compliance, line-of-business managers
- Events: Association meetings, conferences, user groups, continuing education
- Online: Blogs, LinkedIn (community), vendor websites, community-focused publications, business travel, and accounting publications.
- Assets: Research, white papers, slide decks, testimonials, vendor websites, product reviews

Overarching pain points

- Compliance and policies, employee education
- Long hours, work-life balance
- Compiling monthly forecasts and reports, audits
- Inability of management to understand what can and does go wrong
- Unclear reporting structure (site GM/line-of-business manager, controller, and finance)
- Fear of risk-taking/sharing ideas to help resolve problems and quickly implementing to show success
- Staying current on latest trends

Buyer persona – Carla

"I ensure that employees' expenditures meet regulator and corporate policies."

Identifiers
- **Title:** Assistant controller; cost controller
- **Role:** Oversees the T&E process; ensures policies, procedures, and activities are in compliance with corporate standards. Audits reports as needed.
- **Salary:** $50,000–$115,000
- **Company size:** Enterprise organizations with employee base of at least 5,000 (4,000 expense reports annually)

Demographics
- Female, Gen X, 30–50, with bachelor's degree in accounting
- Collaborative, assertive, communicative, analytical, logical, compartmentalizes, risk averse, works long hours
- Thrives in a fast-paced and pressurized environment
- Focused on career growth

Responsibilities
- Reviews expense reports and verifies coding, approval, and documentation to ensure policy procedure compliance
- Conducts audits and provide corporate audit support
- Develops processes to automate data collection and to reduce expenses
- Generates cost reports, recommendations, and analysis of invoices
- Tracks and analyzes cost activities
- Establishes and maintains internal controls and present reports and potential risk areas to senior management

Information sources
- Influencers: Peers, CFOs, controllers, financial operations, compliance, line-of-business managers
- Events: Association meetings, conferences, user groups, continuing education
- Online: Blogs, LinkedIn (community), vendor websites, community-focused publications, business travel, and accounting publications
- Assets: Research, white papers, slide decks, testimonials, vendor websites, product reviews

Overarching pain points
- Compliance and policies, employee education
- Compiling monthly forecasts and reports, audits
- Inability of management to understand what can and does go wrong
- Unclear reporting structure (site GM/line-of-business manager, controller, and finance)
- Fear of risk taking/sharing ideas to help resolve problems and quickly implementing to show success
- Staying current on latest trends

Source: Frank Cespedes and Amram Migdal, "Oversight Systems," Case 9-817-015 (Boston, Harvard Business School, August 15, 2016).

However, it's also important to understand the limits and misuses of buyer persona constructs. Any way of thinking about buyers is only as good as the empirical inputs. Without sales reps trained in the interview and listening skills discussed in chapter 3, it's garbage in, garbage out. Too often, in my experience, firms simply reverse-engineer an alleged persona's pain points based on the capabilities of their product or technology. This gets it backward, turning a persona from a useful market-driven sales heuristic into a product-driven fairy tale. Good salespeople, moreover, don't use buyer personae rigidly. They know that, in any market, the typical or average buyer is an aggregate artifact and that a persona is an initial template for prospecting and messaging, not a recipe. Finally, don't confuse personae with a segmentation scheme or a research study for estimating your total addressable market. Those are different issues that require different data.

Buying Journey

A persona provides a snapshot of your target buyer, identifiers, and their needs in general. The buying journey is a motion picture of the process or key steps a potential buyer or buying unit typically goes through in learning about, evaluating, selecting, purchasing (or not), and using products or services within the relevant category. Ultimately, any effective sales model must align with the relevant buying journey(s) as that process works today, not yesterday.

There are many ways to map a buying journey.[15] In practice, multiple buying journeys are typically relevant because the journey can differ by segment, re-buy, or usage occasion. However, a good place to start is with a simple, generic framework shown in figure 5-3.

Many buying processes start when a prospect discovers a problem or opportunity. For Oversight Systems, this often

FIGURE 5-3

A generic buyer journey framework

- **Awareness stage**
  - Prospect is experiencing a problem or opportunity and may be doing research to understand, frame, or give a name to that problem or opportunity

- **Consideration stage**
  - Prospect has defined the problem or opportunity (rightly or wrongly) and is researching methods, solutions, or suppliers to address it

- **Decision stage**
  - Prospect decides on a solution method or approach, is evaluating available suppliers, and ultimately making a purchase decision

occurs after a major fraud event in a company or when an audit group becomes aware of duplicate T&E payments and worries about identifying and preventing other instances of fraud or waste. Then, the buyer often begins to consider different approaches or possible solutions to that problem or opportunity. It's at this stage that buyers typically develop what marketers call "a consideration set"—a group of brands and vendors they actively consider. Then, the buyer may request multiple RFPs or demos, pilot a possible solution, or negotiate terms and conditions in deciding on which solution to purchase and from which available seller.

A sales model should be informed by answers to core questions about each stage of the journey, as indicated in figure 5-4. Mapping the buying journey helps to keep a prospect's information needs, desired outcomes, and product evaluation criteria central to selling efforts. It's essential for prioritizing marketing investments, including the role of marketing in lead generation and providing sales with relevant content at each stage of the journey. For a buyer at the awareness stage in a financial services category, for example, relevant content might be third-party research or analyst reports about spending, saving, and retirement accounts. At the consideration stage, relevant information is more likely to be white papers, podcasts,

FIGURE 5-4

Sample questions for buyer journey development

Awareness stage
- How do buyers typically describe the challenges or opportunities your company addresses?
- How do buyers educate themselves on these challenges or goals?
- How do buyers decide whether the challenge or goal should be prioritized?

Consideration stage
- What categories of solutions do buyers investigate to address the challenge or goal?
- How do buyers educate themselves on these solution categories?
- What do buyers perceive as the strengths and weaknesses of the solution category your offering is in?

Decision stage
- What criteria do buyers use to evaluate the different offerings in that solution category?
- What do buyers perceive as the differentiator of your offering relative to competitors?
- What do buyers perceive as your competitors' strengths versus your offering?
- Who needs to be involved in the decision? Do their criteria for the solution differ?
- When does the decision need to be made?

---

or webinars focused on understanding different approaches and investment options. At the decision stage, direct vendor comparisons, product literature, referrals, or testimonials are often important. Without up-to-date understanding of the buying journey, marketing then relies on a "spray-and-pray" approach to content generation, and the result is the estimated 70 percent or more of marketing collateral that is never read or used by sales or customers.[16]

The importance of each stage of the buying journey will vary by product category. Table 5-1 outlines research about the percentage of purchases made from brands in the consumer's initial consideration set and the percentage of repurchases from that initial set, versus the percentage purchased from brands added during the consumer's buying journey.[17] The results differ by category, as do the implications for effective customer acquisition. Why do auto companies spend so much money on mass-media advertising? Because it's important to become part of the consumer's buying journey at the awareness stage and in the initial consideration set. Also, variety-seeking behavior and different needs characterize the same buyer over time as their family or other life circumstances change what they seek in a car or truck. There's relatively little repurchasing from a previous consideration set, and auto companies must keep spurring awareness of their latest models. By contrast, auto insurance involves more search and consideration beyond the initial set, and once purchased, a combination of buyer inertia and switching costs drive high rates of repurchase from the same insurance company.

In many B2B sales contexts, mapping the buying journey is essential to understanding the role of a given persona in the *buying center*—the members of an organization involved in a buying decision—and what's relevant for sales navigation of that unit. Figure 5-5 indicates a common set of roles in a buying center. These roles—and therefore the process of awareness, consideration, and evaluation—may be done by different people (a common situation when selling to enterprise accounts), or virtually all of these roles may involve one person and key decision maker (e.g., the owner of a small business). That's an important difference in a sales model.

TABLE 5-1

Importance of stage varies by category

	% Share of purchases			Number of brands	
	Initial consideration	Active evaluation	Repurchase from initial set	In initial set	Added in evaluation
Autos	63%	30%	7%	3.8	2.2
PCs	49%	24%	27%	1.7	1.0
Skin care	38%	37%	25%	1.5	1.8
Telcom	38%	20%	42%	1.5	0.9
Auto ins.	13%	9%	78%	3.2	1.4

Source: Adapted from data in David Court et al., "The Consumer Decision Journey," *McKinsey Quarterly*, no. 3 (2009).

FIGURE 5-5

The buying center: Key dimensions and roles

- **Initiators:** Perceive the existence of a problem or opportunity
- **Gatekeepers:** Control access and flow of information
- **Influencers:** Provide information for evaluating alternatives
- **Deciders:** Have final authority to make or break the purchase decision
- **Controllers:** Set the budget for the purchase
- **Buyers:** Place the order and sign the check
- **Users:** Live with the purchase; may also be influencers

Similarly, knowing whether a contact is a gatekeeper, decision maker, or user—and how their role might change after an initial purchase or as the customer gains more experience in the category—is core to effective B2B prospecting and selling.

There are broader organizational and strategic issues embedded in understanding customer processes. A useful way of thinking about buying, which a journey map helps to emphasize, is that *value = benefits − costs*. Products and services that address a customer pain point provide value, but customers also incur costs at each stage of a buying journey and the costs are not just financial. The costs include their time, effort, and other nonmonetary but real transaction costs in search, purchase, and usage of a product or service. The heart of a superior value proposition is the seller's ability to increase the benefits and/or decrease those costs for the buyer. To do this, however, a company needs a shared view and common language about who buys and how.

⊕ QUESTIONS TO ASK . . . AND ANSWER

Without clarifying the sales model, selling is a set of individual heroic efforts in the field, not a scalable process for growth. Yet as emphasized at the beginning of this chapter, in many companies, the de facto model is often an unexamined collection of practices that have accrued over the years. Examine the components in your current sales model by answering the questions in table 5-2.

A focus on buyers and the buying journey accelerates selling today and helps to guard against being blindsided tomorrow. Business models focused on customer buying processes are what's changing most markets, not simply technological innovation.[18] Most well-known disruptors focus on specific areas of a buying journey, add value to that buying activity, and so lower customer search, purchase, or usage costs. That has implications for maintaining and, when necessary, reconstructing a sales model.

TABLE 5-2

Assessing your sales model

In our company, how well do we . . .

Clarify our customer selection criteria and then communicate those criteria to our salespeople?	1 2 3 4 5 6 7
Have in place lead-qualification processes that our sales managers and sales reps know and use?	1 2 3 4 5 6 7
Discuss and disseminate a deal profile in our training and performance reviews?	1 2 3 4 5 6 7
Develop and use buyer personae in our account or territory assignments and prospecting efforts?	1 2 3 4 5 6 7
Understand the limits of buyer persona constructs and complement them with market research?	1 2 3 4 5 6 7
Track relevant buying journey(s) at our target accounts and align marketing and sales efforts accordingly?	1 2 3 4 5 6 7
Update our assumptions about who buys and how with ongoing information from a variety of sources?	1 2 3 4 5 6 7
Use that information for continuous improvement in our value proposition?	1 2 3 4 5 6 7

MANAGING, MAINTAINING, AND RECONSTRUCTING SALES MODELS

A sales model is not an end in itself. If target customers, their buying criteria, or your products change, you must optimize different aspects of a sales model and perhaps develop a different model altogether. To know whether, when, and what to change, you need relevant analytics and managerial smarts.

In this chapter, we'll discuss managing and maintaining a sales model with customer conversion analytics and reconstructing a sales model when your strategy or product changes, or—as is increasingly common—if your business shifts to a subscription model.

Problems and Opportunities of Customer Conversion Analytics

Every business has a customer conversion dynamic—that is, a set of activities from lead generation to closing and often post-sale service. Some conversion processes are long and complex, while others are short and relatively simple. The time and expense salespeople spend at each stage are key drivers of your go-to-market economics and growth requirements. In turn, the purpose of most sales metrics is to manage behaviors that have impact on customer conversion. But which metrics?

Many companies fudge this crucial issue with unfocused appeals to big data, which is a conveniently vague concept. By 2010, companies with more than a thousand employees already had, individually, *more* data in their CRM systems than in the Library of Congress.[1] The data has gotten "bigger" since then. As a result, managers often lack a clear sense of what is really driving conversion in their business, while salespeople get lost in the day-to-day noise. In fact, most sales organizations are currently a ground-zero example of Nassim Taleb's comment that "there is plenty of information. The problem—the central issue—is that the needle comes in an increasingly larger haystack."[2]

Surveys indicate that "wins"—closed deals—are the most common metric used across industries to track selling activity. One reason is that most CRM software automatically weights revenue expectations by pipeline stage on the assumption that the odds of closing increase in successive stages. On average, firms measure closed deals and rep production against quotas monthly. But a closed deal is a lagging indicator. It tells you where you were, and in running a business, the arrow of time only points forward: what's happened has happened. Conversion analytics uncover leading indicators, which are more often within a rep's or manager's ability to affect via their allocation of time and other resources.

Let's look at an example.

Showpad

Founded in Belgium in 2011, Showpad is both an enabler and example of the issues and opportunities uncovered by conversion analytics.[3] Showpad sells software that generates reports on how sales reps interact with the content available to them, indicating, for instance, what collateral is used, how many times, and even how long the sales rep spends per slide or per page. In turn, sales reps can use Showpad on any computer or mobile device to present content to prospects, with notes or highlighted information; see how the prospect interacts with the material (e.g., did they open the presentation? how long did they spend on each slide?); and have better information for follow-up. Hence, Showpad provides marketers with the ability to manage and improve the content they provide to sales and enables reps to have better sales conversations. One customer noted that Showpad is "a real eye-opener about what actually happens in selling. Also, when reps can track customer interactions with the content, they get better at prioritizing leads, understanding key stakeholders, and allocating their time more productively."

Figure 6-1 outlines the customer conversion process from lead to close in Showpad's early years. At Showpad, marketing generated leads by blogs, emails, webinars, and online promotions to prospects who provided their email address and basic information about their company. Once a lead entered the system, marketing "qualified" it. For example, someone who downloaded a white paper was qualified, while someone applying for a job was filtered out as a prospect. Qualified leads (QLs) were then sent to a sales development representative (SDR), who decided whether that lead was a sales accepted

FIGURE 6-1

Showpad customer conversion activities

1. Lead generation via content marketing, blogs, emails, webinars, other →

2. Qualified leads (QL) → SDRs → Sales accepted lead (SAL) →

3. Sales qualified lead (SQL) → Demo with AE →

4. "DIPS" criteria to evaluate a sales qualified opportunity (SQO) →

5. Booking and close → Postsale customer support (CS)

lead (SAL) and worth subsequent effort. If accepted, the SDR researched the prospect's company and tried to book an online demo meeting between the prospect and a Showpad account executive (AE). A booked demo meant the lead was then a sales qualified lead (SQL) and sent to an AE, who then had a call and demo with the prospect. Demos were held online and lasted about an hour. After the demo, the AE determined whether the lead became a sales qualified opportunity (SQO), using the following criteria (known internally at Showpad by the acronym DIPS):

Device. Does the target organization have devices compatible with Showpad?

Influence. Are we speaking to the right person in the organization?

Pain. Is the customer aware of the need for a solution?

Size of opportunity. What is the potential number of licenses we could sell?

The AE then worked an SQO through to close and booking, and a postsale customer success team handled integration, onboarding, technical support, and training.

FIGURE 6-2

Showpad customer conversion data

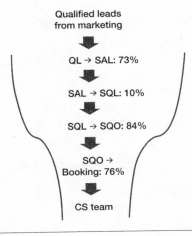

Like many ventures, Showpad grew rapidly, but then growth slowed and there were conflicting opinions about why. The founders eventually analyzed the customer conversion process; the results are displayed in figure 6-2. The big drop is after sales development reps send an SAL to the AEs, who decide that only 10 percent are actually SQLs. Conversion analytics help to isolate the issues, options, and choices—important for improving the productivity of any sales model and vital for managing a venture's cash burn rate.

One possible cause of this leak in the conversion process is the lead qualification criteria used by the SDRs. Note that they pass on three of four leads (73 percent) to AEs. Is this too liberal? If so, Showpad can institute more rigorous qualification criteria or reallocate conversion activities: for instance, make the DIPS criteria part of the SDR's template for passing a lead to the AEs.

On the other hand, notice that the AEs do a demo with over eight of ten leads (84 percent) they do qualify, and close a sale with an impressive three of four (76 percent) of those prospects. Is this great salesmanship, or are busy AEs too conservative and qualifying too few leads? Or, like many new products in a relatively new category, do prospects require a demo before they understand the capabilities, usage possibilities, and kinds of ROI available with Showpad's product? If so, is a one-hour-per-prospect demo the best use of the AE's time, or is it better allocated to SDRs or to the technically proficient customer success (CS) reps? Or are there self-service demos that can be deployed on the website or through one of marketing's lead-generation vehicles?

The point is that many sales outcomes have their root causes in other activities in the sales model, and you won't know that without conversion analysis. Instead of isolating specific cause-and-effect links that you can test and improve, you'll only be looking at outcomes and, like many sales managers, rely on unfocused "sell better" exhortations as your approach to growth. Once you do isolate cause-and-effect links, however, you can improve a sales model along multiple dimensions.

Applying Conversion Analytics

Firms often get their highest returns from conversion analytics when optimizing activity assignments and increasing selling time, reallocating account assignments, monitoring and managing the combination of online and personal selling now required in most sales models, and enabling better coordination between salespeople within and across organizations.

Increasing Selling Time

Clarifying cause and effect in the conversion process generates options for specifying which activities should be handled by sales and by which salespeople (e.g., SDRs or more experienced and expensive AEs), or handled by marketing, shared services, or channel partners with regular access to the decision makers in your category.

The data varies by industry and company, but most salespeople spend the bulk of their time on nonselling activities and much less than 50 percent of their time interacting with customers.[4] Most companies, therefore, have a big opportunity embedded in their sales models. Think about the impact in your business of deploying reps where they have the most impact and so increasing selling time by an incremental 10–20 percent. In most businesses, that represents a very significant gain. Further, when improvements lower the total cost of conversion activities, prospects that were not profitable enough to target become worth it, increasing your addressable market.

This is usually what sales managers seek to do when they design and allocate sales territories. There have long been optimization models used for territory design, and more appear annually. Yet analysts estimate that 55 percent of sales territories in the United States are either too large to be covered adequately or too small, and therefore calls and selling time are wasted.[5] Why? As a character in a Thomas Pynchon novel says, "If they can get you asking the wrong questions, they don't have to worry about answers." Historical outcome data is the typical input to those models, and the result is often the right math for the wrong questions. Conversion activities drive sales outcomes, not the other way around, and should be an input to deployment in a sales model, including territory design and quota setting.

As part of a wider application of analytics in its organization, Microsoft looked at the time sales teams spent interacting with their accounts and the number of individual contacts they were connecting with.[6] There were big differences across different accounts and segments. On average, teams engaged with twice the number of customer contacts in higher-growth accounts and spent double the amount of time with these customers compared to lower-growth accounts. What's cause and what's effect here? Are the accounts higher growth because sales spent more time and attention with those accounts, or did sales spend more time because they are higher growth? Conversion data showed that investing more time and attention with historically lower-growth accounts indeed produced results—in other words, the drivers were the selling and account-management efforts. Microsoft adjusted its sales model, reducing the number of enterprise accounts per seller to allow each team more face time across its account portfolio.

Reallocating Account Assignments

In many firms, established sales-client relationships are driven by legacy assumptions and therefore are susceptible to inertia over time. An important application of conversion analytics is understanding where those relationships do and don't make a difference in outcomes.

Edward Jones is among the most successful financial services firms in the world. In 2017, Jones surpassed $1 trillion in assets under management (AUM), making it one of the top five brokerages in the United States and consistently at or near the top in surveys of both client and employee satisfaction. Like other brokerages, its sales and service model relies on financial advisers (FAs) to acquire, maintain, and grow accounts and AUM with the hundreds of clients for whom each FA is responsible. In most brokerages, these relationships are regarded as sacrosanct, and the broker, not the brand, in effect "owns" the customer in perpetuity.

A key to Jones's success has been its management of account assignments and service levels. In 2001, it established the Goodknight program, named after its originator, Jim Goodknight, a partner at Edward Jones. The program involved an established FA turning over to a new FA the clients that the veteran FA had not contacted for a specified period of time. This freed veteran FAs to spend more time with and increase share of wallet at established clients; it allowed new FAs to work with existing but underserved Jones clients. The success rate in customer conversion of a new FA without the Goodknight program was 36 percent, while new FAs in the program have an 80 percent success rate. Jones therefore conducts thousands of Goodknights annually. Conversely, as it grew, Jones also found that smaller accounts take up inordinate amounts of time and effort in the conversion efforts of individual FAs. Hence, in 2017 it assigned inactive accounts with less than $50,000 in AUM to home-office-based service centers, freeing up time for FAs to focus on getting and keeping clients with more opportunity.[7]

Monitoring Online/Offline Interactions

Even when they do purchase from a salesperson, buyers in many categories now begin their journey online via websites, social media, Google, Amazon, or other vehicles. As a combination of online and personal selling becomes the norm in sales models, conversion analysis is more important.

It's important for understanding the role and efficacy of your online investments. For example, time on site and page views are often associated with positive engagement, when they may be a result of a confusing or slow-loading site. New-visitor counts are often touted as surrogates for growth, but much of this may simply be driven by the proliferation of new devices and disconnected from actual purchases. Or, in certain subscription sales models, a "win" is treated as synonymous with the "last click," when the reality is that the purchase was motivated by a combination of sales and marketing activities throughout the buyer journey. In online activities, conversion analytics shed light on the types of onboarding that spur initial adoption, the features that retain customers, and the offers that are more and less likely to be effective when reaching out to dormant users of a platform. What tech enthusiasts call a "viral loop" *is* the result of these targeted customer conversion efforts.

Conversion analysis is also important for understanding where in-person selling efforts have the biggest impact. What we know about buying indicates that online and offline behavior interact. They are typically complements, not substitutes, so ignore these interactions at your peril. We will look at examples and lessons of these interactions in more detail in chapter 10 about managing a multichannel approach. But, here, consider the relevance of conversion analysis for understanding where and when your salespeople should have a conversation with customers. In early stages of many conversion processes, customers are not ready to transact, and a better use of resources than a sales call is often content marketing (see later in this chapter). At a later stage, ongoing interaction with a knowledgeable and trusted rep is often crucial, and online means, however sophisticated, may not suffice.

The ultimate economic rationale for marketing and sales investments is what some call a "baseline-lift" valuation—that is, a measure of the lift over a baseline of existing sales that is attributable to a specific initiative.[8] You will never know what that lift is (or isn't) unless you can link the investment to the customer conversion dynamic in your sales model. Further, no one has repealed the law of diminishing returns: the lift from a given investment will inevitably alter. You rarely generate three times current revenues and profits by doing three times whatever got you to your current state.

Coordination and a Single View of the Customer

Buyers expect a seller to provide a coherent response. Meanwhile, for sellers, a buyer's order touches multiple functions as it moves from initial contact to purchase to postsale activities.

A typical problem is that each function has its own metrics and priorities. Even within the sales function, CRM systems are usually reporting the aggregate result of what, in reality, is multiple salespeople using different criteria in CRM reports. One rep may tally a customer's request for a price quote as a qualified lead or active account in the CRM system, while another rep may use identifying a known budget as the criterion for qualifying a lead or responding to price queries. Necessary coordination is impeded or even actively subverted because the firm lacks a single view of the customer conversion process across customer-contact and order-fulfillment functions. The problem is even greater when a multichannel effort is relevant to buying and selling.

Conversely, the rewards of getting this right are significant. Pandora, the music streaming service with more than 80 million users, sells media on its stations to local advertisers, small businesses, and corporations.[9] Its more than five hundred salespeople are in thirty-five cities in the United States and are organized in terms of customer size: an inside-sales team for small clients and inbound marketing efforts, field sales teams in each city for smaller agencies and local business prospects, national account teams for large clients and agencies, and a variety of channel partners. Core to its sales model has been monitoring the conversion process from prospecting through closing to billing and post-sale service—a process that crosses multiple functions as well as handoffs from marketing to different sales groups. In most companies, this is a recipe for siloed behaviors and customer confusion. But David Rogers, Pandora's director of business operations, notes that "Every internal system for sales is integrated, so reps don't have to step outside [the system] to pitch or run a campaign for a client. All lead and pipeline information is captured in the system, as is updated content from marketing, interactions between sales teams and legal and finance, as well as commission payouts and billing information."

The last item is noteworthy. In the media business, orders must be custom built to run at selected times and stations in the future. Billing (and sales commission) only happens when the ad is delivered. Pandora's system increases buyer and seller trust in the process, freeing up time for selling rather than checking that client service and incentive payout have occurred accurately. As Rogers explains, the focus on conversion dynamics and the supporting systems provide other benefits throughout the sales process: "Reps spend less time researching answers to questions about campaigns. Onboarding has become easier, and the time in which they can ramp and start selling productively has shortened." Similarly, a classic collaboration barrier is tracking and apportioning credit across channels. At Pandora, as Rogers notes, "If a client hits a certain threshold, they're funneled up to sales teams and client-support groups that can handle more complex campaigns. We can track this, keep it visible, and reward the originating channel with post-pass credit . . . and avoid typical channel noise."

There's no one-size-fits-all form of conversion analysis, and your sales model should not be premised on a search for the perfect metrics. So much depends on context. But a deep dive into the conversion process inherent in your sales model is the prerequisite for a dialogue about its strengths, weaknesses, continuous improvement, and, when necessary, reconstruction of the model.

Reconstructing a Sales Model

The closest thing I know to a law of the marketplace is that, over time, customers tend to get smarter and use that knowledge to become more discriminating buyers. That's why, as explained in the previous chapter, any sales model is like perishable goods in grocery stores: it has a sell-by date, because markets don't stand still, and neither should your go-to-market process. At some point, tweaks will not suffice and reconstructing the sales model is necessary.

A common situation is when a strategy and product shift requires a change in the sales model. Let's return to a company discussed in chapter 5, Oversight Systems, the provider of analytics that monitors corporate purchasing card and reimbursement data for errors, fraud, and operational inefficiencies.

Oversight Systems: Moving from a Field to Inside Sales Model

Oversight initially sold a product customized to individual clients. In that sales model, the target buyer was the CFO or other senior executive at a corporation, the price was $200,000 to $500,000 per year per business process monitored, the buying journey was protracted (typically nine to twelve months), and selling involved expensive enterprise reps (on-target compensation of about $300,000 per rep) who could diagnose specific applications and manage pilots with IT managers. Further, postsale onboarding and systems integration activities took an additional three to six months. Oversight acquired about forty customers, and the market credibility required of a startup, via this approach.

But this sales model is tough to scale. As Patrick Taylor, founder of Oversight, explains: "Customizing the analytics is essentially a professional services business; it takes many hours that decrease margins [and] it's expensive—you can't have fresh-out-of-college people selling customized solutions. We also had a forecasting problem: we did not know if or when a deal would close." Manish Singh, who ran Oversight's sales and client services team, adds that "There was a lot of handholding. If the customer assigned someone who really understood different types of implementations, the end product was good. Otherwise, there were lots of issues."

Taylor and Singh saw advantages in a more standardized product. They noticed that customers tended to focus on a few recurrent themes in using Oversight's software. The firm created modules, branded as Insights on Demand (IOD), each focused on a data-monitoring domain (e.g., T&E spending by region or function, Foreign Corrupt Practices Act compliance, duplicate payment monitoring, and so on). In turn, this change in product required a different sales model, affecting who to hire, how to sell, pricing, and the division of labor across conversion activities from prospecting to ongoing account management. Singh notes that with IOD, "We went from a face-to-face software selling model adapted to individual customer requirements to an exclusively [inside-sales] approach with scripted processes." In turn, that change in sales model meant big differences in price, type of sales person needed, purchase terms and conditions, postsale service, and potential channel partners.

IOD sold at $50,000 per year per module, much less than prices for the custom solution. Enterprise reps were too expensive in this model and not necessary, because an IOD module could be integrated into a client's system in a day. Instead, the new sales model involved demand generation reps (DGs) who used scripted telephone-based outreach to arrange an online demo with a target customer for a given module with an AE. DGs, typically recent college graduates with one to two years of sales experience, focus on getting the first meeting. AEs, more experienced salespeople or DGs promoted after some years of experience, earned a salary about one-third of that paid to the enterprise reps, plus commissions on closed deals that, at target, made up about 50 percent of their total compensation.

In turn, these less-experienced resources were enabled by other aspects of the reconstructed sales model. After a demo, Oversight offered the prospect a free analysis of three to six months of their data, and a one- to two-week trial period for people in the relevant department (compliance, audit, T&E) to use and explore the module's capabilities. Upon sale, customers could cancel at any point. Taylor explains that, with the new model, "we treat our prospects like customers and, once they subscribe, we treat our customers like prospects: we keep them happy every month, or they can cancel and we refund the balance of their subscription payment." It's a process designed to lower entry and accelerate conversion with low-touch and lower-cost salespeople.

Similarly, in the old model, postsale service required a dedicated IT solutions team in addition to the enterprise rep. But the one-day integration of an IOD module allows Oversight to allocate talented DGs and AEs to that activity and also increase upselling of additional modules. Finally, the new sales model facilitates an approach where leads, referrals, and initial business-development activities can be handled by third-party channel partners, extending capacity and market reach.

The Oversight example contains important lessons. First, no sales model is a substitute for a coherent business model in tune with market conditions and growth requirements. As Singh says, "With IOD, we standardized how we price, package, and deliver product. We then could streamline the sales process to fit." In other words, strategy first, and *then* the go-to-market.

Second, the changes in Oversight's sales model are increasingly common, as subscription business models proliferate in many areas. It's therefore worth focusing on some core issues that are typically crucial in reconstructing sales models along these lines.

Subscription Sales Models

One more time: technology is not replacing sales, but it is changing buying and therefore sales tasks. One change is a shift in many industries to subscription-based models. They are now common in many SaaS categories, telecommunications/cable and media companies, health and nutritional categories, digital publishing, and—just starting but likely to grow significantly—in a variety of equipment and device sectors where internet-of-things (IoT) technologies are spreading.

In this model, the first sale is typically the starting point for a land-and-expand approach. The order evolves over time as the customer upgrades, downgrades, or changes the number of users or other specifications. Because the sale is priced as part of a recurring revenue stream, not a single up-front purchase, it often changes who buys at the customer and how the purchase is budgeted (e.g., part of that buyer's operating budget versus a capital expenditure requiring management approval). Hence, changing to a subscription business means reconstructing a sales model in several core ways: an inside-sales group often becomes more prominent instead of—or in addition to—a field-based sales force; marketing and sales interactions increase, and content marketing is a primary form of lead generation; and postsale service becomes more integral to customer acquisition and lifetime value.

Inside Sales

A subscription approach usually requires a lower-cost sales model to align with the lower up-front price and ongoing need to get renewals and upgrades. As with Oversight, this typically means replacing or augmenting a more expensive field-based model with an inside-sales model staffed by less experienced and less expensive people. To make the model work, however, it's important to understand where it applies and the tools required.

SaaS services like file sharing or scheduling software are typically used in a department, and buyers can gather much presale information via online search, which allows them to act more quickly and decisively in purchasing. Inside-sales reps can conduct online demos and provide prospects with a semi-customized proposal with a few clicks on the website. On the other hand, a SaaS platform such as CRM or marketing automation services requires more sophisticated integration with the customer's data and IT systems and often the involvement of engineers from the buyer and vendor. This is a more complex initial sale that is harder to do online or by phone with relatively inexperienced salespeople.

Both types of services are subscription services, and buyers can search online for both. But the applicable sales models are driven by buying and product issues, not whether online search is available. Inside-sales models tend to work best when the buyer is making a stand-alone purchase and has budget authority versus an integrated system purchase with a more complex buying and product-usage process.

When applicable, an inside-sales model requires tools that support and sustain a cadence where salespeople are often making twenty to thirty calls hourly. That's a call every two to three minutes, and a successful inside sale is more likely if a rep can contact the prospect within five to fifteen minutes after that prospect visits the seller's site or downloads product information. Software that automates this high-velocity process is crucial. In 2018, for instance, an estimated $6,181 was spent on technology for each inside-sales rep on software ranging from email tools, social prospecting, sales dialers, call tracking, and activity logging to contract and signature management.[10] That's four times more, per capita, than average sales training expenditures. Performance management and coaching practices that keep a sales cadence on track are also crucial for getting a good return on these investments.

Similarly, salespeople need scripts in making repeated calls or sending emails to prospects. When Oversight changed its sales model, for instance, it developed a cadence of scripted calls for DGs to follow in each of a series of successive calls on a prospect for a given IOD product module. Also, persistence counts in inside sales: research indicates that the average inside-sales rep makes one to three calls before giving up on contacting a prospect, but the required number of calls is typically six to nine.[11]

Finally, when you step outside certain tech categories, inside sales is usually part of a hybrid account-based field sales model. In those circumstances, the conversion analytics discussed earlier in this chapter are a foundation for knowing where and when to allocate the different elements of the go-to-market portfolio. Many sales managers assume that the allocation is simply determined by account size: field enterprise reps for larger accounts and inside-sales reps for smaller accounts. But a more efficient approach is often by stage in the conversion process, with field sales involved in consideration and evaluation portions of the buying journey and inside sales at the start (lead generation) and as an ongoing means for monitoring and managing repeat purchases from customers, big and small.

Marketing

In a subscription model, sales and marketing are more interrelated, especially in lead-generation activities via content marketing initiatives. Subscription businesses have hired writers and chief content officers to create blogs, email campaigns, white papers, and other materials designed to attract prospects to a website, download information, and in the process, generate a lead that is then forwarded to the sales organization.

This practice recognizes that, in many categories, the awareness stage of the buyer journey may often be triggered by relevant content about a problem or opportunity addressed by that seller's product or service. But an estimated 70 percent of the content generated is never used by sales, and an equal percentage of the leads generated this way disappear into what some have called the "sales lead black hole."[12] Further, there are many contradictory assertions about which content marketing benchmarks indicate success and best practices in this growing component of many sales models.

Content marketing (like advertising) is the subject of many opinions but few facts, so it is an area where unexamined assumptions distort allocations of money and effort. The following is what a study of 34 million interactions between customers and content indicates about core aspects of this practice: how much time prospects spend on content, on which devices, when, and the type of content they prefer.[13]

You Have Under Three Minutes to Communicate Content. Buyers are now bombarded with messages, and the average viewing time for web-based content in this study was 2.5 minutes. During that brief period, prospects make many rapid-fire judgments, including whether or not they will move to the next step of that conversion process.

Try to get your content into two- to five-page documents. Prospects spend more time viewing each page and are more likely to view all of it, compared to lengthier content. The data also indicates that much marketing collateral is read by prospects outside of the normal workweek. If initially engaged, a prospect reading a piece on Wednesday often returns for a longer visit on the weekend. This reflects the reality discussed in chapter 1: buyers adopt parallel streams to explore, evaluate, and engage with content and salespeople, and content forms, formats, and sequencing must adapt to buying behaviors.

Mobile Devices Are Important but Overhyped. The proliferation of smartphones, iPads, and other devices has generated a certain folk wisdom about crafting content for the mobile buyer. But the data in this study indicates that it typically makes more sense to optimize content for viewing on multiple formats and devices. Further, when they do engage online with a salesperson, a majority of prospects view sales content on desktop devices, not mobile.

These findings have actionable implications. Avoid needless and often costly optimization for a single device and format. Also, since prospects often return for a closer look outside office hours, effective content campaigns should also help sellers prioritize required follow-up actions. In doing this, recognize inherent differences between marketing- and sales-relevant content. In the former, the goal is often to establish awareness and interest; for sales, the goal is to get the customer to sign a contract.

There Is No One "Best Day" to Send Content. There are many assertions about the best day of the week to send content. Some argue for Tuesday afternoon, while others are loyal to Thursday morning. But data indicates that total visits to sellers' sites are almost evenly distributed across each day of the workweek—slightly more on Tuesday, Wednesday, and Thursday, and unsurprisingly, fewer on Monday morning and Friday afternoon.

Focusing on specific days for sending content probably indicates unused capacity and a lack of cadence in your sales model. It's better to focus on types of follow-up content after initial engagement. This often means linking content marketing efforts to the prospect's vertical segment or industry.

Prospects Prefer One Type of Content More Than Others. The tried-and-true case study is, by far, the content that prospects actually read through more than others. In this research, case studies had an 83 percent completion rate—orders of magnitude higher than other sales and marketing content provided during the buying journey. The implication is that buyers, especially B2B buyers of a subscription service, want to know what others *are* doing with your product, not only what they *might* do to improve a business outcome. Good case-study content does that, while providing compelling reasons for prospects to learn more and initiate a change process from the status quo system they have in place.

Content marketing is evolving and spreading from SaaS and subscription businesses to other sales models as well. But without tools for tracking what, when, and where prospects read content, there is a blind spot in a growing part of the marketing and sales budgets in many firms.

Sales-Service Interactions

In subscription models, service becomes part of the sales process at multiple parts of the buying journey. In response to a content marketing piece, a prospect may be on your website and click on a chat button for additional information. If the product is sold via trials, the service provided during that period is critical. This is a very different interaction than in a postsale service model, and many subscription businesses refer to their service groups as Customer Success (CS) teams, because they are vital in closing a sale and account-expansion efforts after the initial sale.

An example is DoubleDutch, which sells a subscription-based event management app to organizations hosting conferences, trade shows, large meetings, and similar events. Its app, when used appropriately, enables attendees, speakers, and event managers to communicate with one another during and after the event, gathers data useful to all parties, and increases engagement. This is a large, diverse market where customers range from corporations and agencies to nonprofit and trade associations that have differing needs, usage patterns, and levels of technical experience. Before the pandemic of 2020, almost 2 million people in the United States attended over 270,000 conventions and about 11,000 trade shows annually. Globally, over $500 billion was spent on such meetings, and about $30 billion of that expenditure was for event management software of various kinds.[14]

DoubleDutch uses an inside-sales model to make the initial sale, and its CS team is responsible for developing app functionality for the event, technical integration, onboarding and training customers about usage and best practices, and post-event debriefs aimed at making next year's meeting or conference even better. Clearly, the CS team does more than traditional postsale order fulfillment and problem resolution. The CS team is a key to subscription renewals, upsells, and cross-sells to other services. This raises issues in managing interactions between sales and service in this model: How to delineate responsibilities between CS teams and sales in terms of renewals, upsells, and ongoing account management? How to measure each group for these activities? How to manage the cultural issues often relevant to service versus selling?

In answering these questions, it's important to clarify the role(s) of the CS team in your sales process. Consultant Nick Mehta provides a useful typology of possible CS roles:[15]

- **Firefighter CS.** Typically found in early-stage companies, CS is the "one-stop shop" responsible for support, renewals, and other postsale activities. This CS role places much pressure on finding the right multitalented people and is often hard to scale.

- **Sales-oriented CS.** Typically found in companies with low levels of product complexity. The CS team is responsible for upsells, and its metrics are tied to revenue as well as customer satisfaction.

- **Service-oriented CS.** Found in companies with more product complexity. Here, the CS team focuses on customer service with less attention to account expansion, but there are more handoffs as a customer is passed from sales to service and back to sales for upsell or cross-sell efforts.

- **Integrated CSM.** Here, sales focuses on new business, while the CS team works on both presale and postsale activities. The issues are that (a) some duplication of effort is likely, increasing costs, and (b) attributing sales results and quantifying ROI for each group is more difficult in this approach.

Where the CS team reports is also a key decision in a subscription model. One option is that the team report directly to the CEO, because the function is such an important driver of the customer experience, from onboarding to renewals and account expansion. But this approach can make alignment with ongoing sales and product management activities more difficult, and most CEOs already have too many direct reports.

Another option is that the CS team reports to the head of sales or as part of a sales operations function. This places all revenue-generating activities from acquisition to renewal in one function and can help to increase integration across the land-and-expand sales life cycle. But priorities between service and selling are often in tension, and this approach typically raises other issues. At DoubleDutch, for example, the CS team was involved in integration and ongoing usage at clients and therefore in an ideal position to monitor and encourage renewals, upsells to premium packages, and so on. Soon after the sale, the team had stronger relationships with clients than the inside-sales reps who initially landed those clients. But the CS team balked when management sought to have the group monetize those relationships. As one CS manager said, "We're a services function . . . We don't want this dynamic to change. Clients have to fully trust that we're working in their best interest, and it's important that we differentiate ourselves from sales."

Some might argue that good service can continue even as the CS team becomes more aggressive in soliciting upsells, and that appropriate compensation incentives are the fix here. On the other hand, this attitude about service versus sales is common in organizations, which recruit different types of people for those activities (sales versus engineering backgrounds, for example). Selling and servicing *are* distinct skill sets in most businesses. As we'll discuss in the next chapter, moreover, relevant compensation is a necessary but not sufficient cause of getting the behaviors you need in a sales model. As a manager once told me, "When people don't want to do things, nothing can stop them!"

For this reason, some subscription businesses opt for a different approach. InsightSquared sells sales intelligence solutions. In its early years, it had a CS group responsible and compensated for renewals as well as integration and support.[16] But it moved away from that approach as it grew. Fred Shilmover, CEO of InsightSquared, explains that "building renewals, support, enablement and professional services didn't allow the group to have a real identity, and it focused them on things other than customer success." The firm dismantled the CS group in favor of a services department, placed former CS people responsible for renewals and expansion into the sales department, reorganized sales into acquisition and postsales expansion teams (rewarded on net changes in account annual recurring revenue), and assigned service-only personnel to territory-focused sales teams. The objective was to create what Shilmover calls "small, almost nuclear families, where the pre-sale and postsale activity on the same account is managed by the same people in the same team and with the same manager."

QUESTIONS TO ASK . . . AND ANSWER

Maintaining a relevant and productive sales model is a process, not a onetime event. Consider what you do, and should do, in managing and possibly reconstructing your sales model by answering the questions in table 6-1.

TABLE 6-1

Managing, maintaining, and reconstructing your sales model

In our company, how well do we . . .	
Understand and track the customer-conversion activities inherent in our sales model?	1 2 3 4 5 6 7
Have in place and communicate leading indicators of customer behavior, not only outcome metrics like wins?	1 2 3 4 5 6 7
Use conversion analytics to increase customer-contact time in our sales force?	1 2 3 4 5 6 7
Examine established account assignments to identify under-served customers and segments?	1 2 3 4 5 6 7
Track interactions between our online and in-person efforts and place reps where they have the most impact?	1 2 3 4 5 6 7
Enable better coordination within sales and across functions with systems that provide a single view of the customer?	1 2 3 4 5 6 7
Make use of available tools that support and sustain the kind of ongoing cadence required in our sales model?	1 2 3 4 5 6 7
Clarify the role of service in the customer acquisition and retention activities required in our sales model?	1 2 3 4 5 6 7

Despite currently fashionable talk about "predictable revenue" and "growth hacking," no sales model manages itself, and any process is only as good as the behaviors of the people who manage and work within that process. A key management tool is the focus of the next chapter: the role, limits, structure, and how of sales compensation and incentives in linking daily behaviors with your sales model and growth initiatives.

COMPENSATION AND INCENTIVES

Compensation is the single biggest chunk of the money that firms spend on selling. Further, *how* you pay influences the relevant talent pool and therefore *who* you hire and *what* you (should) measure. But compensation is ultimately a necessary yet insufficient cause of getting selling behaviors that align with a sales model. Elsewhere, I have outlined a process for developing a sales compensation plan.[1] Here, I want to broaden the topic because, in a world with shorter life cycles and more information available to customers, it's a mistake to develop a comp plan in isolation from other factors.

Sales managers now face a daily challenge: how to ensure that their people efficiently sell in line with the firm's strategy and sales model and, when necessary, collaborate with others to identify and deliver customer value. This chapter focuses on the what and how of the comp plan: the role and limits of sales compensation in influencing behavior, common problems with compensation practice in firms, tailoring comp plans to stage and type of growth, and important issues in how you pay salespeople regardless of the structure of the plan. We'll then compare and contrast the pay plans at two companies in order to understand how business model economics, competition, and buying behavior affect sales compensation decisions in specific circumstances.

The Role and Limits of Compensation

Those unfamiliar with sales often assume that salespeople are "coin-operated"—a terrible phrase that equates people with vending machines and assumes that money is their only motivator. But there's a robust stream of research in economics and psychology that documents how monetary incentives can come into conflict with other sources of motivation and change how people perceive tasks. A classic example is that paying people to donate blood breaks social norms about voluntary contributions and can result in fewer people who donate.[2] This is called the "crowd-out" effect of monetary (extrinsic rewards) versus nonmonetary (intrinsic rewards) incentives on behavior.[3]

Consider a study of effort and collaboration in an inside-sales organization, the fastest-growing segment of sales jobs.[4] The researchers found that structured meetings, with a free lunch, between high-performing and lower-performing reps yielded larger and more persistent productivity gains than monetary incentives alone *or* conditions in which the reps had both meetings and incentives. Why? The lunches provided a forum for sharing important tacit knowledge about selling that is difficult to capture in a sales methodology or training programs.

As the research indicates, you can sometimes substitute smart management for money, but rarely vice versa. When it comes to money, moreover, a key is typically the incentives in the compensation plan. Take, for example, the sales incentives at Wells Fargo bank, which eventually resulted in hundreds of millions of dollars in fines, the firing of over five thousand employees, the clawback of more than $75 million in compensation from former executives, and long-term damage to the brand. Money matters, and so does ongoing performance management.

About 95 percent of firms in the United States use some form of variable-pay incentive in sales, with commissions and quota-based bonuses being the most common.[5] On average in companies with the one hundred largest sales forces, salespeople have three to four times as much compensation at risk as their brethren in other functions.[6] Clearly, managers believe in the motivational value of monetary incentives. Yet, surveys consistently indicate dissatisfaction with the impact of compensation on actual selling behaviors, and a whopping 80 percent of firms revise their sales comp programs every two years or less.[7]

But these changes are typically alterations to the target numbers, not to the structure and purpose of the plan. Ironically, these frequent quantitative but full-speed-ahead changes may be a contributing factor to misalignment between incentives and desired behaviors in fast-moving and information-rich markets.

Problems with Practice

Dilma Rousseff, the economically disastrous former socialist president of Brazil, once said, "We are not going to set a goal. We are going to leave the goal open but, when we reach our goal, we are going to double it." This was funny—if you weren't living in Brazil. Something similar often happens in for-profit companies in a variety of areas.

Companies routinely confuse "strategic planning" with their annual capital budgeting process, and it's well documented that these meetings result, on the whole, in only modest resource shifts. Within a firm, last year's budget allocation typically serves as a salient and, in the cross-functional battle for limited resources, readily justifiable anchor during the planning process. The usual result is a tweak up or down in the goal, not a meaningful reallocation of resources. As one group of researchers concluded, "Whether the relevant resource is capital expenditures, operating expenditures, or human capital, this finding is consistent across industries as diverse as mining and consumer packaged goods."[8]

The same is true in advertising spending, where the budget is typically set as a percentage of the company's sales. Hence, both the correlation and media allocation between current-year ad spend and the firm's ad programs for the previous five years are often remarkably high. Further, there's a kind of bass-ackwards effect: the ad budget goes up when market demand and sales are high, and it's cut when sales decrease and demand-generating ads are arguably more important.

The same is also true in sales compensation, where inertia is common in many companies' pay plans. An initial burst of energy around the design of the plan is replaced, over time, with tweaks to the numbers, not the structure, and the plan becomes less useful in motivating relevant behaviors or even downright counterproductive.

Further, the plan's structure often relies on conventional wisdom for setting the pay mix (the ratio of fixed to variable pay in the plan). Commonly accepted principles for pay mix tend to look at factors like the selling cycle (the shorter the cycle, the higher the variable pay), the ability to forecast sales volume in a market (the more difficulty in predicting sales volume, the higher the fixed pay), and the rep's ability to control the factors that generate sales outcomes (the higher the level of control, the higher the variable-pay component). Similarly, there are often unexamined assumptions about the effects of pay mix on selling behaviors: for example, higher fixed pay encourages a "long-term orientation" and attention to tasks such as customer service, but also encourages "hunters" to become "farmers" and often results in free riders in the sales organization; higher variable pay attracts "risk takers" and a pay-for-performance culture, but encourages a short-term view and creates a "high-pressure" selling environment that can alienate customers.[9]

These assertions are, at best, broad generalities and are like rules of thumb in language and other living, evolving human activities. "I before E, except after C. Or when sounded as A, as in neighbor and weigh." Did you know this "rule" actually has more exceptions than rule-conforming examples in English? Sales is similar: results often have their root causes in other areas besides compensation.

Developing a Comp Plan

The comp plan should support your sales model, not drive it. So first consider the tasks inherent in your customer-acquisition process. The comp plan should then set priorities among the relevant tasks, and this will vary by market and by sales model. It's the specific realities of buying and selling in your business that should determine the priorities, not textbook rules or organizational legacy.

How You Adapt

Change is incessant in business: markets change, products change, buyers change, and competitors provide alternatives or substitutes. Your comp plan should reflect those changes. Early-stage companies are good examples because, if successful, they go through stages that demand different sales behaviors.

HubSpot, a pioneer in inbound marketing, in its early years redesigned its sales comp plan three times to respond to changing priorities.[10] The initial plan paid reps a base salary and a $2 commission up front for $1 of monthly recurring revenue (MRR) they brought in, but with a four-month claw-back on commissions—that is, if that customer did not remain with HubSpot for at least four months, that commission was deducted from that rep's earned commissions in the next pay period. The good news: this plan helped HubSpot grow to about a thousand customers and $3 million in revenues. The bad news: the level of customer churn was unsustainable in a subscription business.

The data indicated a big difference in customer churn rates by salesperson—more than a 10x difference across the sales force, depending upon the types of prospects the salesperson targeted and the expectations the rep set with accounts. In response, a new plan set commissions based on customer retention rates. The top-performing quartile of reps on this metric earned $4 per $1 of MRR, the next quartile earned $3 per $1 of MRR, and so on. This plan was complemented with training about the importance of retention to the business model and techniques for setting customer expectations and smart usage of inbound marketing. In six months, customer churn dropped by 70 percent.

A third stage was scaling the business, both in terms of number of customers and their up-front payment of MRR. Salespeople earned $2 per $1 of MRR, but the commission was paid as follows: 50 percent on the customer's first month's payment, 25 percent on the sixth month's payment, and 25 percent on the twelfth month's payment. Hence, if a customer signed up month to month, the salesperson waited a year for full payment, but an up-front year's subscription earned the rep their entire commission immediately. Before this plan was in place, the average up-front customer commitment was 2.5 months. In less than a year, the average was seven months, cash flow improved, and the company began to prepare for an IPO.

In startup mode or when introducing a product, acquiring customers quickly is typically important for cash flow but also for market credibility, referral accounts, and making product changes, among other reasons. But profitability and retention become more important as the market matures. More generally, as discussed in chapter 5, over the course of the life cycle for most products and services, there's a shift in buying behavior as product/service design becomes standardized and therefore more easily imitated, competitors enter, and initial segments become saturated. Conversely, as a seller's product line or services increase, upselling and cross-selling become more important goals.

The comp plan should reflect the relevant changes. Notice, however, that not only the comp plan changed in the HubSpot example: training and pricing changes were complementary to the revised structure of each plan. As always, compensation is a means and part of a wider performance tool kit for sales managers. An important tool is communication. Mark Roberge, head of sales at HubSpot during these changes, notes that "Whenever I considered changing the compensation plan, I always involved the sales team in the redesign. To kick things off, I usually held a 'town meeting' with the team [and] would share some of the structures that were being considered and invite people to offer their feedback." Roberge also created a wiki site, explaining the reasons for a change in the plan, outlining the goals, and inviting comments. The lesson here is that *how* you manage compensation matters mightily.

How You Pay

Many managers believe that "we pay for results, not process" and that "money talks"—that is, monetary rewards speak for themselves as motivational cues. Not true. Money is powerful, but it's mute. Without attention to how you pay in a sales environment, you often don't get what you're paying for. Let's consider a few perennial issues about the process of rewarding salespeople.

Transparency

Executives often tout transparency and open-book practices, but compensation is typically an exception. Pay is often an uncomfortable, taboo topic in the workplace. Managers fear that pay transparency will generate conflicts and motivational problems. But as bethanye McKinney Blount, a serial entrepreneur and veteran of Facebook and Reddit in their startup phases, points out, "Comp transparency is a spectrum. [Not] 'I'm going to know how much everybody makes.' A better way to frame it is, 'I'm going to understand *why* I'm paid and *how* I can increase my comp.' It's about making sure employees understand their current reality and see a career development path in front of them."[11]

Research supports this perspective and indicates a more nuanced reality than many managers assume. Like other people, salespeople want to maximize their income and know why they did or didn't achieve incentive goals. They want to know so they can make *more* money next quarter and next year. After a firm informed its workers how they ranked in pay and performance, average productivity increased by nearly 7 percent, and the effect was not a onetime Hawthorne effect: it persisted over time.[12]

Other research indicates a difference when people know the pay of their peers (horizontal comparisons) versus those higher in the hierarchy (vertical comparisons). When the boss was fewer than five promotions away, employees were more motivated and productive because they "became more optimistic about the salaries they will earn themselves in the future. [But] finding out peers get paid more does have a negative effect on the employee's effort and performance. Finding out that peers earn on average 10% more than initially thought caused employees to spend 9.4% fewer hours in the office, send 4.3% fewer emails, and sell 7.3% less."[13] Surveys indicate most employees favor anonymous pay transparency (i.e., average pay by position), but not when specific names and numbers are shared.

The research suggests, again, that it's not wise or easy to motivate solely through monetary rewards. There are interdependent links between motivation → effort → rewards that we will examine later in this chapter in considering the factors shaping two specific pay plans.

The research also suggests that managers often think pay secrecy is in their best interests when it is not, and can lead employees to randomly attribute reasons for their compensation. Blount provides an example that is unfortunately common: "I used to work for a tech company where the way you got raises was that the leadership would decide and money would just show up one day in your bank account . . . They thought it was a fun way to keep things fresh. But the whole team was really thinking, 'Is this a bank error? Should I spend this or not?' It was very confusing and not the least bit fun."[14] I personally know two high-performing salespeople who quit their firms after *receiving* six-figure bonuses in this manner. As one said, "If my boss won't even thank me for all the work I put in to achieve that performance, I don't want to be there and I have other options."

Pay process matters.

Recognition

There's a reason why so many sales organizations display reps' sales numbers on leaderboards in the branch office or on a monthly or quarterly spreadsheet sent via email to everyone on the sales team. People are social creatures and want to know how they perform relative to others.

While cash constitutes the majority of incentive compensation expenditures, companies across the globe spend billions annually on merchandise incentive programs for their salespeople. One study of six hundred salespeople found that, after controlling for salesperson, seasonality, and economic conditions, when a mixed cash and prize reward program was replaced with an equivalent-value all-cash package, both effort and results *dropped*—a 4.36 percent decrease in sales that cost the company millions in revenue.[15] Many reps preferred the prizes (no tax implications), and many just liked having a choice between money and merchandise. Cash is not necessarily king in compensation. Why?

People seek relations and recognition as well as livelihood in their jobs. Include a handwritten note with the sales bonus check. "Ring the bell" and create a buzz in the workplace. Make the reward a public event with a gift that gets displayed and lasts longer in memory than money does. Your mother was right: always remember to say thank-you. Encourage peer-recognition events: some companies run programs where employees get monthly reward points that they can give to colleagues to recognize their effort, help, or outcomes; it's not expensive and it makes a difference.

People often won't talk about the cash bonus they received, but if you reward someone with a nice dinner or trip, they will talk about it with their coworkers, and that can motivate everyone. It also builds social connections and potential peer learning in the workplace.

Fairness

"Life isn't fair," but people's perceptions of fairness affect their motivation and effort. This is true in any area of business, but especially in sales. No other function uses contests, leader boards, or performance-pay plans as much as sales does, and in most companies, no other function has as much total compensation at risk. Further, any sales force is composed of heterogeneous abilities and experience levels, and so a performance-based plan means that paychecks will vary. Meanwhile, social media and organizations like Glassdoor make it easier to access and share information about pay.

There are multiple dimensions to fairness in the workplace. *Interactional* fairness refers to the explanations that people receive about their compensation. *Procedural* fairness involves perceptions of the pay procedures—the mechanisms and metrics used, for example. *Distributive* fairness refers to employees' perceptions of the fairness of pay outcomes. Research indicates that procedural fairness increases acceptance of and compliance with decisions, even when people don't agree with the decision.[16] Meanwhile, the interactional dimension of fairness—that is, whether and how sales managers take the time to explain the pay process and how reps can improve performance and rewards—has more effect than the procedural or distributive dimensions in influencing sales performance.[17]

However, remember that fairness is in the eyes of the beholder as well as in the explanations, metrics, and actual outcomes of the plan. Those perceptions vary by culture and across regions in the same company. For instance, by the second decade of the twenty-first century, five hundred US firms employed about 24 million salespeople across the globe, but US-centric conceptions of pay fairness are not universal. Research repeatedly indicates differences in risk tolerance and risk avoidance by national culture (and, yes, Germany generally scores low on risk tolerance, while England and the United States score high).

What's more, there's evidence that these perceptions can overwhelm the basic economics. It's not just that different cultures have different risk profiles; those profiles affect what people *mean* by "fair." For instance, across sales forces globally, there is a high correlation between the level of variable pay and the total level of net pay. In other words, risk and reward are indeed bedfellows: volatility in pay links to the absolute level of take-home pay in sales. In high-tax countries, however, those taxes tend to reduce the gap in pay between high- and low-performing reps. The economic solution is to increase the variable component in those situations and reflect the gap—artificially reduced through taxes—in individual performance.[18] But cultural preferences about risk often prevent this.

Self-Selected Incentives

Let's push the pay envelope. All sales roles are not the same, any sales force has different skills and motivational preferences among its people, and so identical incentives do not equally motivate all reps. Further, markets and accounts differ, and that's why companies routinely use segmentation techniques to understand those differences and design segment-specific marketing strategies. Yet, the vast majority of comp plans treat the sales force as a homogeneous entity, and the debate is about the relevant pay mix for all people in that group. As an alternative, why not let individual reps select the incentives that correspond to their risk preferences and motivational makeup?

There are usually two core objections to this approach. One is that managers are not good mind readers and lack the required data on salespeople's preferences and risk profiles. The other is that the approach will raise the fairness issues described earlier and perhaps legal trouble.

But there is an actionable use of self-selected incentives that avoids both of these obstacles: offer each salesperson a menu of goal/reward combinations, calculated on the basis of their past performance (e.g., salary plus different levels of variable pay depending upon the percentage or absolute improvement over baseline sales for that rep). Each rep then gets to choose their preferred combination from the menu and is rewarded if and when they attain their selected goal.

At least two types of organizations (dealerships of a major US auto manufacturer, and a US *Fortune* 500 telecommunications company) have used this approach, with well-designed control groups in order to analyze the impacts. In both, the self-selected incentive scheme yielded significantly higher performance (up to 25 percent higher sales in some of the groups) than the companies' established systems of assigning a single quota to all reps (the auto dealers) or tiered quotas (the telecom firm) to the sales force. Further, the reps with self-selected incentives outperformed the control group even when the self-selected option yielded economic payoffs identical to the quota systems. Not only that, the performance effects were durable when offered again and persisted even after the self-selected pay plan was stopped.[19] Participation in incentive selection apparently makes a difference for salespeople.

This approach should attract your attention if you're a sales leader or compensation consultant, especially since regulations and company practices often result in de facto but less effective versions of self-selected incentive schemes. In France, for example, a commission compensation plan is considered a contract, and a company cannot change any aspect of the commission (e.g., rate, payment, threshold, or cap) without the explicit and full consent of the salesperson. Draws against future earnings (i.e., the rep on a commission plan receives an anticipated payment that will be offset with future earned commission) are common in US pay plans—see the HubSpot example earlier in this chapter. But draws are illegal under Japanese labor laws and most union agreements there.[20] In many companies, it's common to offer "spiffs" or special incentives when achieving that quarter's sales goal looks doubtful. In effect, individual reps opt in or out of these incentives by voting with their feet. Why not be more proactive and consider seriously and thoughtfully a menu of relevant self-selected incentives?

A Tale of Two Compensation Decisions

There's no such thing as effective selling if the selling doesn't link to your firm's strategy. Hence, the starting point is understanding what the salesperson can and should do to drive results given your business model, economics, and competition. Incentives should focus on how the salesperson makes a difference with your target customers in your business model and stage of growth.

To understand that difference, and the implications for sales compensation and performance management, let's return to the framework discussed in the previous chapter—the customer conversion process inherent in a sales model from lead generation to closing and postsales activities—and compare the process in two companies: Elmenus.com and Bigbelly.[21]

Elmenus.com

Elmenus is a website that combines restaurant menus, dish descriptions, prices, and information about location and restaurant hours. Consumers can search, "like" their favorite dishes, upload food pictures, and recommend a restaurant or dish to others. Amir Allam founded Elmenus in Cairo during the Egyptian revolution of 2011–2012 when many people were hesitant to go out in unstable security conditions. By 2015 his site contained over 3,200 restaurant menus in eight cities in Egypt, featured over 330,000 dishes, and had about 1.5 million visits monthly.

The firm's source of revenue is advertising on its site—about 80 percent of revenue directly from restaurants and 20 percent from ad agencies that placed ads for their restaurant, food, and beverage clients. Elmenus provides value to restaurants in multiple ways: the ability to reach consumers when they are exploring food options; a means for targeted advertising by category, location, or dish; and the ability to advertise on a platform with broad reach and so increase patronage via promotions. Elmenus charged the equivalent of $400 per month for advertising on specific restaurant pages, and a premium option to advertise on all of Elmenus's pages within a category group for $3,000 per month.

Allam had plans to expand within Egypt and to neighboring countries. His issue at the time was deciding on a sales compensation plan. Under the current plan, sales reps received a fixed monthly salary plus a 4 percent commission on all sales they generated if they met their monthly volume sales goals, which Allam set by reviewing the previous month's actual sales and increasing the target goal. The commissions, when received, made up about 50 percent of total monthly compensation for each rep, and salary was 50 percent. Does this type of plan make sense for a business like Elmenus.com given its market conditions, competition, and growth plans? Consider the sales tasks in this platform venture and the selling behaviors that a comp plan should motivate.

Buying Behavior and Buyer Assumptions

Restaurants in this market had limited budgets, placed ads at different times depending upon budget and current sales results, and viewed advertising as a onetime expense for a specific purpose. Moreover, despite the fact that internet penetration was increasing rapidly and already included 50 percent of Egyptian households by 2015, many restaurants had never advertised online and were skeptical because, as one owner said, "Most consumers search by restaurant name which implied that consumers decide on the restaurant before using the platform." More than 50 percent of Elmenus's customers advertised there for one month and then stopped after obtaining a desired result such as increased orders.

Elmenus is in a relatively new category in its market. Sales tasks here include customer education (the ability to identify and articulate the purpose of online ads for that type of restaurant), encouragement of trial, and persistent follow-up. The compensation plan should therefore motivate frequent, multiple calls on target accounts, both for initial sales and, with 50 percent account turnover monthly, for account management. But note that the current plan provides no incentive for account maintenance and, in fact, may provide a disincentive: sales reps currently get another commission if they sell customer X, then X leaves after a month, and the rep then "resells" customer X some weeks or months later. This type of unintended consequence is not uncommon in sales compensation plans.

Business Model Economics

On the top line, Elmenus charges $400 to $3,000 per month, depending upon the ad category chosen by the customer. The plan should contain incentives for upsells to the higher-priced offering and for package deals for multiple sales to chain restaurants.

On the cost side, a platform business like Elmenus.com has low marginal costs once a restaurant is on the site, and as in any two-sided platform, more restaurants mean more choice for the consumer and more consumers mean more value for the advertiser. Allam should consider incentives—for example, volume discounts, sales contests—to call on and bring in as many restaurants as possible for a given city.

There are links here, as in many businesses, between pricing, customer-acquisition tasks, and sales incentives. But note that the current comp plan, by linking variable pay to volume sales targets based on the previous month's results, also provides an incentive for the rep to "save" bookings for the next month once the rep has met this month's goals. This negatively affects cash flow (especially important in an expanding startup like Elmenus) and is a common defect in many comp plans.

Linking incentive pay to targets based on previous results is also often the source of complaints—typically by the people who established the plan in the first place—that sales reps "play games" with the incentives embedded in the plan. Well, of course they do: it's called maximizing income while minimizing effort. The managerial issue in sales compensation is not whether reps will play games. The issue is establishing a win-win game for the rep and the selling company.

Competition and Strategy

At the time of Allam's decisions, Elmenus was the early mover in providing online menus and restaurant advertising. But aggressive competition was entering its market: a larger and better-resourced European firm had recently acquired Otlob.com, a pioneer in Egyptian online food-ordering services. Elmenus did not provide a food-ordering capability on its platform, but Allam was considering adding this feature for restaurants, as well as data analytics that could provide tailored restaurant recommendations to consumers. Further, remember that his strategy was to scale operations in Egypt and expand to neighboring countries. With that goal in mind, Allam explained that he was seeking a sales compensation plan that would "motivate better close rates and increased customer retention."

Note the impact on sales tasks and relevant incentives if Elmenus adds the ordering and recommendation features. While Elmenus had 50 percent churn in its customer base, its selling cycle was only two to four weeks on average. Sales tasks become more complex if reps have a wider portfolio to explain and promote, and that probably means a longer selling cycle and more interactions between sales and product management. In turn, that means a change in the pay mix, with a higher proportion of fixed salary to sustain rep motivation in a longer selling-cycle model.

The market expansion goals and increased competition also raise an important choice that can be reflected in sales compensation structure: (a) should Elmenus provide incentives to sign as many prospects in a market or city as possible before bigger competitors enter? Or (b) given the high churn in the customer base, let bigger competitors educate the market, and Elmenus then competes with lower prices in a business where both consumers and retail customers have low switching costs?

The chosen route will have very different implications for sales force deployment, metrics, motivation, and relevant incentives. These interactions are inherent in any comp plan. It's like the interconnected aspects of the weather: wind depends on air temperature and temperature depends on air pressure and pressure depends on wind. With pay, think of the links this way:

Goals → Motivation → Effort (how much? what type?) → Results → Metrics → Rewards

Given your business goals, what type(s) of effort should you make to motivate your sales force? What will affect desired motivation besides the pay plan? What are the key metrics or other criteria for judging sales results at this stage of the business? How can you reward the desired results through the structure and process of your pay mix? There is a feedback loop along this chain of cause and effect. Motivation affects effort, results, and rewards, but how you pay and measure sales will also effect motivation and effort.

The founder of Elmenus wants his sales comp plan "to motivate better close rates and increased customer retention." Well, who doesn't? These criteria are cited by sales managers around the world as their motivational goals. But note the inherent tension: almost any combination of salary and incentives will put more emphasis on one of these goals to the detriment of the other, even in a relatively simple business like Elmenus.com. This is ultimately a set of strategic, not just sales, choices, and it's a mistake to develop and manage sales compensation in isolation from those choices. This is one reason why thinking and managing beyond compensation are so important in sales management, and why trying to substitute compensation alone for ongoing performance management typically won't work.

Bigbelly

Bigbelly sells solar-powered waste and recycling stations with software to manage the stations and a cloud internet connection for monitoring and control of the system. Typical trash cans in public spaces suffer from waste overflow, pest access, windblown litter, little recycling, and inefficient collection due to lack of information about waste generation patterns in different locations.

Bigbelly stations address these shortcomings. Solar cells mean its stations have more than five times the capacity of an average trash can, lowering the frequency of collection, labor costs, fuel, and other pickup and disposal costs for municipalities and institutions. (In 2016, a typical garbage truck in the United States involved an average cost of nearly $50 per hour just for fuel and maintenance, and then there's the cost of the sanitation workers.) The stations separate waste from recyclable materials, better protect the container from pests and water, and provide a cleaner, safer, and more ecologically friendly space. Meanwhile, the software collects real-time data from a network of stations, allowing a municipality or college campus to manage waste and recycling more efficiently based on actual usage patterns.

It's a high-tech solution in a rote pick-it-up-and-throw-it-out world, and in a few years Bigbelly's customers included malls, businesses, universities, sports stadiums, and some hospitals for nonmedical disposal. But most customers were cities and towns where, according to the VP of sales, the customer conversion process typically involved multiple steps and a long selling cycle. It typically took up to eighteen months to initiate active conversations with the many influencers involved in these decisions at prospects, and then an additional nine months to gather and map the necessary data about their current waste-disposal systems including locations, collection frequency, and other relevant information. At this point, Bigbelly would then submit a formal proposal concerning purchase and implementation, and prospects on average needed about six months to discuss that proposal with the multiple stakeholders involved. Then, with many customers, even an approved proposal required a change to their extant budget and more time to do the associated work within their procurement process. In all, the selling cycle between initial contact and a shipped order was often thirty-six months or more.

Traditionally, Bigbelly had sold its stations for $4,000 per unit plus an optional fee for the software. Sales reps received a base salary and a commission based on a percentage of the total contract value of that sale and any add-on sales to that customer. As one sales rep noted, "There's always initial interest in our product. No municipality is 'against' better trash collection. But a mistake is to confuse that interest with actual buying behavior. Our issue is not generating awareness: municipal officials talk to each other. Our issue is [to] actually convert interest into a sale." In fact, most customers purchased a few stations as a trial. In turn, a successful trial depended heavily on the quality of implementation, and Bigbelly found that many municipalities and institutions lacked knowledge of where to place the stations and how to use the information from the software. As CEO Jack Kutner explained, "Our thinking was that once they buy 50, they will love it and buy 500. But that transition rarely happened."

Hence, Kutner decided to change the business model and sales strategy with the introduction of a new software platform called Connect. What had previously been sold as separate hardware and software products was now fully integrated. It was an opportunity to reposition Bigbelly from a vendor often perceived by customers as selling expensive trash cans to a provider of waste management and value-added services. Connect would be offered as a subscription with the stations for $125 per month per unit on a three-year contract, including installation and maintenance. The issue facing Kutner was to craft a sales comp plan to support this strategy. What are the relevant factors in this context?

Change in Business Model and Value Proposition

Bigbelly is moving from selling units of equipment to selling a SaaS service and integrated system. This means different buyers, purchase criteria, and metrics that customers use to judge the success of the product. With its new approach, Bigbelly is also selling a change in behavior at its customers, not only a product/service package. Its salespeople must identify the right customers—not only initially enthusiastic prospects—and work with them to make changes in their approach to waste collection.

This is a more complex sale than that of Elmenus.com and involves both selling and postsale tasks. Other factors besides pay mix are relevant here.

> **Deployment.** How can Bigbelly focus reps on the segments most interested in purchasing at the critical mass required to demonstrate the value of the integrated system?

> **Organization.** Should sales reps be responsible for both selling and postsale usage tasks, or should Kutner split those tasks between separate sales and postsale customer success groups?

> **Training.** What new skills will be required? However you organize a sales force, always remember that no sales force is a blank slate. The legacy land-and-expand sales approach in this venture (sell a few stations and incrementally try to sell more) can undermine the value proposition and actual value delivery; sales reps will need training in new selling skills as well as a comp plan that encourages use of those skills at the right prospects.

Diverse Customer Base and Budgeting Processes

The repositioning also means that for many customers the purchase of Bigbelly products has moved from a capital expenditure to a current operating-expense decision, and at other firms, it moves in the opposite direction, depending upon the volume purchased. This affects who buys (operations? finance? environmental managers?) and the kind of justification relevant to that buyer. Further, Bigbelly prospects are a wide variety of types (malls, businesses, universities, stadiums, hospitals, and municipalities). Their funding for waste management will range from fees to utility charges to property taxes. Customers in different sectors also have different alternatives and constraints: the necessity to work with a sanitation workers union versus use of private contractors versus the political as well as physical benefits of a more ecologically sound waste collection system in a city, business, or university setting.

Sales reps need to have this customer-specific knowledge to make the sale at required scale, and the comp plan should support their ability to acquire and apply that knowledge. In addition, pricing plans that accommodate different budgeting processes in target segments are an important part of the selling tool kit in this situation. Also, note that another, complementary approach here is to work with channel partners that do have this knowledge and access to the relevant buyers. That would involve a compensation plan aimed at motivating efficient and effective channel management (see chapter 10).

Selling Cycle

Bigbelly's situation is a stark contrast to that at Elmenus (see figure 7-1). Bigbelly faces a long selling cycle, covering forty months and multiple checkpoints. At Elmenus, the selling cycle was two to four weeks, and frequent calls on restaurants in a neighborhood or city helped to amortize selling expenses. But once a prospect is in the funnel at Bigbelly, it is very expensive to pursue and close a deal. In other words, this is a business (like many others) where selling, general, and administrative (SG&A) expenses and the lengthy time-to-cash cycle can kill the company if not managed properly. Further, because no one is against better trash collection and nearly all prospects are for a better environment, it's a context where it's crucial to minimize chasing false positives.

A strategically effective comp plan here must support reps through the selling cycle and encourage their use of customer-qualification criteria for finding and making the right type of sale. The plan might involve clawback provisions, staged commissions, or other means to do this. The current plan—a commission based on top-line contract value—does not do that. In fact, as in most compensation plans that link variable pay to volume sales goals, there's no such thing as a bad prospect for the revenue-maximizing salesperson. Reps therefore have an incentive to chase all prospects, bringing in many costly false positives that drive up SG&A expenses and sap time and attention as well as money.

Elmenus versus Bigbelly

Comparing the Elmenus and Bigbelly situations is instructive.

For Elmenus, building awareness and usage in a fragmented market is a core selling task. The comp plan should provide incentives to feed the funnel and for reps to make frequent and repeated sales calls. Because there are low marginal costs to setting up and maintaining a customer on Elmenus's platform, one can adopt a highly leveraged, commission-driven, mainly variable-cost compensation plan in this context.

Bigbelly is different. There's a protracted buying process, where both customer and channel relationships are important. Initial enthusiasm for Bigbelly's service can be deceptive and expensive. In contrast to Elmenus, lead generation is less important than ensuring that salespeople pursue the right leads. Moreover, Bigbelly's margins are mainly in contract length, renewals, and the ancillary services that its data collection can provide *if* its reps get the right scale and scope in the initial sale. Here, the comp plan should encourage reps to do a few things:

1. Vet the sales pipeline carefully, so they don't spend months chasing the wrong prospects, and

2. Spur best-practice dissemination about selling the integrated system—for example, useful techniques for iden-

tifying, early in the selling cycle, which prospects are worth it and which are not, while

3. Providing reps with an incentive to manage the sales and renewal process when they *do* pursue the right prospects.

As in many sales situations, it's not easy to accomplish all of that solely through the comp plan. At Bigbelly, a clear strategy about where to sell in a large, diverse market will be crucial to customer selection. Pricing and channel management will be important for executing strategy effectively. Whatever the plan, contract policies set in nonsales areas will help or hinder selling: for example, what customers must do to qualify for a trial, perhaps pricing by stage of implementation during the long selling cycle, incentives for channel partners to work with your reps, and so on.

These examples illustrate how compensation plans affect selling behaviors, but also why Pavlovian assumptions about salespeople—"they're coin-operated": push this pay lever and get this behavior—are often complicated by other factors and can lead to the land of unintended consequences.

⊕ QUESTIONS TO ASK . . . AND ANSWER

Pay plans are always part of ongoing management practices (good, bad, or indifferent) in your firm. It's a mistake to decouple rewards from performance management activities in your sales model. Studies indicate that employees' attitudes toward their firms' management processes are primarily influenced by three factors: a clear line of sight that links performance goals to business priorities, compensation that supports the motivation → effort → rewards linkages discussed in this

TABLE 7-1

A sales compensation diagnostic

In our company, how well do we . . .

Understand and update the role of our sales compensation plan in our business model?	1 2 3 4 5 6 7
Link incentives to activities in the customer conversion process where salespeople have the most impact?	1 2 3 4 5 6 7
Manage compensation and incentives so they align with our current growth plans?	1 2 3 4 5 6 7
Examine our process of rewarding salespeople in terms of transparency and fairness?	1 2 3 4 5 6 7
Augment compensation with visible recognition events, activities, and awards?	1 2 3 4 5 6 7
Clarify the type(s) of sales efforts that our compensation plan is intended to motivate and support?	1 2 3 4 5 6 7
Have in place metrics to track the desired efforts?	1 2 3 4 5 6 7
Complement monetary incentives with relevant performance reviews by our sales managers?	1 2 3 4 5 6 7

chapter, and active coaching by managers.[22] Does your current pay plan support or sever these links (see table 7-1)?

Among other things, I hope that part I of this book has reminded you of the centrality of people and performance management in establishing an effective sales effort, and that part II has convinced you that money, motivation, and management interact in influencing and channeling selling behaviors. But people and process in a company's go-to-market strategy must also be executed in pricing and, increasingly, via multichannel activities—two areas where sales execution lives or dies. That's the focus of part III.

PART THREE

PRICING AND PARTNERS

PRICING AND CUSTOMER VALUE

Pricing builds or destroys value faster than almost any other business action. Warren Buffett said it well: "The single most important decision in evaluating a business is pricing power. And if you need a prayer session before raising price, then you've got a terrible business."[1]

When you lose a deal, how many times have your sales-people said, "Our price is too high"? Few customers wake up in the morning *wanting* to pay a higher price. In fact, research repeatedly finds that consumers believe that the selling price of a good or service is higher than its "fair" price. They also tend to underestimate the effects of inflation, and fail to take into account the full range of vendor costs in providing products, services, and a product-service bundle.[2] But most customers do seek value, and it's the responsibility of the sales force to frame and deliver the value proposition, including price.

The focus of this chapter is on the strategic choices inherent in pricing and selling value. The next chapter focuses more on tactics and implementation: price testing, the links between pricing approaches and different sales models, and the alignment of selling behaviors with pricing goals.

Price Pressures, Costs, and Value

More firms now face the following situation: their customers have online access to product and price comparisons from multiple suppliers; they face global competition with companies that may have labor, exchange-rate, or other cost advantages; and shorter product life cycles seemingly mean that commoditization (like the expansion of the universe) is accelerating. In categories where digital business models have come to dominate, pirated or past copies of a song, film, or video game are often easily accessible online, and as my colleague Anita Elberse notes, "Some people may feel that paying a full price for media products is somehow unfair, old-fashioned, or just plain stupid."[3]

Not surprisingly, surveys regularly find companies bemoaning the pricing situation in their industry. In one comprehensive study, about 80 percent of respondents said they were under price pressure, and 60 percent said they were in an ongoing price war.[4] In this situation, pundits urge firms to go lean, go online, cut costs (especially SG&A costs), avoid customized products and services and so simplify operations, and then price low to gain volume and scale. Indeed, this advice became conventional wisdom during the economic crisis caused by the coronavirus.

Most firms use cost-based pricing. Price is easier to explain when it's based on input costs, and cost is the salesperson's default option in justifying price to a prospect. This pricing approach is often seen as being transparent with customers.

Clothing retailer Everlane, for example, supports its slogan of "radical transparency" by providing for every garment it sells a detailed breakdown of costs for materials, labor, duties, and transport, along with its markup. In retail, chemicals, and other businesses with multiple products, fluctuating cost inputs, and frequent promotions and price changes, it's administratively easier to do simple cost-based markups, especially if the seller doesn't know or can't demonstrate, before actual usage, value to the customer.

Some firms compete successfully in this manner. But realities typically allow only a few firms to build a sustainable low-cost/low-price business model. Once established, the very success of these firms makes it difficult for others to duplicate.

Look at the data. A study of more than twenty-five thousand companies listed on US stock exchanges between 1966 and 2010 compared financial performance, measured in terms of return on assets (ROA). It found that the share of companies that achieved long-term success (measured as above-average ROA for the years the company was listed) was much lower for firms pursuing low-priced strategies than for firms with a premium-price strategy. As the researchers conclude, "Very rarely is cost leadership a driver of superior profitability."[5]

Also, in the rough-and-tumble of competition, many managers lose sight of a core fact: *lowering cost* does not necessarily mean *low cost* versus competition or substitutes, and in any industry, there's ultimately only one *lowest-cost* competitor. Never confuse these distinct positions. A classic example for years was in the US airline industry. As American, Delta, and United slashed prices in the 1990s, Southwest Airlines placed advertisements saying, "We'd like to match their new fares . . . but we would have to raise ours." Throughout the decade, Southwest had a business model and cost position that the others could not duplicate, and the aggressive discounting was a race to the bottom for all involved.

More recently, most newspapers (78 percent of those with a daily circulation of over fifty thousand, according to the American Press Institute) have launched low-cost digital editions with paywalls between their print and online editions. Research finds that the results vary, but for most papers, the net effect is negative because the digital subscription revenue is offset by bigger decreases in ad revenue due to reduced website visits. Indeed, when this pricing approach works, it is usually because a bundled print-and-online offering increased print subscriptions.[6] Similarly, Kraft Heinz for years cut costs, especially selling costs, but that approach can take you just so far and can alienate powerful channel partners: its PE owner, 3G Capital, slashed the value of its brands by more than $15 billion in 2019, and Kraft Heinz expanded its sales and merchandising teams by 80 percent to boost its presence with key retailers.

In fact, cost-plus pricing can discourage continuous improvement and innovation. While Kraft Heinz was cutting costs, other consumer packaged goods firms were devising more expensive sizes, flavors, and other versions of their products: fudge-dipped Oreo Thins for $.56 per ounce at Walmart, compared to $.30 per ounce for standard Oreo Thins and $.18 per ounce for traditional Oreos; Eggo Waffles flavored with vanilla for $.28 per ounce compared with $.23 per ounce for the standard version. Hostess Brands, producer of Twinkies and Ding Dongs, created new snack cakes called Bakery Petites to attract new consumers at higher price points and sold them at Walmart for $.47 per ounce, more than double the price per ounce for Twinkies.[7]

The antithesis to cost-plus is value pricing where the firm competes on the basis of product and/or service performance initiatives for which customers willingly pay higher prices. In consumer goods, brands like Belvedere Vodka, Nutro Dog Food, and others sell at prices 60 percent to 200 percent or more higher than their competitors. In B2B selling, the heavy-duty truck industry has big, price-sensitive fleet buyers. Yet, Paccar, the producer of Kenworth and Peterbilt trucks, has for decades been a successful premium-priced supplier with superior financial returns.

Ink for fountain pens sounds like a commodity in a declining—indeed, terminally declined?—industry. But J. Herbin from France sells ink for love letters at $28 for 50 milliliters, while Sailor Pen from Japan sells Kobe Ink #4 Kitano Ijinkan Red at $30 for 50 milliliters (the ink has a slight gold sheen) and other inks at more than $40 for a 50 milliliter bottle—more than five times the cost, on a per-milliliter basis, than Glenlivet's eighteen-year-old Scotch.[8] There are zero-fee mutual funds available, but the majority of US equity fund assets are determined by fee-based money managers, and the amount has grown over time: according to Federal Reserve data, the asset management industry had more than $51 trillion under management in 2018 or about 250 percent of gross domestic product; in 1968 that ratio was 80 percent.[9] Every day, some companies manage to extract price advantages that others do not.

Linking Price and Value

Successful performance pricers have a business model and sales management practices for identifying customer value, understanding how value varies across customers and purchase contexts, and clarifying the opportunity criteria so their salespeople compete for the relevant business.[10] They do not adopt a one-size-fits-all average price, but use data and sales processes to determine the attributes and benefits that each customer truly values. They then actively communicate that value.

An analogy can be helpful. Ted Williams, the last baseball player to hit .400, was a student of his craft: "My first rule of hitting was to get a good ball to hit. I learned down to percentage points where those good balls were." Williams charted the results and used the term "happy zone" for that area of the strike zone where "I could hit .400 or better [versus] the low outside corner where the most I could hope to bat was .230." Williams also emphasized the demand side of his discipline: "Learning the zone, because once pitchers find a batter is going to swing at bad pitches he will get nothing else."[11]

The same applies to pricing and selling value. Performance pricers are adept at identifying the optimal zone between their product/service offerings and their target customers' preferences, and then configuring their offerings and value propositions to dominate, not their industries, but their particular zone of value. Consider some historical examples and contemporary counterparts:

- On the Erie Canal in the early nineteenth century, boats carrying bulky freight paid lower prices than those moving more valuable but lighter goods, allowing canal operators to pitch their services to different types of customers while maximizing utilization. Something similar happens today in the pricing for online ad rates, and via algorithms this approach is spreading to other markets. For instance, download the Chrome extension Keepa, which shows the price history for any item on Amazon. Even for seemingly simple products like marshmallows or Duracell batteries, you will see "wild pricing gyrations [that] resemble a penny stock during heavy trading."[12]

- Later in the nineteenth century, railroads sought to get the most profit from a line of track and maximize ROA. They began with a set price versus their major alternative at the time: canal rates. But this approach did not extract the higher prices that many riders and shippers were willing to pay, depending upon the distance traveled (in shorter times than by canals) and the products shipped (copper versus coal being the standard examples at the time). Today, you see this in yield-management pricing whenever someone next to you on an airplane paid more or less than you did for a ticket. You also see this in tech markets where companies manage prices and the product line to achieve similar goals. In 2018, Apple released its iPhone XS and XS Max models, with prices starting at about $1,000, followed weeks later by the XR with a starting price of $749. As an analyst noted, "It's sort of a Dutch auction. The people who are most committed will pay to get early access. Then you get to the people who . . . settle for the $750 phone."[13]

- Futures contracts have been common for centuries. Wheat delivered in May had a different price than wheat delivered in August, allowing for pricing according to different customers' particular usage needs and risk tolerance. The same applies in the pricing of financial options, many professional services, and surge pricing at Uber and toll booths in cities like London.

The zone of profitable pricing can vary by customer, product, order (e.g., the same customer on business versus leisure travel), space (distance traveled or shipped), time (futures contracts), and other variables. It's the confluence of particular customer preferences and your economics that establish the relevant variables and optimal zone.

Conversely, a single price to the average customer is usually a suboptimal approach for both the seller and many buyers.[14] When different customers derive different value from the same product or service, then one price means that some customers are, in effect, subsidizing others. Sooner or later, competitors, a purchasing consultant, or a good CFO will tell those customers what is going on. Or, depending upon where you set a single price, other customers pay for features they don't want when an à la carte model would give them the option to save money.

Online channels, Wi-Fi-enabled products, and data analytics are increasing, not decreasing, the performance-pricing options available to companies. Software for dynamic pricing—adjusting price as customer preferences and demand patterns unfold—is now available from multiple vendors. Managers are therefore enthusiastic about "pricing analytics" and charging by customer value. But most have only a vague understanding of what's involved: how to identify that value, where to look, the relevant unit(s) of analysis, and the implications for pricing. As usual in business, the important levers for seizing opportunities are leadership and customer-management practices, not the technology.

In the Zone: Identifying Value

Optimal pricing zones are typically tied, not to industry supply and demand curves, but to the relevant piece of business (POB). A POB is *not* the same as an account, which is a basis for many firms' segmentation efforts but too broad a unit of analysis for performance pricing. Neither is a POB always the same as an order, which is the focus of most sales efforts but is usually an output of a POB situation.

Rather, a POB is *a separable buying decision, driven by a customer's buying unit and its needs in a specific context, and made in relation to your perceived performance versus competition and substitutes.*

- **Separable buying decision.** A POB occurs when a seller locates a customer need and a solution that increases willingness to pay and/or lowers a buyer's total costs (see later in this chapter).

- **Driven by a buying unit.** Performance pricers target buying units within accounts. Selling premium-priced solutions to purchasing, for example, rarely works.

- **In a specific context.** The value of a product or service varies for different customers, different buying units, or the same buyer at different times or usage situations. Same product but different values. For years in the paper industry, the paper stock purchased by a magazine printer for the articles and for ad inserts was the same in composition and weight. But the value for the ad-inserts paper was much higher because the paper couldn't be ordered until a few days before the print run as ad sales closed, while the other paper could be ordered four to eight weeks in advance. As a result, the POB for ad inserts carried a higher customer willingness to pay.

- **In relation to perceived performance.** Delivering performance versus alternatives is key and perceptions matter, which is why framing and communicating value are so important. Further, performance is not only quantifiable product performance; it can be emotional, identity, or status value tied to the brand as well as functional benefits tied to product features.

Figure 8-1 illustrates a POB transaction and pricing parameters. The gray portion represents a supplier's total cost of providing a product or service. The highest horizontal line represents the total value of that product or service as perceived by the customer. These lines bound the space of possible prices or, using negotiation terminology, the zone of possible agreement (ZOPA). The difference between price and cost is supplier profit. For most companies, this is a driving force to sell more and part of everyday commercial language. Interestingly, however, there is no common phrase in business for the difference between perceived customer value and price. Economists call this difference "surplus" or occasionally "consumer welfare"— terminology that suggests it is discretionary or simply a choice by suppliers to lower price and increase customer value. For

FIGURE 8-1

Pricing a piece of business

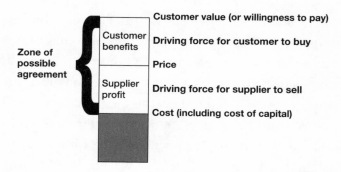

Source: Frank V. Cespedes, Benson P. Shapiro, and Elliot B. Ross, "Pricing, Profits, and Customer Value," Case 9-811-016 (Boston: Harvard Business School, August 2011).

good reason, these terms never caught on in business lingo: try selling something at a price equal to the customer's perceived value and you will probably fail. The essence of a deal and the driving force to buy is the perception that the value exceeds the price. In figure 8-1, this difference is "customer benefits."

Performance pricers mine the differences between value and price and between price and cost to identify opportunities. To do that, you must adopt a certain mindset. In my experience, most pricing discussions concern incremental changes designed to respond to competitors' pricing moves or to maintain volume or share. These are not irrelevant discussions: a given percentage increase or decrease in realized price has a much bigger impact—up and down—on net income, and for many firms a net price increase or decrease of as little as 2 percent is the difference between a profit and a loss. But this approach doesn't deal with the core issue in selling and extracting value: how to create more benefit and profit simultaneously by increasing the ZOPA.

In addition to monitoring competitors' prices, you should focus your market research, the generation of creative options, and sales approaches on how you can (1) create more customer value, (2) increase customers' perceptions of value, and (3) cut costs without decreasing customer value (e.g., pruning inessential product features, or finding a different sales model or distribution channel to deal with currently high cost-to-serve accounts or segments). The most profitable and sustainable pricing opportunities are usually the result of examining POBs with these questions in mind.

Too often, however, managers talk about "value" as a kind of spiritual or theological concept. It's not. Business is about this world, not the hereafter. The availability of information as well as the increased sophistication of supply-chain and purchasing departments mean that the requirements for documenting and quantifying value in sales conversations have also increased.[15] One way to do that is to begin by recalling Adam Smith's comment in *The Wealth of Nations*: "The real price of everything . . . is the toil and trouble of acquiring it."[16] Especially if you sell in a B2B market, extend Smith's comment to include cost of capital and operating costs. When a customer buys something, that customer always incurs acquisition, possession, or usage costs (see figure 8-2).

Acquisition costs include price, but also the search and administrative costs involved in finding, qualifying, buying, and processing a purchase. Most products and services are items in a wider usage system at that organization or household. Somebody must put that system together: the customer, a supplier, or a value-added reseller. One-stop-shop suppliers can often be lower acquisition-cost choices even at premium prices. Conversely, suppliers with poor order fulfillment or siloed sales efforts by product unit can mean higher acquisition costs for a customer. In its tens of thousands of categories, Amazon is a good search and buying experience if you know what you want, but it's not a great shopping experience if you don't because you do that search, not a retail salesperson.

FIGURE 8-2

Identifying total value (illustrative example)

Acquisition costs	+	Possession costs	+	Usage costs = Total customer cost
1. Price		7. Interest cost		13. Field defects
2. Paperwork cost		8. Storage cost		14. Training cost
3. Shopping time		9. Quality control		15. User labor cost
4. Expediting cost		10. Taxes and insurance		16. Product longevity
5. Cost of mistakes in order		11. Shrinkage and obsolescence		17. Replacement costs
6. Prepurchase product evaluation costs		12. General internal handling costs		18. Disposal costs

Source: Frank V. Cespedes, Benson P. Shapiro, and Elliot B. Ross, "Pricing, Profits, and Customer Value," Case 9-811-016 (Boston: Harvard Business School, August 2011).

Possession costs include financing, working capital, payment terms, storage, handling costs, and other money and effort required to keep the purchased product or service available for use. For many maintenance, supply, and operating items in industrial markets, the "toil and trouble" of possession costs greatly exceed purchase price. In hospitals, possession costs of many products are a portion of a hospital's total operating costs that is exceeded only by labor costs (doctors, nurses, and others), which is a hard-to-change number without damaging health care. In retail, automated replenishment systems, and suppliers that can work effectively within that system, lower possession costs. More generally, just-in-time inventory systems, which originally began to lower possession costs, have over the decades evolved into a wider approach to managing a business for velocity or inventory turns.

Usage costs are the time and money spent by customers to get maximum value from their purchased products or services where and by whom they are used. This can include costs associated with product defects and returns, employee training required to use the product or service, or (in many environmentally sensitive categories) costs of product disposal. Usage costs are often hidden or opaque for customers, because they are spread across different departments (so the CFO may not have a single line item that aggregates these costs), and in a household they may simply be attributed to "how it works." But smart buyers tally these costs as they consider make-versus-buy decisions, examine suppliers, and evaluate prices. Product quality lowers the usage costs of defects and returns; smart product design and onboarding can lower a customer's training costs and efforts; product materials, postsale service, and channel design (e.g., the reseller that stocks and empties the coffee-and-snack place in the office; the retail partner that accepts and disposes of the used ink cartridge for your printer) are often key in lowering or even eliminating disposal costs in some categories.

Customers incur these costs whether or not they explicitly acknowledge them. They always pay not only money but also their time and effort. Different customers have different priorities across these costs, depending upon the POB and their trade-off criteria. Consumer research indicates that, as a general rule, younger people and those with lower incomes tend to be more price sensitive, while older and higher-income consumers tend to be less so. Keep that in mind when you hear another glittering generalization about how generation X, Y, Z or whoever has transformed buying: whatever else happens to young people, they get older.

The Product Is What the Product Does

Value is ultimately in the eyes—and behavior—of the beholder. Consumers who are more price sensitive tend to be less effort sensitive, and this trade-off typically remains true whether they shop online or in a brick-and-mortar store. In fashion categories, for instance, online shoppers seeking the highest discounts will expend more effort browsing and clicking, while less-price-sensitive shoppers expend many fewer clicks. Research about consumer behavior on websites shows that you can limit discounting off list price by deliberately "hiding" highly discounted products on a site and having visitors perform additional clicks to find those items.[17]

Priorities vary by country and culture. Everyday low price has been a winning approach in the United States for many retailers, because one-stop shopping saves time for busy professionals and dual-income households. In many other countries, households are constituted differently, shopping is a daily activity, and consumers trade time for low price and the emotional as well as monetary benefits of bargain hunting across outlets. This is one reason why retail formats that are a big success in their home markets are often difficult to export. Across cultures, however, the value of a product or service *is* what it *does* for a customer—functionally, emotionally, or in terms of perceived social impact or risk reduction.

Price is a quality signal in many consumer markets, sometimes to an irrational extent. In the US health care and higher education markets, where insurance and loans are ubiquitous and outcome information is lacking or hard to understand, many consumers assume high price means high quality and they seek out the higher-priced institutions. Suppliers can be penalized for *lowering* their prices. Why? Brand and price are linked. In the downward spiral of the magazine business, the *New Yorker* and the *Economist* have maintained their higher subscription prices. The former brand says you are a cultured person, and the latter says you think broadly about global political and economic affairs. Their content is certainly part of their value propositions, but the brands also add value by reinforcing and projecting an identity.[18] They are vehicles for what marketers call aspirational value, so for instance, most firms project a younger image in their clothes or cosmetics ads even when the target market is decades older.

In business markets, the qualitative emotional benefits are typically less salient for customers, but still there. As in buying health care or evaluating tuition prices, "No one ever got fired for buying X" still pertains in many categories. Signaling your commitment to innovation, either to customers or to employees, applies in evaluating suppliers in other categories, not only in what magazines (if any) are in the conference room or the visitors' waiting area. But value documentation in B2B selling more often means documenting tangible impacts on customers' economics. Figure 8-3 outlines the components of an ROE calculation. Often called the "DuPont formula," it's a standard tool and closely watched number among stock analysts because this kind of analysis helps to locate the source(s) of ROE outcomes.

B2B performance pricers add value by helping customers improve their profit margins through total-cost reductions,

FIGURE 8-3

Value delivery and customers' economics

$$\text{ROE} = \frac{\text{Profit}}{\text{Sales}} \times \frac{\text{Sales}}{\text{Assets}} \times \frac{\text{Assets}}{\text{Equity}}$$

$$\text{(Margins)} \times \begin{pmatrix} \text{Asset} \\ \text{turnover} \end{pmatrix} \times \begin{pmatrix} \text{Financial} \\ \text{leverage} \end{pmatrix}$$

- **Value: Helping customers improve their margins**
  - Cost reduction in category acquisition, possession, usage costs
  - Differentiation and price premiums due to your product/brand
  - Process improvements via their relationship with your organization

- **Value: Helping customers improve asset turnover**
  - Working capital management
  - Reduction (or elimination) of assets required
  - Process outsourcing and/or balance sheet benefits

Source: Frank V. Cespedes, Benson P. Shapiro, and Elliot B. Ross, "Pricing, Profits, and Customer Value," Case 9-811-016 (Boston: Harvard Business School, August 2011).

by the ability to differentiate their products and charge a higher price in their end-use markets, or by process improvements in important areas of the customer's business model; and/or they help customers improve asset turnover through better working capital management, reducing or eliminating the assets required by customers, or by enabling customers to outsource tasks and use that money, time, and effort in other areas of their business. As figure 8-3 indicates, these types of performance improvements translate directly into core drivers of enterprise valuation: customers' margin improvements, operating efficiency, and the ability to increase asset turnover. In contemporary markets, data analytics not only improve targeting for sellers and advertisers but also increase buying firms' abilities to calculate these impacts before they buy.

Managing the Zone: Extracting Value

Firms make money where the spread between their costs and customer willingness to pay is greatest. The relevant cost for pricing decisions is not just COGS, as in most cost-plus pricing approaches. Rather, it's fully burdened costs, including selling, service, delivery, and customization for a given POB. Clarifying the cost to serve by POB is crucial for effective pricing.

To simplify, consider a single dimension of product performance (e.g., speed, mean time between failure, bandwidth, or processing power). In most businesses, the relationship between product performance and cost is not a smooth curve. Rather, as in figure 8-4, that relationship at a point in time is typically "bumpy," meaning that value and costs are not symmetric, although they are usually monotonic, meaning that value rarely decreases as performance increases. These discontinuities are pricing opportunities. You can add value for less than commensurate cost and profitably mine the gap.

FIGURE 8-4

Bumpy performance curves: Pots of gold

Find discontinuities in the spread between customer value and cost

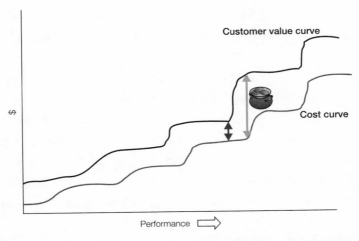

Source: Frank V. Cespedes, Benson P. Shapiro, and Elliot B. Ross, "Pricing, Profits, and Customer Value," Case 9-811-016 (Boston: Harvard Business School, August 2011).

Performance pricers do this in diverse ways. Sometimes the bump is tied to time. What's the value of flowers delivered on or the day after Valentine's or Mother's Day? Some in the flower business sell very profitably by managing price, delivery, and their supply chain to target those times when the bumps between costs and value are greatest. In the music business, Taylor Swift and Jay-Z pioneered "slow ticketing"—releasing concert tickets in increments with the price rising as the concert date gets closer—and increased total gross for their events.

Sometimes the bump is tied to financing. For years before the financial crisis unmasked other deficiencies in its business, GE's corporate credit rating allowed GE Capital to borrow at rates estimated to be up to 2 percent less than a pure financial company. GE Capital then financed customers and helped to drive sales for the corporation's industrial units with financing terms that competitors could not match.

Sometimes it's product design. Modular design can enable a big bump in performance at low incremental cost. IKEA offers ready-to-assemble furniture for young buyers seeking style and assortment at low cost. Modular design allows IKEA to extract higher prices where semi-customized assortments drive willingness to pay without proportional increases in costs. In the restaurant business, The Cheesecake Factory lists over two hundred items on its menu, including forty kinds of cheesecake. This choice, and the fun associated with the choice, helped Cheesecake regularly rank among the highest chains in average check size and return visits per store, while a modular menu design in the kitchen (revised every six months) kept costs lower than delivered value. Modular design is now a tenet in software development, and as software becomes integrated into more products, so do performance-pricing opportunities.

Even everyday-low-price approaches, and performance during economic downturns that increase customer price sensitivity, can be improved by identifying and managing the relevant bumps. During the recession, Walmart distinguished "win, place, and show" categories. In "win" categories such as toys and TVs, Walmart priced lower than competitors and doubled its share of retail sales in those categories while increasing the average sale size. "Play" applied to categories like apparel where Walmart matched price on a narrower range of items than competitors offered but did not seek to dominate that zone. "Show" referred to items like hardware, which are important to carry at a one-stop-shop retailer, but in small assortment: as Walmart's chief merchandising officer noted, "It's important we have hammers and tape measures, but not 28 tape measures."[19] These distinctions among POBs apply to other businesses where profitability and sales effectiveness are closely tied to the realized price of a basket of goods sold and serviced at different individual price points to the same customer—for example, many chemical companies, distributors, and others.

How you then extract value can also vary, and you have more options for doing so. In grocery retailing, for example, slotting fees from suppliers for additional or end-of-aisle shelf space have become the top source of income for the average US supermarket chain, and float (i.e., the money between the time a supermarket sells an item and when payment is due back to the supplier of that item) is the second largest source of income.[20] Profit on the actual goods sold is in fourth place, but what goods are stocked and how they are priced are part of a value-extraction mechanism that goes beyond the accounting margin on those items. Similarly, at Costco, value extraction is not the result of individual product profitability, but its membership fees. In fact, Costco loses money in its supermarket retail business, but more than makes up for that loss with membership fees.[21]

So-called razor-and-blades pricing extracts value by identifying the bump between performance and cost in the relevant postsale market: selling cheaply or even giving away the initial product or platform, but pricing the consumables or add-ons at a premium price. This was true over a century ago for King Gillette, and it's true today for printers and ink cartridges, video-game consoles and games, e-readers and ebooks, and many "freemium" pricing approaches in software and other categories.

Choosing the Unit of Value

Some companies are very good at getting price commensurate with the performance value of their products and services, and others are not. A key is to tie price to a unit or metric that frames and makes visible the value to the customer in the relevant POB context. This will vary, but it's usually worth your effort to examine this issue in depth and by product or market segment.

Why do ski resorts charge the same price for lift tickets instead of a usage fee, and why does Disney charge a single fee to enter the park, after which all rides are "free," even when lines are long? What's the logic?[22] The relevant price in these POBs is not the price of the daily lift ticket or park entrance fee, but the price per ride. This depends upon the number of customers: if a lift ticket cost $10 and lines allowed five runs per skier, the price would be $2 per ride; if few people showed up because of bad weather, and short lines allowed twenty runs per skier, the effective price is $.50 per ride. For ski resorts and Disney, pricing by ride is more expensive to set up, manage, and monitor; for customers, the cost of waiting in line is small compared to the fixed cost of getting to the resort or theme park. The lines automatically adjust the *real* price that customers pay (in money, time, and effort), incentivize a self-selection process that allocates different customers to different rides, and so maximize profit for the supplier. In other words, pricing can flexibly play the spread between value and costs even when it appears to be fixed.

In other cases, the relevant unit of value and pricing may be a different bundle altogether. For a century, movies were released according to a "windowing" model of pricing that captured different buyers' willingness to pay. The initial release at the highest price in selected theaters attracted those who valued that movie most highly, and this was followed by release at smaller theaters at lower ticket prices, and then renting (now streaming) the movie for viewing on the smaller screen at home weeks later but at lower prices. Studios extracted maximum value from each group without cannibalizing sales to the others. The time frame of windowing shortened in the

twenty-first century, but this remained standard industry practice before enforced shelter-in-place conditions closed theaters
during the pandemic. The major exception was Netflix which,
even before the crisis, released its movies in theaters on the
same day it made them available for "free" on its streaming
platform. Why?

Netflix is dealing with a different POB. It's not in the business of selling individual movies to multiple customers; it sells
bundles of movies to individual customers. More generally, as
Michael Smith and Rahul Telang point out, not every consumer assigns the same value to individual movies in a bundle,
but in a large-enough bundle, the differences average out. If a
seller can accurately predict the average value a subscriber is
willing to pay for the bundle, then (as explained in connection
with figure 8-1) it can set a price slightly below that threshold
and extract maximum value from its customers.[23]

Similarly, as platform models disseminate more widely, identifying the relevant unit of price becomes essential for effective
selling, and this too varies by POB. Inbound-marketing firm
HubSpot initially charged a flat per-month subscription fee,
but then tied its pricing tiers to the number of contacts in a
customer's database. This removed a cap on extracting value
because as a customer company grew its database, the value of
HubSpot's platform at that company increased (it was managing more data) and so did HubSpot's ability to share in that
success via performance pricing.

For other platform businesses, the relevant unit is different. Fintech firms typically charge a fee for each transaction
processed through their platforms. Usage tends to be episodic
and hard to predict and not, as with HubSpot and a number
of other inbound-marketing platforms, part of a marketing or
sales cadence at customers. The sharing economy is rife with
POBs with different pricing implications. Consider mobility
business models. Zipcar, Maven, and others price on a stan-

dard by-the-hour or by-day rental structure from a choice of supplier-determined pickup and drop-off locations. But Turo, DriveShare, and other person-to-person car-sharing platforms have pricing based on time, distance, auto brand, and other variables that are often part of a bundle with ancillary services.

Identifying the relevant unit for value and pricing also affects how the firm must sell and to whom. The length of the sales cycle often shortens as you move from an up-front payment to outcome-based performance. But the buyer, relevant value documentation, and the sales conversation also change. When software firms move from selling licenses to cloud-based subscription pricing, that also means a change in buying. Software licenses are typically purchased as part of capital budgets, while annual or monthly subscription payments are usually funded from operating budgets. The former usually means high up-front costs, but low annual maintenance costs and unlimited use within the customer organization. But subscription pricing means payments over time and, depending upon the supplier, usage-, contact-, or features-based packages that sales must learn to justify by desired outcomes with operating personnel as well as finance or purchasing people at that customer.

How to Do It: A Step-by-Step Process

Firms can identify and extract value when they have processes that analyze information in their customer portfolio, and then craft and communicate a value proposition that the relevant buyers, and their own salespeople, can understand and embrace. Because value extraction is about the ZOPA between cost and willingness to pay, this must be an organizational process, not only a sales initiative. In most firms, the best understanding of the value performance curve is held by a combination of people in sales, marketing, service, and operations; meanwhile, costs are managed in procurement, product groups, manufacturing, and finance. How often in your firm do these people come together to discuss value versus cost in a disciplined way? Here's an example, from a tough B2B market, of how to do that.

Zolam (disguised name) is a chemical firm serving diverse markets characterized by fluctuating demand, industry overcapacity, and capital-market pressures to increase earnings—conditions facing many other firms. For some years, Zolam stressed new technology complemented by reduced service levels and other cost-cutting moves. In sales, the rule was to take any order at an acceptable price. But this approach did not yield good shareholder returns or growth, and leadership sought other ways to win profitable business. Zolam's pricing was overhauled in terms of four key elements and a core prerequisite: a mindset that stresses the search for specific buyer benefits across all functions of the firm.

Step 1. Identifying Value Opportunities: Analyzing Buying Data

Zolam leaders started with a consistent message: "We must understand what is valuable to customers in order to be valuable." They repeatedly asked how product, service, or other benefits impacted customer outcomes, including but not limited to their financial success, and took a new look at available buying data via a POB approach.

Zolam's customers included firms that packaged pharmaceuticals and to whom it sold rubber stoppers to cap injectable drugs, a product long viewed as a low-price commodity. But Zolam found a hierarchy of benefits in this product. The base level was to minimize the customer acquisition costs of the stopper; the next level was to reduce the possession and usage costs through design and delivery initiatives that increased customers' packaging line speeds, lowered their inventory requirements, and aided manufacturing capacity planning. A third level was to help customers increase *their* product's performance: for instance, stoppers molded in unique colors helped hospitals and doctors reduce errors and lower insurance costs, yielding higher price and less customer churn for the packager.

Adopting this approach across its product line, Zolam developed metrics, customer profiles, and new ideas about value. Different customers, or the same customer at different times, had different purchasing criteria and price elasticities. In Zolam's case, the distinction among POBs was generally the usage application. Customers buying base performance in a category were viewed as commodity POBs, while buyers at other levels were specialty POBs.

Step 2. Prioritizing Opportunities: Value Delivery and Competitive Requirements

At this point, many executives would focus on specialties and avoid commodity POBs. But Zolam (like most firms) served customers across POB transactions. Further, even if a POB started as specialty, it generally moved through a classic life cycle, and another analysis indicated that, in its industry, there simply were not enough specialty POBs to support Zolam's growth targets. Yet, Zolam was not positioned to serve all POBs, and like any firm with limited resources, it had to decide what offerings to provide, at what prices, and how to invest in required product, sales, and other capabilities.

To do this, Zolam also analyzed POBs in terms of Zolam's ability to deliver the required product offering profitably. For example, Zolam had a proprietary product that improved performance of dental filling material. But the total market was only a few hundred pounds, and the investment included expensive human-testing procedures. In this case, Zolam could own the market at a high price but still not cover its total costs. Dialogue between R&D, product, and sales found the same could be true for other POBs that, historically, had driven Zolam to proliferate features and generate costs across the organization. But with a shared understanding of value-delivery requirements, Zolam could set priorities for product and sales units. High-priority POBs included applications for makers of protective maskants and others where the bumps in the performance and cost curves were especially attractive, while low-priority POBs included many powder coatings applications where investments in R&D, manufacturing, and inventory were evaluated with different screening criteria.

Zolam also found many situations where seemingly commodity POBs could be profitable if sold appropriately. For example, Zolam's plant in Spain produced a chemical used by customers across Europe. This analysis provided sales with tangible direction: be aggressive with Spanish customers because shipping costs were low, but very selective with customers for this product in Germany and Scandinavia. Those latter POBs had different pricing terms.

Step 3. Aligning Value and Price

The next step was to ensure that product offerings were aligned with what the customer was willing to pay and how the sales force sold. Zolam developed an offering tracking system that, on an ongoing basis, documented the relevant product features and benefit in the value proposition, the cost to Zolam, and the pricing options. Table 8-1 is a sample matrix (with specific data deleted) created to provide guidance on whether each value element should be offered for a POB.

TABLE 8-1

Zolam offering tracking system

Potential value proposition elements per market/application

Category	Value proposition element	Benefit type	Explanation	Are they eligible? Will we charge separate for it?								
				A1	A2	A3	B1	B2	B3	C1	C2	C3
Commercial	Minor product modifications	Higher revenue	Possibility of slightly modifying our products to fit the customer	Y/N	Y/Y	N	Y/N	Y/Y	N	Y/Y	N	N
Commercial	Toll manufacturing	Lower RM cost	Available but potential and costs to be discussed with the customer	X	X	X	X	X	X	Y/Y	Y/Y	N
Commercial	Exclusive product codes	Easier, lower risk	Special name only for that customer. Can be similar to relabeling.	Y/N	Y/Y	N	Y/Y	Y/Y	N	N	N	N
Commercial	Supply agreement—change notification requirement	Low risk	This can be discussed with customer. Rejection is always possible	Y/N	Y/N	N	Y/N	Y/N	N	N	N	N
Customer service	Out of hours contact	Easier	Extra phone number	Y/N	N	N	Y/N	N	N	Y/N	N	N
Customer service	Pre-sampling	Low risk	Yes—Usually organized by customer service. No charges	Y/N	Y/Y	N	Y/Y	Y/Y	N	Y/Y	N	N
Supply chain	Lead times	Faster	Shorter than standard lead times	Y/N	Y/N	N	Y/N	Y/N	N	Y/N	N	N

Category	Service	Benefit	Definition								
Supply chain	Rush orders (includes airfreights)	Faster	Delivering faster than agreed- includes both freight cost and effort	Y/Y	Y/Y	N	Y/Y	Y/Y	N	Y/Y	N
Supply chain	Special manufacturing (filtration, machine, raw mats)	Low risk, lower operating costs	Are we willing to modify our manufacturing process	Y/N	Y/N	N	Y/N	Y/N	N	Y/N	N
Supply chain	Special packaging	Easier	Yes	Y/N	Y/Y	N	Y/Y	Y/Y	N	Y/Y	N
Supply chain	Safety stock	Easier, faster and low risk	Defined with customer	Y/N	Y/Y	N	Y/Y	Y/Y	N	Y/Y	N
Technical	Direct access to technical support	Lower operating costs, higher revenue	Dedicated resource	Y/N	N	N	Y/N	N	N	Y/N	N
Technical	Priority access to new technologies	Higher revenue	Technology Showcase	Y/N	N	N	Y/N	N	N	N	N
Technical	Technical seminars	Easier, faster, higher Revenue		Y/N	N	N	Y/N	N	N	N	N
Technical	Product safety and compliance support	Easier, faster, higher revenue, low risk	Access to our HSE resources globally	Y/Y	Y/Y	N	Y/Y	Y/Y	N	Y/Y	N

Source: Frank V. Cespedes, Benson P. Shapiro, and Elliot B. Ross, "Pricing, Profits, and Customer Value," Case No. 9-811-016 (Boston: Harvard Business School, August 2011).

The offering tracking system facilitated communication between the field and the factory *before* sales negotiations, and improved win/loss analyses *after* sales results. It allowed Zolam to clarify target price, reservation price, and price negotiation strategy. Target price was what Zolam needed to attain on average for a given offering; reservation price was the level where Zolam walked away from that POB. Price negotiations by salespeople were now informed by data about where to start in promoting the product, how to frame a price for different value components, and when to get more aggressive or walk away. This is crucial: in industries with fluctuating demand and overcapacity, offering very low prices in a competitor's happy zone can start a price war, and offering low prices in your happy zone may maintain volume for a season but trains customers to expect continuing discounts.

Step 4. Communicating Total Value

With this approach, Zolam's salespeople were calling on different decision makers at customers. Because the approach required documenting the impact on customers' performance metrics, an important change was getting sales and service personnel to work *with* the customer in quantifying the benefits and doing regular reviews with accounts to audit the results. A key addition to the sales reporting system was the customer impact statement that detailed the agreed-upon cost savings or other benefits attributable to product features, delivery terms, service levels, or other factors associated with an order.

Over the next five years, Zolam grew profits 10 percent annually in a market growing less than 2 percent per year. The approach also allowed Zolam to weather tough times better than competitors: after the financial crisis in 2009, industry volume declined over 20 percent versus 14 percent for Zolam (due to better positioning across its POB transactions) and, despite less volume, Zolam's return on sales *increased* due to its ability to identify and communicate value to cost-conscious customers.

Good pricers make the kind of process illustrated by Zolam, and the dialogue which supports that process, a part of their organizational cultures. One result is more precision about where to compete, how to prepare for and conduct sales calls, and better understanding of the true causes of wins and losses. So much pop advice about overcoming price resistance is empirically unsupported and can turn your sales force into a kind of cargo cult, believing that if they perform certain actions or say certain things, the heavens will open and objections will disappear. Don't believe it. The best way to deal with price objections is to lessen the likelihood of objections by identifying value by POB.

⊕ QUESTIONS TO ASK . . . AND ANSWER

Your pricing approach shapes perceptions of what you are as a company, educates customers about when and how to buy, and over time, can become your primary customer-selection mechanism. You can choose customers based on the value they place on the product or service being delivered. Or you may be rewarding high cost-to-serve customers that purchase primarily on low price, and these customers then receive too much attention by the sales force and consume too many resources in operations and service. Evaluate your current pricing approach by answering the questions in table 8-2.

In an information-rich world, moreover, buying criteria and responses to price can change for lots of reasons beyond

TABLE 8-2

A pricing diagnostic

In our company, how well do we . . .

Understand the basis for our pricing: Is it primarily cost-plus or value-based pricing? Why?	1 2 3 4 5 6 7
Have processes in place to track how the value of our products or services varies across customers and contexts?	1 2 3 4 5 6 7
Have and use software that can provide dynamic pricing abilities by customer, product, or order?	1 2 3 4 5 6 7
Track and analyze the relevant piece of business in evaluating willingness to pay?	1 2 3 4 5 6 7
Focus on increasing the relevant zone of possible agreement in our sales training and account reviews?	1 2 3 4 5 6 7
Work with customers to understand the acquisition, possession, and usage costs that are incurred in our category?	1 2 3 4 5 6 7
Have in place an offering tracking system that helps us to clarify target price and reservation price?	1 2 3 4 5 6 7
Have a cross-functional team to help identify price versus cost opportunities in delivery, financing, product design, or other areas?	1 2 3 4 5 6 7

your control. In addition to a process for identifying customer value and value-extraction opportunities, you also need to test prices regularly and link pricing to your sales model and selling behaviors, which is the subject of the next chapter.

TESTING AND LINKING PRICE WITH YOUR SALES MODEL AND SELLING BEHAVIORS

Price is a dynamic variable in a business, affected by changes over the course of a product life cycle, as markets and buying behavior change due to competition or substitutes, or as a company moves into new segments. Hence, testing prices should be, but rarely is, an ongoing part of effective selling.

In today's information-rich markets, inertia is costly. A price often has multiple dimensions: base price, discounts off list price, rebates tied to volume, special offers, price for additional services, different prices by package size or product variant, and so on. These dimensions are increasingly visible to prospects and customers. Sites like Edmunds.com, Kayak.com, and others facilitate this in multiple categories. Further, the default option is not necessarily a profit-maximizing option. Notice, for instance, how Amazon distills thousands of stock-keeping units for consumer packaged goods products into price-per-ounce comparisons on its website.

This chapter first looks at the role of price in certain sales models and requirements for linking pricing and selling behaviors, including how your sales force frames value in conversations with prospects and customers. It then discusses why, given the changes discussed in earlier chapters, price testing is especially important, and via an example, tools for testing prices and the mindset relevant to using those tools and interpreting results in a world that never stops changing.

Linking Price with Your Sales Model and Selling Behaviors

Pricing affects the prospects approached by sales, the resulting orders that operations must deal with, the onboarding or other postsale issues encountered by customer service, the working capital and cash-flow dynamics measured and managed by finance. Hence, it's important to understand how a pricing structure fits with your sales model and, because the sales force is the major vehicle for implementing price realization in most companies, how to link price with ongoing selling behaviors.

Here, I'll discuss some common situations that are often misunderstood: pay-per-use and freemium pricing models; when pricing to capture first-mover advantages is and is not warranted; and because so much of price realization is linked to account management, issues in framing price and a value proposition to the right people at accounts.

Pricing and the Sales Model: Pay-per-Use and Freemium

Many people associate pay-per-use pricing with tech companies of the past decade, but it has long been used in multiple industries.

In 1959, Xerox introduced its 914 copier at a purchase price of $29,500 . . . and sold almost nothing. It changed to a lease model where, for $95 per month, customers got the machine and two thousand free copies, after which they paid $.04 per copy. Xerox sold over ten thousand machines via the lease model and, as customers quickly surpassed the two thousand copy allotments, became a $1 billion company in revenues (not just valuation, as with current "unicorns") by 1968. For years, Michelin used pay-per-use pricing in selling its tires to truck fleets, which pay Michelin per mile of tire performance. Michelin tires provided a 25 percent performance improvement over comparable tires, but fleet buyers resisted a 25 percent price increase. Pay-per-use linked the price paid with the tire's performance while minimizing sticker shock. In their engine businesses, GE and Rolls-Royce sold by-the-hour performance to airlines. Durr and BASF, leaders in automotive paint, offer a price per car painted to auto OEMs.

In all of these instances, the pricing structure transforms the seller from a product to a service provider, and that affects buying processes and sales tasks. In the up-front purchase model, buyers must justify capital-expenditure decisions, and salespeople must know how to support and navigate that process at their accounts. In the pay-per-use model, the buyer can often make the purchase as an ongoing operating expense, and salespeople must now know how to identify and justify a different category of benefits (e.g., reduced complexity and elimination of fixed costs and personnel, lower risk of product obsolescence, etc.) to different buyers at their accounts.

The role of price, its fit with the product, and the management requirements differ by sales model. Consider the freemium pricing model where a customer can get a basic version of the product for free—either for a limited time or for a limited number of uses or users. Then, continued use means paying for that product or a premium version. This approach has three core requirements:

1. An introductory offer that can attract a lot of users

2. The right fencing between the product tiers to encourage conversion from free to paid to premium versions of the product

3. A customer-loyalty or usage gate to generate repeat usage and motivate renewals, trade-ups in price and functionality, and thus customer lifetime value (LTV) that's higher than CAC

Notice the tension between items one and two: you need an attractive basic offer, but not *too* attractive or it becomes difficult to differentiate premium versions from the basic. In that case, you get lots of free users but too few paid conversions—the plague of many SaaS and consumer internet business models. Conversely, if the basic version offers too little value, it's hard to attract enough prospects: you may get high conversion rates but in too low absolute numbers to scale a business.

The fencing between the offers can be achieved through product features, differences in usage, capacity, or other dimensions. Without relevant fencing, and sales incentives linked to that fencing, a freemium model can produce a sales force that generates high initial customer acquisition but also high churn that is more costly than the revenues generated.

A key assumption in a freemium model is that, if users become comfortable with the basic functionality, a land-and-expand sales effort can motivate them to pay for more capacity or features. Hence, this pricing approach lends itself to certain experience goods, where value becomes apparent with actual use, and especially products where the experience depends on multiple users using the same product—for example, Dropbox, Skype, online gaming, and social networks—and where the marginal costs of the free offer are very low (e.g., internet platform businesses). But it is less appropriate in many other subscription categories where the model is often used but in fact is less applicable—for example, the struggle by many newspapers to get paid for their online content, or the swift rise and fall of MoviePass where $9.95 per month pricing for an unlimited number of movies attracted heavy users that were negative-LTV customers and forced the venture to place a cap on usage.

The relevance of freemium pricing depends on many factors.[1] A key factor is that this pricing requires a low-cost sales model. That's the lesson from the success of companies like Atlassian, Basecamp, Drift, Slack, and others: the complementary fit between the target market, product design, marketing, and the sales model.

Later in this chapter, we'll look at Basecamp in more detail in connection with price testing. But note here that Basecamp was an early entrant in a fast-growing category; its collaborative-software product has inherent virality; and the company explicitly managed its successive products to maintain a simple, easy-to-use, largely self-service product. Basecamp uses some content marketing and Google Ads. But its marketing has been primarily word of mouth and a form of thought leadership via the company's provocative blogs and its reputation in the software community: Basecamp's cofounder David Hansson is the inventor of Ruby on Rails, the popular coding methodology. All of these factors allowed Basecamp to grow with what is, compared to other firms, minimal and low-cost marketing and selling efforts that support its freemium pricing structure.

Pricing for First-Mover Advantages

Freemium pricing is often part of a sales model designed to capture alleged first- or early-mover advantages. The rationale is that first movers can "buy" customers through low prices because network effects will then build the brand, attract more users, make customers sticky as more users make that product the standard, and generate scale economies in the business. It's a go-to-market approach that emphasizes growth and market share, not profitability. It was the rationale behind experience-curve pricing in the 1970s, and with different language, it's again a mantra in many circles today.

Tech companies routinely cite network effects and first-mover advantages in fund-raising pitches and press releases. The argument is that long-term vision, an entrepreneurial mindset, consumer awareness, and early-mover advantages make the deal attractive despite prices that fail to cover costs. It fueled the initial enthusiasm about Groupon in 2009, and a decade later, Lyft's IPO filing in 2019 emphasized that "Network effects among the drivers and riders on our platform are important to our success."

But it's not only tech companies that now routinely assert first-mover advantages: investors in real estate provider WeWork pointed to alleged early-mover advantages, and even companies selling marijuana make this argument. Canopy Growth Corporation, the cannabis company founded by Bruce Linton in 2013, justified its pricing and unprofitability because (according to Linton) "The way the company operates is an aggressive entrepreneurial company not managing for profit at this point . . . but managing for market share and growth."[2] Linton was fired as CEO in 2019, but, hey dude, that was *after* he sold Canopy to Constellation Brands in 2018 for $4 billion.

The data does not support easy assertions about first-mover advantages. Table 9-1 lists examples from the 1980s to the present where first movers failed and later entrants (often third, fourth, or even tenth entrants) became market leaders.[3]

Even Amazon, the poster child for first-mover advantages in tech pitches, is in fact a counterexample: BookStacks Unlimited was founded in 1991 and launched online as books.com

TABLE 9-1

First movers and later entrants, 1980–2020

Product category	First mover	Later entrant
Social networks	MySpace	Facebook
Ride sharing	Sidecar	Uber/Lyft
Laser printing	Xerox	HP
Hybrid car (US market)	Honda Insight	Toyota Prius
Smartphone	Nokia	Apple/Samsung
Web search	Infoseek/AltaVista	Google
High-end electric cars	Fisker	Tesla
CRM	Siebel	Salesforce.com
Music downloads	Diamond Rio/Apple	Spotify

in 1992, while Jeff Bezos was still working on Wall Street. Yet Amazon and other later entrants cited above succeeded, while the first movers failed despite alleged network effects. Why? Business schools use the term "fast follower" to describe this pattern. But that's more a post hoc description of outcomes, rather than a managerially useful explanation of the market reasons and the implications for pricing and sales. To do that, you need to identify and make distinctions about when pricing for share is and isn't worth it.

Networked Market versus Network Effects

Many managers (and investors) confuse a networked market with network effects. Many markets are networked in the sense that people in that market watch each other's behavior, speak to each other, and collaborate, and that give-and-take affects buying and selling. Investment banking, syndicated deals in venture capital, private equity, commercial real estate, aerospace, and many other markets where finished products require integration across suppliers and buyers are examples of networked industries. But these markets do not necessarily have significant *network effects* where the product or service is more valuable if more customers use it.

The classic example of network effects in the economics literature is landline telephone service: a telephone was useless if nobody else had one, and its value increased with the number of people a user could call. This is called a direct network effect. Similarly, in two-sided platform businesses, the more suppliers there are, the more customers are attracted to the platform, and vice versa. This chicken-and-egg dynamic is called an indirect network effect. Both direct and indirect network effects are independent, however, of whether the people using the phones or platform are part of any ongoing collaborative network. Don't confuse networks with network effects.

Multi-Homing

Even in markets with genuine network effects, early-mover advantages are typically overstated. In many markets, people can and will use multiple platforms—what's called multi-homing. It's not difficult to install Lyft *and* Uber *and* other ride-sharing apps on your phone or communicate with friends via Facebook and Twitter and WhatsApp and Snapchat, and so on.

Besides Lyft and Uber, for example, you have later entrants like Grab (operating in multiple countries in Asia), 99 and Easy Taxi (in South America), Hitch carpooling in Australia, Olacabs in India, Gojek in Indonesia (weaving in and out of Jakarta's traffic on the back of a small motorbike—not for the faint-hearted or a middle-age professor, but less expensive than competing ride-hailing services and growing fast), and (until its acquisition by Uber in 2019) Careem in the Middle East, Africa, and East Asia. Pricing below cost in order to build share is usually a perpetually money-losing sales approach in such markets.

More generally, precisely because early adopters are more willing to experiment and take risks, they are typically the *least loyal* customers in the category.[4] The Nokia 900 smartphone was there before Apple, but those customers were among the quickest to switch when a more exciting product appeared. Then, when Spotify entered the music market in 2011, Apple already had more than 50 million iTune users and was selling about a billion downloaded songs every four months, but Spotify surpassed Apple as a leading source of digital music globally. No seller truly "owns" early adopters or other customers in a market; they're just renting them.

Customer Selection

Pricing to capture network effects is not simply being able to outspend your competitors on customer acquisition because of access to capital. It's about knowing what drives product value and therefore *which customers* you need. PatientPing is a Boston-based firm that sells a software platform which allows health-care providers to receive real-time notifications ("pings") when one of their patients is admitted to or discharged from a health-care facility.[5] The platform facilitates coordination across providers to reduce costs and help ensure that patients receive more timely, better-quality health care from the relevant provider. Under the Affordable Care Act (ACA or Obamacare), moreover, providers benefit economically by keeping patients within their network of care organizations. PatientPing sells to a range of customers, and its product clearly displays network effects and early-mover advantages: the platform provides escalating value as it attracts more customers in a region, more data about patients, and therefore more information to a growing group of users. Does this mean PatientPing should price low, or even below cost, to gain share fast? No.

Not all customers are created equal in any market, including one with network effects. Certain customers have significant spillover effects and disproportionate value. For PatientPing, big hospitals in a region are a key source of data and platform value. In fact, until the big hospital(s) in a region is sold, it's difficult to attract other facilities at any price because the value of the platform is low. Conversely, once the big hospital signs, it's much easier to sell to other facilities. A low price to those initial big customers makes sense, but not to others. This is reflected in PatientPing's pricing and its sales organization: it has a "new market" field-based sales team focused on large hospitals and other facilities that provide the relevant data feeds, and a "live market" inside-sales team focused on signing other facilities after the key initial accounts have signed onto the platform.

It's about the right customers—those who influence subsequent purchases and adoption—not any customers. This is true in many markets, offline and online. PatientPing's situation is analogous to what a mall developer encounters when building and populating a new mall: find and woo the anchor tenant(s) that attract and legitimize the mall space for others. In high-end malls in Asia, Louis Vuitton is a desired anchor tenant and receives very favorable terms if it agrees to place a store in that mall. It's also true in consumer categories where social media has become a prominent marketing tool. In the beauty industry, popular influencers like Jaclyn Hill, Katie Jane Hughes, and Jeffree Star attract hundreds of thousands of followers via Instagram, Facebook, and YouTube. Their value is analogous to that of big hospitals for PatientPing, and brands pay influencers to promote their products so that they *don't* have to discount prices to consumers. Estée Lauder now reportedly spends 75 percent of its digital marketing budget on influencer marketing, and studies show that in other online markets, it's also a minority of users who generate virality, not simply volume of customers.[6]

For that matter, even before anyone could spell "digitize," health-care firms understood the importance of the right customers. It was and is called a "hierarchy of influence" in a market. Selling diagnostic equipment to large teaching hospitals had longer-term advantages and merited special sales attention, because medical students use and disseminate the product to other institutions. For years under Steve Jobs, Apple pursued a similar sales approach when it focused on schools for its computers.

Value Proposition

Table 9-1 also illustrates that the right value proposition for the right target buyers trumps broad share. In China, eBay was the first mover, with a dominant share there by the early 2000s. But Alibaba surpassed eBay largely because of an escrow payment system more suited to the buying behavior of Chinese consumers. In the United States, OpenTable initially focused on signing up as many consumers and restaurants as possible to reap perceived first-mover advantages. But diners cared about finding the right restaurant in their neighborhoods, not any restaurant. On the brink of bankruptcy, OpenTable pivoted to focus on relatively high-end restaurants in specific locales, and—before the pandemic closed restaurants—became the leading reservations platform for fine-dining establishments in the United States and a number of other countries.[7]

The successful leaders are typically the first provers in their markets, not necessarily the first movers. Never forget that when setting prices, allocating sales resources, and equipping your sales force to frame and articulate the value your firm provides.

Framing Value and Price

A price must be made part of a coherent value proposition that communicates, and that largely happens in sales conversations. Your reps must know how and when to present value to the right people at their accounts. For some decades now, work in psychology has demonstrated that choices are heavily influenced by how the choice is framed.[8] The lessons include:

- **Focus on the positive outcomes.** Doctors and patients are more likely to recommend and accept a treatment when it's presented as having a 90 percent survival rate than when told the treatment has a 10 percent mortality rate.

- **Take advantage of loss aversion, or the fact that people weigh possible losses greater than possible gains.** Companies will often offer a credit to stay with the service when a customer calls to cancel, but a telecom company found that its cancellation rates dropped significantly when, instead, it informed customers that they had already been issued a credit for a hundred calls but would lose the credit if they now canceled.

- **Anchor the price to your advantage.** People are more likely to give more when the fund-raising circular suggests options like $75, $100, $300 rather than $5, $20, $50, and the same is true in price negotiations and product-line pricing.

These are fundamental insights. But years before the current vogue for "behavioral" economics (buying and selling happens between people, not abstractions: who knew!), retailers long framed prices and the value proposition according to these tenets. The meat isn't 25 percent fat; it's 75 percent lean. It's not just a 30 percent discount for off-peak diners; it's the "blue bird" or "pre-theater" menu. It's not a surcharge for dinner on Valentine's or Mother's Day; it's the "special" menu for that occasion. Stores' sale prices routinely anchor shoppers on "discount off original prices," and most items sold on Amazon have a struck-out price next to them for similar reasons. It works: a study of clothing and accessories sold in outlet stores found that for every \$1 increase in the posted original price for an item, consumers were willing to pay, on average, an extra 77 cents for that item—even when the original price listed was fake.[9] As Daniel Kahneman summarizes the research, "Unless there is an obvious reason to do otherwise, most of us passively accept decision problems as they are framed."[10]

In B2B markets, finding the relevant frame is more complicated and often account specific. The commercial buying process is typically more complex than the process for consumer goods and can involve more people with multiple perspectives, and buyers usually have standard operating procedures in place. If you do not alter their current frame, either the sale will fail or the value price will not be attainable. In these situations, reframing is crucial for price realization. Here are guidelines for selling value in that context.[11]

Know Who

In general, the higher the contact a salesperson calls on at a company, the more framing in terms of industry insights matters. If your reps call on a mid-level IT director (as in many SaaS models, for instance), they will probably want to frame the value and price in terms of comparative product functionalities and ask questions about operating systems at their accounts. If calling on a C-suite or line-of-business executive, however, it's typically more important to frame the value in terms that relate to trends, opportunities, challenges, or evolving best practices in that market, not only at that company. Or as one senior executive says to sellers who call on him: "Your job isn't to ask me what keeps me up at night. It's to tell me what should be."

Choosing the right approach is important. Gong.io has recorded and analyzed sales meetings from thousands of deals made on web conferencing platforms. At meetings with an SVP-level buyer or higher, the data indicates a strong *negative* correlation between asking discovery questions and closing deals. Once you've asked a few questions, every additional question with a busy senior buyer decreases the odds of success. On average, successful meetings here involved about four questions, while unsuccessful meetings averaged eight. For meetings at lower levels, however, successful sales calls averaged eleven to fourteen questions.[12] One role played by less senior managers is to be the gatekeepers and vet vendors so that meetings up the chain *can* focus on business issues *because* the product fundamentals have been scrutinized. At that more senior level, other frames are usually more salient than additional information about a product already on the prospect's short list.

Here's an example from a rep—call him Eric—who sells data-analytic tools for an IT firm. He called on a large US retailer shortly after a storm had shut its largest distribution center, which represented about 25 percent of inventory shipped to its stores. In conversations with Eric, lower-level managers framed the issue as a logistics problem, so Eric explained how his firm's tools could provide data relevant to optimizing flows and reducing delivery costs while the center was being repaired. But at subsequent meetings with more senior executives, Eric framed the issues and solution differently. This retail chain was also in the early stages of implementing an omni-channel bricks-and-clicks strategy, and in this context, logistics costs were just one element in a larger story. For the senior meetings, he brought examples illustrating how markdowns and out-of-stocks have a bigger impact on margins than logistics costs, why it's important to make pricing and other elements of the in-store and online customer experience as seamless as possible, and how others in the industry utilized data-analytic tools to do this. Senior executives approved the sale and at a scope wider than a purchase for logistics software.

Assess When

The relevant frame also differs based on where you are in the sales cycle. In an early meeting with a senior buyer or influencer, it's typically important to credential yourself: demonstrate that you understand and can articulate how your product relates to that customer's business and market. This can take the form of indicating who you know (people and companies using your product to drive business value and financial benefits) and/or what you know (your firm's viewpoint about industry trends and the implications).

This is important for a few reasons. Most products and services sold to businesses are part of a wider usage system at the buyer, so adoption means changes to the system. Senior buyers must also justify a significant purchase versus alternative uses of capital, and this is typically done by addressing a market challenge or opportunity, not just product performance comparisons. As one salesperson emphasizes, "Start with something that demonstrates you understand how people make decisions in that sector. At this stage, it's typically not competitors you should worry about; it's the status quo because 60 percent of all buying 'decisions' are to postpone a decision. So in initial meetings, I look for an industry issue or example they need to know about to make a decision." This rep is putting into practice what multiple studies demonstrate. Framing value in terms of what others are doing provides "social proof"—that is, people are more likely to take action when they know others already have. Demonstrating knowledge and empathy for their current decision criteria helps a rep to leverage existing beliefs in motivating assent to change—a practice shown to be important in political campaigns and other areas.[13]

Later in the B2B sales cycle, the issue is often credentialing your implementation capabilities. Here, relevant framing often takes the form of articulating (a) your recognition of the organizational processes affected by adoption of the solution (e.g., how adoption of a sales productivity tool will affect other parts of the business such as capacity planning, operations, delivery, or postsale service), and (b) how your organization has managed that process at other relevant customers. A senior partner in the consulting practice of a Big Four accounting firm emphasizes that "our associates can leverage the reports we produce and the content on our website earlier in the sales cycle with functional managers. But C-suite executives have little time to read that material, and by the time I speak with them, we're credentialed in terms of relevant experience. The selling difference then is typically how we can uniquely frame and implement a solution for *their* organization—how it applies to their strategic goals, and how we can help execute required initiatives in their company with their people."

"Sell higher and call on the C-suite" is a common refrain in sales, because that's often crucial for effective price realization. But, as always in sales, influence is bestowed by the buyer as well as earned by the seller. Achieving influence depends on how the salesperson frames the value and when in the sales cycle. How many in your current sales team have this ability? What are you doing to develop their ability to get access to the right buyers? Are you educating your reps on the discussions they are ultimately going to have with different people at their accounts, and helping them frame the story?

Price Testing: Why It's Important and Difficult

Price is a core profitability driver. The impact varies by industry, but studies indicate that for a global 1,000 firm, a 1 percent boost in price realization—not necessarily by getting 1 percent more on every order; perhaps higher or lower on different orders, but averaging out to 1 percent and holding volume steady—means a gain of 8 to 12 percent in operating profits. These results have been consistent for decades—before the internet became a factor in buying and selling, since it became a factor, and for both online and offline firms.[14] A 2018 study of SaaS companies, for instance, found that pricing changes—increases either to the subscription price or to usage fees—accounted for nearly all of the growth in annual recurring revenue(ARR) for those SaaS firms that did grow.[15] Similarly, research has long shown that a percentage change in price typically has a bigger and faster impact on sales than a comparable change in ad expenditures: according to some studies, "on average the price elasticity is about 20 times the advertising elasticity."[16]

Because price is such a potent weapon of value creation or destruction, price testing must be a deep and ongoing practice at firms, right? Wrong. In my experience, not that much has changed in many companies since David Ogilvy's observation made in 1963: "It is usually assumed that marketers use scientific methods to determine the price of their products. Nothing could be further from the truth. In almost every case, the process of decision is one of guesswork."[17] In fact, price is often primarily an emotional rather than economic issue for both buyers and sellers.

On the buying side, note the language used. Consumers, politicians, and regulators talk about "price gouging" (as in gouging out eyes) and "predatory pricing" (as in business = wolf and

customer = lamb). Note the reactions in the press and blogo-
sphere to surge pricing by Uber and others. A classical economist would defend this practice as legitimately allocating finite
supply to those who value the service the most. But the emotional reaction was overwhelmingly negative and caused the
companies to retract this mechanism in many markets. Behavioral economists have long documented how, despite market
logic, many buyers instinctively react negatively to many pricing
scenarios.[18]

Emotion also applies on the selling side. Many managers
and most salespeople have a fear of changing price, especially
if the change is an increase. One reason is that one can rarely
know with certainty how customers will react, and meanwhile
next quarter's quota is looming. Hence, common company
practice is to stick with the devil you know, despite market
changes. Because pricing is a visible moment of truth in business, many managers take refuge in the herd.

Testing prices is important to resist the downward forces
of gravity as a market matures, the inertia of legacy prices
that reflect obsolete circumstances, sales's common fear of
price increases, and setting price either by gut feel or simply
in line with category competitors. Further, the impact of pricing on selling is usually multidimensional. Price determines
revenue per customer, but can also drive win rates, retention,
and (with cost to serve) the LTV of customers the sales force
acquires.

In a business context, however, price testing presents challenges that are qualitatively different from the circumstances
surrounding academic research or clinical trials in medicine.
There are few opportunities for randomized controlled trials
in a competitive market. You must typically change or repair
the pricing ship while it's in full sail on the open waters of buying, selling, and price negotiations. This remains true in the
era of big data and artificial intelligence. The issue is not the

amount of data available for tests, but the nature of that data in the context of buying behavior.

Hermann Simon, cofounder of pricing consultancy Simon-Kucher, points to the work decades ago of Lester Telser, an economics professor who emphasized that past market data usually has only limited relevance for determining the actual shape of the demand curve today and tomorrow. In a market with high price elasticity, there are typically few changes in relative competitor prices.[19] With or without big data, managers know that a price change can cause major shifts in volume among price-sensitive buyers. So in these markets, competitors tend to follow each other's changes, and relative price positions don't vary much over time. Hence, the independent variable (price) stays within too tight a range to allow valid estimates of the demand curve at different price points. Conversely, in markets with low price elasticity, you will likely see more price differences, but they often yield only slight shifts in volume among differentiated competitors. Here, the dependent variable (sales volume) moves too little to determine what the underlying price elasticity really is.

Simon also points out that most companies pay little attention to pricing when times are good and markets are stable. It typically takes a structural change (e.g., a new competitor or technology, expiration of a patent, or a deep recession or demand collapse caused by a pandemic or financial crisis) to motivate a rigorous pricing test. But when such a change occurs, historical data offers only limited insights into future customer behavior precisely *because* of a structural change in buying criteria.

When you look at their actual workings, nearly all big data and AI approaches to price setting rest on historical data—more data than in the past, but still past data. Yet customer responses to prices are determined by dynamics as they work today in your market, not yesterday. You therefore need to approach both the process and interpretation of price tests with an awareness of the inherent limitations and with a different mindset than that preached by most vendors of this software. Managerially actionable price testing will rarely have a "scientific" result. But it can still yield insights, options, and influence. The following section provides an example.

An Example and Its Lessons

In 1999, Jason Fried cofounded 37signals, a web design agency in Chicago. In 2004, 37signals launched Basecamp, an early entrant in the project management software market that has grown exponentially in this century and spawned firms like Atlassian, Slack, and others. Fried soon focused on his software business, rebranded the firm as Basecamp LLC in 2014, and during this time launched multiple products with different pricing structures.[20]

Basecamp Classic (BCC), the original version, provided one free project with no time limitations, but no file storage or other features available in paid versions where subscription prices ranged from $24 to $149 per month, based on the number of projects and size of file storage. Average invoice values for BCC continued to show monthly growth more than ten years after launch. Basecamp 2 (BCX, for "Basecamp Next"), released in 2012, did not offer a free tier; instead, it offered a sixty-day free trial. BCX charged based on the number of projects and storage only. Plans ranged from $20 to $150 per month, with the top end including unlimited projects and storage. BCX's pricing attracted many customers who might have otherwise stayed with the freemium offer. But account upgrades and invoice value growth were slower than for BCC.

Basecamp 3 (BC3) was launched in late 2015 with feature-based pricing tiers. All plans began with one free project. Teams with two or more projects on the platform could then choose (a) the $29 per month "For Us" plan with internal collaboration features only and 1,000 GB of storage, or (b) a $79 per month "With Clients" plan that included external collaboration tools and 100 GB of storage, or (c) Basecamp Big, which provided a dedicated support manager, an uptime service agreement, onboarding training, and 2 terabytes of storage for $3,000 per year. Because BC3 was the first major product release after the firm's rebranding as Basecamp, in early 2016 Fried asked Noah Lorang, a data analyst, to test and evaluate pricing for the products a few months after its launch. Their process illustrates some important lessons, limits, and benefits of price testing in many other markets as well.

Why Test?

Lorang believed that useful pricing tests should shed light on both pricing and product options for creating and extracting customer value. He noted that by 2015, Basecamp was used at groups "ranging from our initial core of web and software developers to marketers, health professionals, accountants, folks in agriculture, and many more. They also span group sizes, from individuals to more than one hundred people in a user group, and over ten thousand job titles. There are big differences in usage patterns, both aggregate usage and feature usage." Like other Basecamp products, moreover, BC3 was sold via the web in a low-cost inbound model without any sales outreach or personal contact to place an order. This model had allowed Basecamp to reach millions of customers with a lean team, and Lorang was clear about the role of price in that model: "Optimal prices [are] those that result in maximum lifetime value (LTV). We'd generally accept a lower purchase rate if a higher average value offset that, and vice versa. We'd also accept a lower average invoice amount if it led to higher retention and thus greater LTV."

It's worth pausing here, because Lorang's comments empha-size some core purposes of price tests that are often ignored when, in contrast to this process, firms use tests in an unfo-cused fishing expedition:

- Identify reactions to different prices in a changing mar-ket with more competitors, more choices, and increas-ingly knowledgeable customers in the category of project management software.

- Understand factors that drive willingness to pay among diverse customer types whose different usage patterns present segmentation and multiple pricing opportunities.

- Do the above while treating price as linked with a firm's sales model and evolving product line.

Lorang was also clear about criteria to use in evaluating results: "It's hard to test LTV directly [because] that's a long-term outcome sensitive to elements beyond price, especially cancellation rates (churn). Instead, impact on LTV is estimated by evaluating conversion rates (free accounts who upgrade to a paid plan) and initial monthly revenue (average price a user pays after conversion to a paid plan)." By contrast, many man-agers are good at asking questions about prices ("how much will they pay?"), but bad at articulating what criteria they will use to evaluate responses and the implications for selling.

Test Constraints

Lorang and Fried then placed certain constraints on the tests. By 2016, Basecamp was adding more than seven thousand accounts weekly and engineering daily supported products with millions of users. Given this scarce resource, no develop-ers were available to alter a product offering for pricing tests.

This is not an uncommon practicality in managerial decision making: the accuracy and precision of predictive information versus the cost and complexity of acquiring it. But notice the implication: a common method of testing prices is a conjoint test, a statistical technique commonly used in large-scale market research that helps to determine how people value different attributes of a product or service and the price-feature trade-offs they are willing to make. Without changes in the product, however, a conjoint analysis won't say much about preferences. Basecamp recognized this, but many companies do not and so waste time and money with tests irrelevant to their business conditions.

Also, because Basecamp's products, including BC3, were already priced lower than competing products, the team decided to test the impact of price increases. Within these constraints, many potential test ideas were then discussed, and the team finally focused on a few, including the following:

- Doubling or tripling the price of the tiers: to test the impact on conversion rates and churn.

- Making the current $29 tier limited to five users and the $79 tier unlimited: this would resemble competitors' per-user pricing structures and test whether a form of per-user pricing would be better for Basecamp in terms of the LTV goal.

- Pricing both the "For Us" and "With Clients" product packages at $79. Current prices segmented users by features that enabled internal collaboration (the "For Us" product) versus collaboration between a customer and their clients or suppliers ("With Clients"). But many internal teams could be as large as client-facing teams. This test was intended to see if those using Basecamp primarily for internal project management would adopt at a higher price.

The lesson here is to clarify the evaluation benchmark for a given test. There's more to testing prices than generating a spreadsheet of price-volume interactions. Price tests require up-front understanding of how to evaluate resulting data versus a baseline. Testing in business is a broader process than textbook hypothesis generation followed by data. It involves evaluating alternatives. For tests to matter, firms must generate new ideas and be willing to make changes. This also applies to evaluating marketing initiatives in general, and there's a big difference between using profit increase or revenue lift, for instance, as the metric. Further, changes in price and sales methods typically have an impact over multiple time frames, not just in the short term, and Basecamp's churn and LTV criteria recognize that.

A/B Tests

The team began with an A/B test to see how customers reacted to a price increase with no other change to the marketing mix. Randomly chosen users to Basecamp's website were shown pages or messages that differed only in price, the "stimulus." The "treatment" group received a new offer the team wished to evaluate. All others, the "control" group, received the current price and offer. Impact was measured in differential rates of conversion, defined as an action like clicking a button, filling out a form, or making a purchase. Prices shown to the treatment group were double the standard price: $59 (versus $29) for "For Us," $159 (versus $79) for "With Clients," and $6,000 (versus $3,000) for "Basecamp Big." The test was simple to implement, with no changes needed to the style of the page. If doubling current prices resulted in fewer sign-ups and less total revenue, the team could try smaller increases; if it improved revenue by enough to compensate for fewer sign-ups, the team could try even higher prices.

The test ran long enough for thousands of users to see and evaluate the double-price offer. But Lorang realized that this procedure did not qualify as a statistically significant test, as defined in academic and clinical research. That would take much longer. Lorang wanted a test that gave meaningful results, while creating the fewest extra hours of work for the already-busy customer support team, which would have to answer questions or complaints from shoppers. The lesson here is that in price testing, you should focus on tendencies and validity, not precision. As noted earlier, because so many factors affect customer responses to price, there's an inherent imprecision in measuring results. But that doesn't undermine the validity of tests that are well constructed, used with an awareness of their limitations, and thus incrementally improve your ability to better separate signal from noise.

By the end of the test, 5,011 users had signed up for a free Basecamp account: 1,573 in the treatment group and 3,438 in the control group. The team then waited five days for freemium accounts to convert to paid. (Experience indicated that 50 percent of paid accounts converted within the first week, giving the team confidence in the result.) It calculated the A/B test results as follows: *Conversion percentage* was the number of paying customers in each cohort divided by the number of registrations. This indicated the willingness to pay when presented with an offer. The test group had 28 of 1,573 registrants convert to a paid plan (1.8 percent), a decrease from the control group that converted 120 of 3,438 (3.49 percent). *Plan value*, calculated by averaging the monthly price paid by a cohort, indicated willingness to choose a more or less expensive plan when presented with a given offer. When multiplied, the conversion percentage and plan value produced the *value per sign-up*, or the expected value of a new account (free or paid) in the cohort.

Price-Sensitivity Survey

The team augmented A/B tests with a Van Westendorp Price Sensitivity Meter (PSM), a survey method common for consumer goods. About twenty-six thousand randomly chosen Basecamp customers received an email invitation to a survey. In addition to questions about metrics that Basecamp collected monthly (e.g., net promoter score), the team included four about pricing. Sliding scales, with prices ranging from $0 to $500, were presented below each of the questions in figure 9-1.

FIGURE 9-1

Basecamp price survey

Help us make Basecamp even better. Thanks for taking a few minutes to share your feedback about Basecamp.

We'd like to ask you a few questions about the price you might pay for Basecamp. This will not affect the price of your current account.

At what total monthly price would you consider Basecamp to be priced so low that you feel that the quality can't be very good?

Your selection:
$0 ———————————————— $500

At what total monthly price would you consider Basecamp to be a bargain—a great buy for the money?

Your selection:
$0 ———————————————— $500

At what total monthly price would you say Basecamp is starting to get expensive—it's not out of the question, but you'd have to give some thought to buying it?

Your selection:
$0 ———————————————— $500

At what total monthly price would you consider Basecamp to be so expensive that you would not consider buying it?

Your selection:
$0 ———————————————— $500

Submit

Source: Frank Cespedes and Robb Fitzsimmons, "Basecamp: Pricing," Case 9-817-067 (Boston: Harvard Business School, April 2017).

FIGURE 9-2

Price Sensitivity Meter: Method

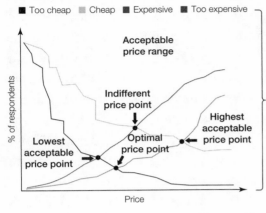

■ Too cheap   ■ Cheap   ■ Expensive   ■ Too expensive

Van Westendorp Price Sensitivity Meter (PSM) asks four price-related questions to **identify upper, lower, and optimal price points.**

1. At what price would you consider Basecamp to be priced so low that you feel that the quality can't be very good?
2. At what price would you consider Basecamp to be a bargain—a great buy for the money?
3. At what price would you say Basecamp is starting to get expensive? It's not out of the question, but you'd have to give some thought to buying it?
4. At what price would you consider Basecamp to be so expensive that you would not consider buying it?

Source: Frank Cespedes and Robb Fitzsimmons, "Basecamp: Pricing," Case 9-817-067 (Boston: Harvard Business School, April 2017).

The survey collected 895 responses (3.4 percent response rate). The team created percentage charts like the PSM in figure 9-2. Each line corresponded to the number of responses indicating a given price point was, for example, "so low" that it affected quality perceptions (question 1), or "a bargain" (question 2), and so on. The intuition behind this chart, Lorang explained, "is that at some price points, all respondents agree that prices are too high or too low. The chart tries to identify the points, as well as the percentages of respondents who say that a given price is, for example, 'too expensive.'"

Another cut of the data expressed respondents' answers as a function of the price they were paying for their current plan. In other words, users saying $5 was too low would be expressing a 0.17x multiple if they paid $29 per month on the "For Us" plan, or a 0.06x multiple if they paid $79 for "With Clients."

A majority of respondents believed that two-thirds or more off the current price was too cheap—that is, free, or close to it, did not signal quality. Customers indicated that an average discount of about one-third from their current price paid would be "a bargain," and 25 percent indicated that the price they were paying today was already low. "Expensive" was a price that was "not out of the question, but you'd have to give some thought to buying it." The median here was 1.4x a user's current price, but many responses extended beyond 2x toward 4, 5, and even 6 times the current price. The median response to the "too expensive" range was double a user's current price paid, similar to the A/B test results.

Notice the different information contained in the A/B tests and the survey. An A/B test provides information about behavior: people click, buy, or not at the prices in the test. By contrast, surveys generate information about expressed attitudes and preferences, not behavior, and there's often a big difference between what people say and do. In a survey of more than a thousand companies across industries, for example, respondents said their most important purchasing criteria were price and product features. But follow-up analysis indicated that services and the sales experience mattered more in their actual buying behavior.[21] Anyone familiar with market research can cite similar studies. The same is true in online interactions. In analyzing Google data, Seth Stephens-Davidowitz shows repeatedly the basis for his conclusion: "Don't trust what people tell you; trust what they do."[22] With surveys, moreover, there's inherent ambiguity about how customers interpret wording like "a bargain . . . starting to get expensive" and so on. Also, when surveys ask customers about price directly, the process itself tends to make respondents anchor on price independent of other value-package components. Hence, the results in Basecamp's survey, where many respondents indicate a willingness to pay more, are indeed noteworthy.

Surveys have advantages: they are easy to administer, generate data quickly, and are a good first step in generating ideas for further testing. But the lessons are, first, combine and use multiple methods (including, when possible, conjoint tests). Second, while surveys remain the most common method of price tests, online A/B tests are increasingly available and fast, and show what people do in response to different prices, but are underutilized by most firms. Meanwhile, your salespeople must deal with actual buyer behavior, not espoused preferences in surveys or conjoint scenarios.

So What, Now What?

Basecamp did not use the price tests as an "answer." Instead, as managers in a dynamic market should, it used the results to generate options, the rationale behind them, and dialogue about how they relate to strategy goals. As one team member noted, the results generally indicated that "consumer surplus is very high for our product with most users. How much more would some customers pay but can't be charged under our current pricing model?" Alternative options included:

- **Onetime user-onboarding charges.** BC3's prices might include a onetime fee for different sizes of user groups (5, 10, 20, 100+, etc.). Some argued that this fee would indicate the size of user groups where customers derived the most value from Basecamp and would help the growing firm to target its marketing messages more precisely. But others questioned whether the number of users is a good proxy for willingness to pay in an experiential-goods product category where many customers probably don't know how many will use Basecamp until they use it.

- **Monthly fee per number of external contacts.** The "For Clients" product allowed BC3 users to include external parties in projects managed with Basecamp. These features were highly valued by users like ad agencies, design firms, and others. BC3 could set prices based on the number of external clients. Some at Basecamp argued that this approach avoids per-user charges that might inhibit adoption: an important factor as competition increased and in a category where initial adoption is critical because, once customers use a given collaborative-software product, it's tough to get them to switch. But others at Basecamp noted that it was often the inherent complexity of a project, not just the number of external contacts, that motivated adoption of "For Clients."

- **Reduced annual subscription fee for an up-front payment.** Unlike most SaaS firms, Basecamp did not offer a discount for up-front payment of an annual contract. This common practice improved cash flow, reduced the number of accounts that churn after using the software for another project or two, and improved forecasting as well. But others noted that having no annual payment was one reason why Basecamp added more than seven thousand accounts monthly, and an annual fee might inhibit initial adoption in an increasingly crowded marketplace.

This dialogue is essential to crafting price changes and clarifying the trade-offs involved. In a business like Basecamp, for example, there's a trade-off between the pricing opportunities uncovered by the tests and maximizing initial customer acquisition. Different functions will have different views on that trade-off, and in most firms, valuable options are often stopped by managers who optimize their function's procedures, not enterprise value. Yet once a decision is made, implementation requires a coherent cross-functional effort.

For Basecamp, that dialogue resulted in the approach that Jason Fried ultimately adopted—a hybrid among the options discussed. In place of its three-tier price structure, Basecamp instituted one $99 price plan for BC3: $20 per month more than the previous second tier of $79 per month. But it grandfathered the previous pricing structure for current accounts. Basecamp did reduce the annual subscription fee for customers who paid up front for an annual contract, while maintaining the monthly payment option for others. Finally, it made these pricing changes while repositioning BC3 to focus primarily on SMB owners as the buyer, not project managers, and changed its website and other communications to articulate how the product allowed an SMB executive to manage multiple projects and tasks more efficiently.

The results over the next six months were as follows. Conversion rates from free to paid were lower under the $99 plan. But average invoice value for new BC3 customers increased more than 25 percent, and more than 25 percent of new customers signed up for annual contracts. Lorang notes that simplifying buying choices for customers was the key driver in offering the annual payment option: "Instead of monthly decisions, it's now a once-yearly choice" for customers. The lower but higher-value conversion rates also reduced the need for commensurately bigger and bigger customer service teams as Basecamp grows. Another result is ongoing price testing and revised pricing for BC3 and other products since then.

⊕ QUESTIONS TO ASK . . . AND ANSWER

A price is the most visible strategic choice that firms make and a signal to competitors as well as customers. In most firms, price perceptions and price realization are shaped by the sales force. Be vigilant about linking your pricing approach to desired selling behaviors. Consider the questions in table 9-2.

TABLE 9-2

Linking price and selling behaviors: A diagnostic

In our company, how well do we . . .

Understand how our pricing approach affects sales prospecting, orders, and working capital requirements?	1 2 3 4 5 6 7
Have processes in place to update assumptions about the role of price in our customer acquisition and retention efforts?	1 2 3 4 5 6 7
Align pricing with what we know about willingness to pay by product or market segment?	1 2 3 4 5 6 7
Track and analyze whether our pricing is meant primarily to drive volume and gain share or maximize profits or margins?	1 2 3 4 5 6 7
Focus on educating our salespeople about how to frame our value proposition and justify price?	1 2 3 4 5 6 7
Understand the links between our pricing approach and customer-segment selection criteria?	1 2 3 4 5 6 7
Test prices on an ongoing basis?	1 2 3 4 5 6 7
Use new tools and a cross-functional team to conduct and interpret test results and generate options?	1 2 3 4 5 6 7

The previous chapter explained how pricing and value are linked. This chapter examined how to keep that link relevant to buyers, your sales model, and conversations with customers and prospects. The next chapter discusses distribution, a key component of selling in an omni-channel world.

You may be familiar with the so-called "4Ps" of marketing: product, price, promotion, and place (i.e., distribution channels). Of those, price is typically the easiest to modify. Meanwhile, for reasons discussed in the next chapter, channels are usually the hardest to change. Yet selling value in contemporary markets requires attention to building long-term relationships with customers *and* with the channel partners that also deal with your current customers and with prospects in new segments that may be vital to profitable growth.

BUILDING AND MANAGING A MULTICHANNEL APPROACH

A theme of this book is that the most important thing about a go-to-market approach is the buyer. As explained in chapter 1, buying is now a continuous and dynamic process where a prospect and an order touch multiple points in the distribution channel for most products and services. Hence, selling also means working effectively with channel partners that are influential during the buying journey and after the sale—or, to use the fashionable term, building and managing the relevant "ecosystem." It's not only listening to customers and providing value. Sales effectiveness requires success at the intersection of company and channel capabilities with target customers throughout the buying journey (see figure 10-1).

To deal with these opportunities and requirements, managers must rethink the role of channel partners in their sales programs, choose and manage partners so they align with buying realities and strategic goals, and utilize the broadening array of tools now available for these selling tasks.

FIGURE 10-1

Aligning company, customers, and channels

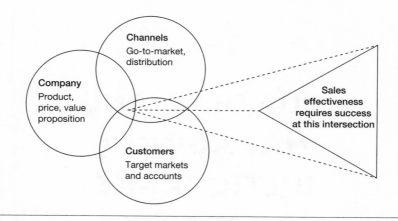

Components and Choices: It's Not Either/Or

In many companies, too much time and energy are wasted on debating whether to be online or in person, interacting via the web or through sales reps. These are false dichotomies.

Multichannel selling is usually the required norm, even in areas that are typically discussed as "disrupting" traditional channels. For example, in 2019, almost 60 percent of US Amazon marketplace merchants also sold on eBay; 47 percent also sold on their own sites; and about two-thirds (66 percent) also sold through Walmart, Sears, and other brick-and-mortar stores.[1] Amazon itself is a reseller in many categories, a platform for other firms in other categories, both a reseller and a marketplace in a number of categories, and it is opening stores. In many industries, competitive strategy now involves rivalry between competing channel systems, not only between individual firms. If you're a retailer competing with Amazon, you are competing with that supply chain, not just price and product on a website.

"Channels" refers to the way in which a product or service reaches its users, and firms have more choices in the means they use. These options can open up new segments, increase levels of order fulfillment and service, and create new business models. Meanwhile, customers are unbundling traditional channel arrangements in many industries along their journey from search and shop to purchase and postsale service. Over the past two decades, many companies called "disruptors" have basically been channel plays (not product innovators) that take advantage of incumbent inertia in industry distribution channels.

The components of any channel are the activities utilized to move the product or service from the point of production to consumption. Those activities typically include some or all of the following:

- Promotion and demand generation: making prospects aware of your product

- Presale education, applications support, and/or product customization: educating the buyer and seller about relevant uses of the product in that organization or household

- Price negotiations, financing, and/or carrying of inventory (where applicable)

- Logistics and order fulfillment

- Postsale services of various kinds

In getting its product to market, a producer must assume these functions or shift some or all of them to intermediaries. A firm's channel may now include the company's field and/or inside-sales force; wholesalers, distributors, and retailers; value-added resellers; third-party agents like manufacturers' reps (who usually sell multiple products in a category and typically work on commission); social media channels; influencer blogs; your website, Amazon, or another website; a call center; webinars for promotion, education, or postsale service; mail-order channels that have been in place since catalogs disrupted nineteenth-century retailing (and which, in the twenty-first century, still garner close rates superior to social media channels in many categories); and others. Companies now have a bigger channels playbook.

But the strategic and managerial complexity has also increased. For one thing, a channel is not only a collection of activities or functions. It's also a go-to-market system that encompasses often implicit and legacy assumptions about:

- **The product and the brand.** What it is and is not, depending upon, for instance, if it's sold via a self-service channel, a systems integrator, or as part of a product-service bundle from a given entity in the distribution chain.

- **The nature of customer value.** For example, a channel that's a one-stop-shop location for that product and other products the customer needs. Industrial distributors, for instance, typically carry an array of goods ranging from capital equipment to supplies and consumables. That array is key to the value provided to the industrial buyer and individual producers: the distributor breaks bulk and reduces inventory, financing, and other transaction costs for both parties.

- **Selling requirements and service needs.** Sales and service models change if you sell direct versus an intermediary versus a multichannel mix. For decades, life insurance executives repeated a mantra: "Life insurance is sold, not bought." The point was that most people don't wake up pondering their mortality; it takes field agents to promote awareness of the need and the product. Accordingly, for years, most life insurance companies were skeptical and static in their channel policies when direct-selling companies entered the market via the internet.

The broad array of channel choices also often outstrips the seller's capacity or willingness to change. Most companies must manage channel relationships across several product-market boundaries or segments, and the relative importance of different channel activities and partners tends to change over the product life cycle or as competition develops. Hence, as we'll discuss later in this chapter, there's a tension at the heart of many multichannel relations.

There's channel design and then there's ongoing channel management. To align components and make these choices effectively, you must think through the implicit assumptions in your go-to-market system. Then, use the right channels for the key sales and service tasks.

Channel Design: What You Sell and What They Buy

Determining the optimal channels for your business is a complex process. But the core issues in channel design involve placing a given function where it can be performed most effectively, managing the trade-off between control and resources inherent in multichannel selling, and clarifying the channel partner's role in your business-development strategy.

In designing channels, bear in mind an important distinction. As I've discussed in more detail elsewhere, people pay for satisfactory responses to perceived problems or opportunities: they don't buy two-inch drill bits; they buy two-inch holes.[2] This distinction underlines the difference between what a firm sells (features of a product or service) and what customers buy (the problem solved or satisfaction desired). Designing an effective multichannel sales program starts by understanding this distinction and its implications for channel functions throughout the buying journey.

In the apparel business, for instance, the majority of consumer shopping journeys now have an online component for either product research or transaction. An estimated 25 percent of US apparel shoppers visit Amazon early in their buying journey, but the majority of those visitors buy elsewhere.[3] This suggests that online channels and Amazon, in particular, are important for the search and discovery phases, but less so for specific product evaluations and the purchase itself. Moreover, research also indicates that the omni-channel customer in this category spends about a third more on apparel annually than offline-only shoppers. If you're managing an apparel brand, your go-to-market system should reflect these distinctions during the buying journey, and the interactions between online and brick-and-mortar channels, that are essential in selling to these valued, high-LTV customers.

In other categories, you may sell the same product to multiple segments, but each segment is buying qualitatively different benefits in distinct ways. As a result, the product's value, adoption criteria, and go-to-market requirements differ significantly. Consider Formlabs, a producer of 3D printers founded in 2012 with technology developed at the MIT Media Lab.[4] 3D printers have been around since the 1980s, but in the past twenty years, they've become smaller, more powerful, easier to operate, and less expensive. In 2001, the cheapest 3D printers cost about $45,000 and required trained technicians to operate them. In 2015, Formlabs introduced its Form2 product for $3,499 with functionality relevant for an array of users: engineers, designers, product managers creating prototypes, jewelry makers, digital artists, architects, medical researchers in labs, surgeons, orthodontists, and—in the United States alone—two hundred thousand dentists and seven thousand dental labs where the 3D printer could perform milling, design, and other tasks core to dental work.

How did Formlabs reach and activate this market potential?

It followed the buying processes and relevant product uses. Jewelry designers typically are concerned with product specifications like castable resin, print precision, and other issues particular to a finely crafted product. These customers buy their supplies, equipment, and materials from a few large distributors, so purchasing directly from a manufacturer like Formlabs was an unfamiliar process. Architects and digital artists typically use a 3D printer with CAD software. They rely heavily on value-added resellers (VARs) and those VARs' recommendations before deciding to purchase. Dentists purchase hundreds of supply items and equipment from large, multiproduct dental supply distributors that provide one-stop-shopping convenience to these busy small-business professionals. Engineers and product designers at corporations are a core market for 3D printers, but their buying processes differ by circumstance and department. Finally, the $3,499 price made Formlabs's product also accessible to consumers and hobbyists who often purchased via Amazon and other websites.

In this situation, product value and adoption criteria depend upon the applications, and third-party channels of various sorts are crucial for educating buyers. Meanwhile, the producer, Formlabs, also needs to provide product support and build awareness of product uses at the intermediary and end-user levels, especially because in the 3D printer business, there's a razor/blade dynamic: resin (the "ink" for a 3D printer) has higher margins than the equipment, and Formlabs made resins for different use cases. But resin sales depend upon the extent and usage of the printer in the installed base of customers. In other words, the business model—like many others in the twenty-first century—is an interdependent triangle: resin sales require equipment sales; equipment sales require vertically specific channels that address a segment's application, usage, and purchasing preferences; the producer must design and support those multichannel efforts, and that requires cash from the resin sales.

This example raises issues central to multichannel selling requirements. One issue is how to balance the trade-off between resources and control over product distribution, and another is how to choose and enable the relevant channel partnerships. CAD resellers, for example, traditionally focus on selling software and might not be as committed to selling hardware like Formlabs's 3D printer, which costs less than high-end CAD software and so offered CAD reps a lower commission. Dental supply distributors are key to a big segment, and in contrast to CAD VARs, Formlabs's $3,500 product price was higher than that of many other dental supply items. But those distributors sell hundreds and often thousands of products. How much time and selling effort could Formlabs expect from this channel? The exact path a company pursues depends upon its products and target customers, and which mix of direct and indirect channels will yield the highest returns. But choose you must.

Control versus Resources

In most marketing situations, the producer faces a trade-off between its ability to control important channel functions and the financial and/or human resources required to exercise that control.[5] The more intermediaries involved in getting a producer's product to market, the less control that producer can exercise over the flow of its product through the channel and the way it is promoted and presented to customers. As the number of intermediaries increases, so do the opportunities for differing levels of service and delivery by various channel partners and overlapping sales efforts. In addition, the producer's ability to set prices to end-user customers generally tends to decrease.

On the other hand, reducing the length and breadth of channels typically requires that the producer perform more channel functions itself and allocate more financial, sales, or support resources to activities such as warehousing, shipping, credit, or service. As one of the oldest aphorisms in business puts it, "You can eliminate the middleman, but not the middleman's functions." Hence, as depicted in figure 10-2, there is generally an inverse relationship between control and resources (especially financial resources like working capital) in many multichannel sales situations.

With this relationship in mind, we can make two important managerial distinctions. First, some business units have the resources to perform most or all required channel functions for their products, *if* management so desires. Other businesses, with more constrained resources (or, like Formlabs, in markets where a dispersed customer base simply increases the resources required for adequate market coverage), lack the ability to perform many important channel functions directly.

FIGURE 10-2

Inverse relationship between control and resources

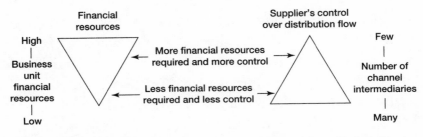

Source: Frank Cespedes, "Channel Management," Case 9-590-045 (Boston: Harvard Business School, revised November 2006).

Second, depending upon the product or market, the need to control a given function may be more or less important for selling effectiveness. That is, because of the product technology, its usage or service requirements, the training or applications development required, the mission-critical importance of the product at the customer (e.g., a "line stopper" item at a manufacturing plant versus a component added at the finished inventory stage), or because of required ongoing company-customer information flows, the multichannel seller will find it more or less important to have control over a function.

Formlabs is an example that's relevant to many other firms. Formlabs's original product, the Form 1, won high praise and sold quickly via the firm's website and its inside-sales organization, primarily to design engineers. But the product had defects, which the firm fixed with input from customers via its direct-sales channels. The Form 2 was a much-improved product in terms of functionality, reliability, and easier setup and service for end users. The Form 1 required Formlabs's service people to train users on repair, but the Form 2 was simpler to use and had few parts that could break. These product features created the multiple market opportunities noted earlier and tend to support a go-to-market based on third-party channels, especially since the Form 2's low price made it economically difficult to support a direct-sales approach. Formlabs's founder, however, was adamant about maintaining a direct-sales channel (in addition to intermediaries) because "When the early Form 1 ran into problems, we got a huge amount of helpful feedback direct from users." Unlike software, hardware cannot be updated online if it malfunctions, and channel partners—selling the products of multiple firms—have no big incentive to defend your firm if and when your product breaks. Direct company-customer interaction is especially important when a company enters new segments with an

FIGURE 10-3

Resources and channel design

Business unit financial resources

	Low	High
High	Resources as *limiting* factor in channel design	Control as *determining* factor in channel design
Low	Control as *minimal* factor in channel design	Cost efficiencies or access as *determining* factor in channel design

(Left axis label: **Need for control of channel functions**)

evolving technology—an interaction and source of information inhibited by third-party distribution.

The more general point is that businesses differ in available resources, and so their *capacity* for assuming important channel functions, as well as their relative *need* for direct control over different functions. A matrix helps to illustrate the selling implications (see figure 10-3).

In the upper-right quadrant, where financial resources are high (i.e., adequate to perform directly important channel functions) and where the need for control over those functions is also high, a direct-sales channel is likely to be the predominant and preferred mode of distribution. This is the case for many engineered products and for products where profit margins or subsidies from other business units in a corporation augment go-to-market resources. In the lower-left quadrant, where resources are more constrained and where the need to control channel functions is relatively low, then multi-tier distribution is predominant. In this situation, the producer can more easily delegate functions to channel partners and conserve its resources for other purposes (e.g., R&D and product development), because the incremental value of a direct relationship with user customers is less important.

In the twenty-first century, however, most of business life occurs in the other quadrants, where a calibrated mix of direct and indirect channels is required. In the lower-right quadrant, where resources are available but the need to control important functions is relatively low, then third-party channels are a *determining* factor in a go-to-market program. You start with a presumption of third-party distribution of some sort in the multichannel mix, and where a function is performed (by you or the channel) is determined primarily by cost-efficiency or market-access criteria rather than direct quality control over those functions. This is often the case in product categories where specifications are well established and where price competition has producers focused on reducing costs, including go-to-market costs. Or think about businesses that, in effect, outsource their promotional, marketing, and order-fulfillment functions to Amazon, Alibaba, or another online channel.

Conversely, in the upper-left quadrant, where resources are low but the need to control channel functions is high, financial and other resource considerations act as a *limiting* factor in channel design. The producer should try to do directly as many important channel functions as possible within its resource limits. This is often the case early in a technology life cycle where there's a high need for customer education and the producer knows more about the product technology than end users or resellers but has constrained financial conditions. Resellers are then often used to achieve market coverage and initial access to prospects, but the producer is involved in many sales conversations. Here, channel costs are a constraint, not determinant, of multichannel design, and this will affect the terms the producer negotiates with its channel partners about ancillary sales (e.g., supply items like resin required for product usage), rebuys, and other contract terms.

One way to think about the choices is to consider alternative uses of your people, time, and capital—that is, the business imperatives that can and should preempt resources for purposes other than selling and distribution. In some situations, the firm's strategic priorities (e.g., achieve a low-cost position or fund new product development) can affect how high or low a priority distribution investments are in the capital-budgeting process. In others, third-party channels focused on target segments can be attractive for a business with limited resources and under pressure to get its product to market quickly. The principle here is to identify those functions where the highest possible levels of quality control are needed versus those where "good enough" will suffice. As with Formlabs, these choices can be crucial, especially for early-stage firms that find that channel partners offer established contacts at prospects but may or may not devote sufficient attention to any one product.

Enabling Channel Partnerships

It's not enough to choose a coherent go-to-market mix. To monetize a multichannel system, you must form relevant channel partnerships. There are three key elements in doing this: reciprocity, tools and metrics, and the role of channel managers.

Reciprocity

Why do companies do business with each other? Because each believes it can accomplish more together than it can separately. Reciprocity is at the heart of channel interactions. Robert Cialdini's studies of persuasion are relevant here. Cialdini emphasizes that the rule of reciprocation—what he calls "the

FIGURE 10-4

Successful channel partnerships: Reciprocity

We give to channel partners	We get from channel partners
• Product knowledge	• Customer access/information
• Responsive product changes	• Responsive promotions
• Ongoing attention/support	• Sales attention and incentives
• Pricing and presentation support	• Sales forecasts and results
• Market research data	• Account information
• Emerging best practices about the above	• Emerging best practices about the above

old give and take"—drives influence and assent. He cites evidence that most societies subscribe to the rule, "and within each society it seems pervasive also; it permeates exchanges of every kind."[6] This includes exchanges between channel partners. Figure 10-4 outlines some of the reciprocal factors that are typically crucial for successful channel partnerships.

Sellers who fail to specify these expectations handicap their ability to drive value with and through their partners. Channels are composed of people, not just institutions. Many big and desirable channel partners for tech firms are companies like Accenture, Salesforce, SAP, and global systems integrators. In their daily operations and allocation of resources, however, those companies are really decentralized collections of regions, branch offices, or individual vertically focused units. Channel partnerships typically occur branch by branch and unit by unit by nurturing and then promoting joint success.

Clarifying the give-and-take helps to increase understanding between interdependent groups about how to interact to support business development, effective selling, and mutual growth. The rules help busy people understand how to prioritize behaviors to support each other *and* to hold each other accountable. End-user customers rarely see or care about these rules of reciprocity among their suppliers. But their presence or absence ultimately affects what those customers *do* care about in areas like product customization, delivery, service, and responsiveness.

Consider Oversight Systems, a firm discussed in earlier chapters. Recall that Oversight sells an analytics platform that allows companies to monitor their travel-and-expense (T&E) spending for errors, fraud, and operational inefficiencies. A key channel partner for Oversight is Concur Technologies, a leading vendor of T&E reporting systems to large corporations.[7] Why has the partnership been successful? Concur is focused on Oversight's core target market, and so both companies reap mutual value. Concur gives Oversight access to important accounts, data relevant to Oversight's software analytics, and thus highly qualified leads. Conversely, Oversight gives Concur's salespeople the ability to augment their value proposition, close deals faster, and so move on to the next prospect sooner.

There's also a clear give-and-take in the financial terms of the channel agreement. Oversight pays a referral fee on first-year revenues for each Concur-referred deal it closes; Concur account managers receive a bonus for each deal they close involving Oversight, and a portion of their quota is tied to such deals. In other words, there are mutual growth incentives, which minimizes conflict about who "owns" the deal. Finally, Concur has a partner-management system in place where leads are logged in and tracked, and its partners have access to the system. The result is transparency and data that help to make channel partnerships work—a key reason to invest in channel-management tools and metrics.

Tools and Metrics

By tools, I mean data and analytics relevant to the channel functions delegated to a partner. Make it easy for partners to access this information because, as is usual in sales, time is money. If you sell through broker channels, for instance, low friction and easy communication are often as important as commission dollars in getting brokers' attention and commitment to your products. Often, however, sellers ship products to a channel partner, but the material and information needed for effective selling are not provided. As an experienced sales executive puts it, "Being ready-to-sell is as important as ready-to-ship. Too many firms do not have a channel-centric list of what is needed for their channels to be ready to sell."[8] As a result, their cost of selling is higher, the percent of sales capacity available is lower, and the number of deals won is lower than it could be.

Here, technology is the seller's friend. The means for establishing, maintaining, and utilizing partner sites that provide white papers, case studies, online demos, deal registration data, and other relevant sales tools are decreasing in cost and increasing in scope. Channel marketing software is a growing sector that enables partners to leverage your content, messaging, branding, and demand-generation knowledge in their selling efforts for your products.

Multichannel selling is complicated but necessary. Trying to do it without smart use of these tools makes it unnecessarily complicated and burdensome. Yet, that's what many sellers currently do. They focus on their product or platform and ignore the wider channel ecosystem in their business. One estimate, for example, is that for every dollar a company spends with a SaaS platform, it will spend four times that amount with third parties like systems integrators and other channel partners.[9]

The rewards of getting this right are significant. A key reason for multichannel selling is increased buyer expectations for timely knowledge and ideas relevant to their particular needs. Buyers may credit your company and salespeople with being smart about products and solutions, but they also know you probably don't have a monopoly on the relevant smarts. At Brooksource, an IT staffing company, President John Causa notes that "Our customers want new ideas and approaches to perennial problems. Having partners that complement our services allows for true solutions." Sales reps work with channel partners across an array of human capital issues through systems that make the interaction productive within the short time frames relevant in the staffing business. Causa emphasizes that "Nobody does cartwheels for software. The payoff comes in the form of collaboration. We had no way to share ideas and track this across our 20+ offices and multiple partners. Now we can. It's meant a 30% increase in call volume and productive leveraging of the tribal knowledge in this ecosystem."[10]

Channel Managers

Enablement tools are increasingly abundant, and smart companies use these tools where multichannel selling is required. But no channel partnership manages itself, even when enabled by excellent systems. You must translate that information into knowledge and relationships that drive the time, attention, effort, sell-through, and support required. That's the role of channel managers, a role that is often undervalued and misunderstood.

First, consider the value. When asked which resource they would add to increase top-line growth, most executives cite an additional salesperson or marketing manager. But research on companies looking to grow in emerging markets found that hiring a dedicated manager for third-party distribution relationships yielded a much bigger increase in revenue growth.[11] In this research, "emerging" markets meant a variety of geographical markets where in-country distributors often have the local contacts, market access, and relations with buyers. But as the previous examples in this chapter illustrate, the same is true in many companies' developed markets when buyers can search across supply channels or when the firm introduces a new product or enters a new segment of its core market.

Second, because sales managers mainly focus on what they can control most directly—their own sales force—channel partners are generally undermanaged. The role and activities of a channel manager are allied to but distinct from those of a sales manager. Channel managers may not be directly responsible for sales, but they facilitate information flows, contracting, invoicing, joint events with partners, and other activities that help to drive business development with and through the channel. They often qualify leads generated by channel partners and work to develop the business case within their own organization. They typically need proficiency in areas like logistics, regulatory issues in a market, an understanding of that reseller's business model, and how their firm's products add value to that model as well as their own. They are often involved in educating partners about the relevant target customer profile, buyer personae, and buying journeys for the producer's product or service at customers. Finally, they help to manage the channel relationship over time and across functions, branches, and regions.

People manage people and, in multichannel efforts, it's typically salespeople who are asked to be the key players where it counts: in ongoing interactions with relevant channel partners and end users. But when sales reps must work with channel partners, their tasks change significantly. For one thing, reps who have been successful individual contributors now have managerial responsibilities as well as selling tasks. That's a big change for many reps, and channel management usually suffers unless the seller takes proactive steps. The Oversight-Concur partnership is an example.

Concur had hundreds of account managers, and Oversight had multiple salespeople. But having multiple people throughout Oversight devoting time on an opportunistic basis to interacting and following up with Concur reps would not have optimized the partnership. Oversight's CEO created a full-time position and promoted Rachel Ware (a sales rep at Oversight) to be the go-to person and manage the Concur relationship. Her activities and mindset are instructive.

Concur's account managers organized client events to promote Concur's product and allied services. But as Ware explained, "The challenge was learning to navigate the Concur organizational structure. Sometimes they have several people attached to a single account, and I had to figure out who could put me in touch with a potential buyer." Within a year, she had established contact with more than 150 Concur account managers and secured speaking slots at multiple user-group events that generated quality leads for Oversight: the prospect was interested in T&E analytics and already qualified by Concur. Ware found that, with attention to reciprocity, Concur's reps were generally open to introducing her to their clients because she could help them increase the speed and scope of a sale: "Oversight helped them sell the Concur ecosystem to their customers, because they could now offer T&E monitoring as well." In turn, Ware then supported the selling process, which typically took about six months from the initial meeting with the client to closing. She conducted demos of Oversight's product for clients with Concur and Oversight reps, and facilitated a subsequent free trial for interested prospects. Perhaps most importantly, her efforts created individual champions for Oversight's product among Concur's account managers, and she then evangelized sales successes within Oversight and at additional locations within Concur, celebrating what was working and talking openly with her company about what wasn't.

Ware rightly approached the channel manager role as a combination education and sales job, and she recognized that there are important interpersonal and time-dependent dimensions to partnerships. There must be trust and rapport between key individuals in both organizations, followed by visible commitments and results.

As always in life, you get one chance to make a first impression. The first year of a channel partnership is often critical for establishing attention and mind share. In any organization, salespeople talk to each other about where their limited time is best allocated. In this situation, initial champions are invaluable because, if properly promoted, success breeds success as more salespeople at both companies pay more attention. Conversely, without that attention, the partner's reps are likely to gravitate to what they are familiar with, presenting your product less often or on an ad hoc basis.

Managing Multichannel Relations

Beyond sales, a multichannel effort can also provide insights about technology, applications, market trends, and usage requirements that create new revenue opportunities. But you must be proactive in developing the relevant relationships and interactions. That usually requires dedicated channel managers and a realistic understanding of the tensions built into channel relations.

No distribution agreement, however detailed and thoughtful, can foresee all the circumstances that are likely to arise during the course of a partnership. Markets change, demographics alter, and customers learn, value, and do different things in their buying journeys. In multichannel systems, these changes must be addressed by separate business entities with shifting objectives, capabilities, and constraints. How should you manage these relations over time and across markets? At least four factors are relevant to maintaining an effective multichannel sales effort: (a) recognizing the tug-of-war inherent in partnerships and the implications; (b) dealing with the entangling alliances that current go-to-market requirements involve; (c) managing channel conflict; and (d) resisting channel inertia.

Tug-of-War

Certain facts condition channel relationships. On the one hand, both parties have mutual interests in maximizing the sales of the products and services in question. On the other hand, each party is in an implicit struggle to retain a larger share of the profits and control of the process. Also, the goals and operating priorities of producers and resellers often differ as markets change. For example, when Microsoft launched its Surface product, it adopted a direct-to-consumer strategy and began to compete with the PC suppliers that, for decades, had been its distribution partners for its operating systems: Acer, Dell, HP, Lenovo, and others. But by 2020, the Surface product line had a greater share in the US market than some of these PC manufacturers.

Because suppliers and resellers have mutual interests and shifting perspectives and needs over the market life cycle, the term "adversarial collaboration" aptly describes these business relations.[12] The rhythm of these relationships is analogous to an ongoing tug-of-war with implications for the capabilities and mindset required. Producers selling through intermediaries must develop capabilities at two levels: as sources of relevant products and revenues for their resellers *and* as the locus of brand preference with user customers. In the former role, producers are marketing partners with their distributors, building levels of trust and reciprocity that motivate resellers to carry and actively support their product rather than competing products carried by that reseller. In the latter role, however, producers seek to have their products preferred and specified by user customers, and as in the Microsoft example, this often requires terms or initiatives that can conflict with resellers' preferences.

At the same time, resellers act simultaneously as selling agents for their suppliers *and* as purchasing agents or sources of supply for their customers. In the former role, resellers seek to develop with the producer reciprocal agreements and marketing programs that can build demand for particular brands or products at user customers. In the latter role, however, resellers seek to assemble a package of products that serve their selling needs with a particular group of customers. This motivates the reseller to give preference, first, to the generic package of products for that customer segment, not the selection and promotion of particular brands capable of completing the package.

How this tug-of-war plays out depends on the supplier's ability to develop and maintain brand pull with user customers, the reseller's other sourcing options in the category, and the margins available to each party through one or another mode of supply and market access. But these are shifting variables that must be managed, not only specified in an initial agreement inevitably subject to market changes.

Entangling Alliances

In practice, producers and resellers are usually members of multiple and possibly competing channel systems. Given how buying behavior has changed, producers often are obliged to sell through multiple intermediaries, while resellers carry the products of competing producers to satisfy different types of demand in a category. The tug-of-war therefore occurs within entangling alliances among suppliers, resellers, and user customers, and that affects selling.

For example, a supplier's pricing decisions must often be considered not only in terms of the impact on customer demand and the factors discussed in chapters 8 and 9, but also in terms of the impact on reseller margins and the continued support of the distribution network in relation to other suppliers that sell competing lines through those resellers. The reality of entangling alliances also affects market access. A reseller's decision concerning whether to carry and support a given supplier's product line must be considered not only in terms of customer demand and that product's margins and working capital requirements, but also in terms of the impact on that reseller's relations with other suppliers.

These factors can make or break a sales effort. It's an omnichannel world, but when a customer moves among channels in a buying journey, partners can feel threatened. The standard ways of managing this issue involve the supplier setting product, market, or account-size boundaries on distribution of its products. Equipment suppliers like Caterpillar, Toro, and others segment their channels based on the size, functionality, or application of the product—for example, a residential channel serviced by home centers for low-end, lower-functionality equipment; an industrial distribution network for sales of more sophisticated equipment to professional users and businesses. Similarly, suppliers can set channel agreements that specify the market boundaries within which a set of resellers can and should sell. These boundaries are often tied to vertical applications: dealers focused on the automotive market versus those focused on other verticals. Each channel then is expected to specialize in the buying, selling, and service requirements of that market. Other suppliers try to separate channels by account size: larger distributors or VARs are franchised to sell to larger end-user customers that presumably have more sophisticated applications or service needs, while smaller dealers and distributors "own" SMB accounts.

Suppliers in a multichannel system often need a combination of these demarcations, but they are difficult to maintain. In the United States, antitrust laws put limits on the reseller restrictions permissible for suppliers, and in most markets no one really owns a customer in a multichannel world. Customers have easier access to a variety of product sources. Resellers have an inherent incentive to grow by pushing the legacy boundaries. Suppliers find that, over time, a product, market, or account-size demarcation no longer reflects buying realities. Entangling alliances are inherently fluid.

Channel Conflict

You can probably see the implication of the tug-of-war and entangling alliances involved in multichannel relations: conflicts will happen. My colleague Kash Rangan provides a wry take on these relationships where business conversations can be like the dialogue in the Eugene O'Neill play *Strange Interlude*, with the unspoken thoughts in parentheses and italics:[13]

SUPPLIER: You must carry our full line of products. No cherry-picking. We must be a full-line supplier to cater to the wide range of market requirements.

(Selling our specialized products is easy; they're so good that anybody can sell them. But the standardized end of our line is more difficult to sell because competitors' offerings are similar, so that's where our distributors must show their mettle.)

DISTRIBUTOR: There is no point in pushing the full line. We should concentrate on our strong points.

Through hard work we have established a market leadership position for the top end of the product range. Why dilute our effort and attention?

(We make no money on the rest of your products. Besides, our other suppliers have much better programs to support their equivalent products.)

SUPPLIER: We need you to concentrate on our products. That's the only way to be true partners.

(How can you flirt with our competitors right under our noses? One day you will take on lines aimed at the core of our product range.)

DISTRIBUTOR: We need exclusive territories.

(For a company that makes such a big deal of being a "real partner," your management is highly insensitive to our needs. You are killing our margins by doing business with our long-time rival, which makes a living by calling on our customers.)

SUPPLIER: We must know about your customers—our customers—in greater detail; that is the only way we can develop products and services they need.

(You don't let us access valuable customers to understand how the whole value equation works, but when a customer complains, we are the first to hear about it.)

DISTRIBUTOR: We track our customer information on an aggregate basis. We don't keep records in a way that's likely to be helpful.

(Not a chance; you'll start selling directly.)

SUPPLIER: We must work together.

DISTRIBUTOR: We agree.

Even with the best channel design and incentives, ongoing market changes mean that conflict is inherent in a multichannel sales effort. Many managers, however, believe the principle is to avoid conflict. That's wrong. The key is to manage the conflict profitably. In fact, whenever you hear that "all our channel partners love us; our dealer satisfaction rates are like body temperature—98.6 percent," ask questions aimed at figuring out who is leaving money or valuable market-segment access on the table.

There are functional and dysfunctional conflicts in channel relations, and research finds that an increase in functional conflict can *improve* channel performance in areas like innovation and revenue growth.[14] Think of channel conflict along a U-shaped curve: too little, and the go-to-market is inefficient, static, or otherwise not assertive enough; too much, and the reciprocity, trust, and mutual interests binding channel partners are destroyed. There's no algorithm for determining exactly the right mix: channels must be managed. A multichannel approach is about increasing the size of the pie and then—almost always—arguing over how to divide the pie. The correct principle here is first focus on making the pie as big as possible, so you are then arguing over something worth arguing about.

Channel Inertia

When a market is entered or a product introduced, elements of channel management tend to cohere around the circumstances and objectives held at the time. As markets evolve, new channels and policies are required. But each dimension of the existing arrangement tends to cement established patterns, making it difficult to change, even as change becomes necessary. So there's a widespread tendency in this aspect of selling to stick with the devil you know.

Channel inertia enables new entrants, competitors, and substitutes, while change risks retaliation or lost support from established channel partners. The first two decades of the twenty-first century saw this play out, repeatedly, in many consumer product categories. Razors, razor blades, and other items for years enjoyed high margins for the established manufacturers and retailers. Once those margins were embedded in investor presentations and the stock prices of those companies, the incumbents faced a tough choice in responding to channel innovators like Harry's or Dollar Shave Club. Cut prices and you cut profits and earnings; develop new online channels for your products and you antagonize retail channel partners. Hence, the inertia and half-hearted moves in this industry for years. Within five years of Dollar Shave Club.com's entrance in its market, Gillette had lost an estimated thirteen points of market share. Bad news and a market change that demanded a response. Yet when Gillette finally responded to channel innovators by introducing its "Our Shave Club" subscription service in 2014, it required customers to sign up with a retailer rather than directly with Gillette. Consumers in this category bought the way they wanted to buy, not how Gillette and its channel partners wanted them to buy.[15]

Many distribution arrangements lag market developments because of systemic causes. One is the difference between potential longer-term benefits of channel change versus the measurable short-term costs. Managers looking at quarterly metrics often know what their established channels can deliver in the short term. Meanwhile, a change in channel structure means transition costs. Also, most producers' accounting systems are set up to measure product profitability, and they often lack the information required to capture cost to serve and profitability by channel.

Uncertainty plus lack of information then lead to a third cause of inertia: management by assumption—assuming that "they" (e.g., a new type of intermediary) "can't sell this product" or that "only they" (e.g., the established service-intensive but higher-priced channels) can sell the product. These assumptions were often true to buying criteria when the product or service was new and required channels capable of providing customer education, applications development, postsale services, or other factors that applied at that stage. But as a market develops, product features and uses become well known and integrated into buyers' business or house-hold processes, and low-service/low-cost channels can and will sell the product—if not your product, then a competitor's product.

You see this repeatedly in tech categories. Long before the cloud and SaaS firms disrupted enterprise software business models, Michael Dell understood this. When Dell started sell-ing PCs by phone in 1984, the established suppliers (Apple, Compaq, HP, IBM, and others) sold through VARs and retailers that provided and charged for various services. The manufacturers, generally coming from a mainframe or mini-computer legacy, believed these services were essential for a tech product like PCs: it had only been a few years since the first models became available in the late 1970s to techni-cally proficient early adopters. Dell sold direct, understanding that in just a few years, PCs were no longer a specialty tech product according to established producers' and resellers' assumptions, but more like TV sets and susceptible to lower-cost channels catering to more price-conscious, self-service buyers. He then did this again in the 1990s with other tech products via a build-to-order supply chain. As one observer noted at the time, "Dell has commoditized low end computers and had them supplant high end proprietary technology (and) used this strategy to dominate PCs—and, again, to attack the server business."[16]

More generally, as customers gain familiarity with a product category, they develop other means of performing functions previously handled by the producer or distributors. A common symptom of this change is the emergence of gray markets where products are sold or resold through unauthorized dealers. Gray markets come and go in products like consumer durables, electronics, and others.[17] At times in India and Malaysia, gray markets have accounted for an estimated 70 percent of smartphone sales. Regulators periodically put in place rules aimed at curtailing this kind of distribution, and political leaders typically label it as "dumping" or "stealing intellectual property," but the practice persists. Why?

Notice what customers are saying when they buy in this manner. A gray market usually reflects the maturation of a product in its life cycle. Customers are placing less value on the support offered by authorized resellers and more emphasis on price. What customers once purchased as a bundle of product and service, they unbundle into discrete purchases and welcome channels that sell on low price with little service or support. If producers and the authorized channels continue to require customers to buy the package of product and support features, the gray market just gets added impetus.

Beware of channel inertia. As customers' buying criteria change—and they will change—you must think through the implications for current channel value-added and act accordingly.

⊕ QUESTIONS TO ASK . . . AND ANSWER

In this chapter, I alter slightly the form of diagnostic used for other topics. Rather than providing a scale for you to evaluate, I list some questions and explain their relevance. The questions are linked and provide a template for an ongoing channels dialogue with your team (see figure 10-5).

First, clarify a channel partner's role in your business-development strategy. Is it primarily about cost efficiency—that is, that partner can perform some important tasks less expensively than we can? Or is it about market access—that partner provides us with access to certain sectors or decision makers at target customers? Or is the partner a necessary part of the solution that customers buy—that is, channel partners provide necessary complements in that system? These are very different roles in a go-to-market program with different implications for required interactions, terms and conditions, and other aspects of channel design and management. Distinguish "sell-with" partners that deal with the same buyers at target customers versus "sell-through" partners that fill a gap in your product or service offering.

FIGURE 10-5

A channels diagnostic: Key questions to consider

- What is a given channel's role in your growth strategy and sales initiatives?
  - Cost efficiency? Market access? Supplement to scarce resources? Necessary part of the solution package?
- What levels of quality control are required for each major channel function?
  - Do terms and conditions reflect the required levels?
- What are the options for shifting a function to a different, more cost-effective channel?
  - Are purchase or usage criteria changing and does our current go-to-market system reflect buyer criteria as they exist today, not yesterday?
- How many target market segments and go-to-market partners can you realistically manage and support?
  - Trade-offs between focus/depth and access/breadth?
  - Trade-offs between control and resources?

Second, specify and keep up to date the levels of quality control required for a channel function. Too often, managers speak of distribution as an undifferentiated category in their marketing plans. But distribution always means a set of discrete activities including demand generation, perhaps carrying of inventory, delivery, aftersale service, and so on. Depending upon your strategy and buying behavior at that stage of market development, different channel functions require different levels of quality control. Some activities must be performed flawlessly, and others just need to be good enough. Effective selling reflects these differences in channel design and management.

Third, evaluate periodically the options available for shifting a given function to a different point in the channel. As products mature and become more standardized, many suppliers find that postsale maintenance and repair, which initially required full-service partners with technically trained personnel, can be performed more efficiently and just as effectively by generic service providers or even self-service. It's usually better to anticipate these shifts rather than react after the fact.

Finally, recognize the trade-offs. Working with channel partners can increase access to more segments and customers, but no channel manages itself. So consider how many segments and partners you can realistically support and work with. A trade-off between control and resources is inherent in a multichannel approach. Don't deny this trade-off. Instead, as outlined in figure 10-3, consider its implications for the best uses of time, people, and capital in your go-to-market programs.

Like most important things in business, the questions posed by this diagnostic may seem simple, but they are hard to answer and do in practice. Changes in selling always have wider implications. These are leadership as well as sales issues, and that's the focus of the final chapter: what changes in selling requirements mean for C-suite executives and for economic growth and opportunity.

CONCLUSION

WHAT SENIOR EXECUTIVES
SHOULD KNOW ABOUT SALES

"Leadership" is a growth industry. As I write, Amazon lists over ninety thousand results for books about leadership. Once you get beyond the snack-crackle-pop genre, most focus on emotional intelligence, charisma, avoiding narcissism (usually your problem, not their problem, according to the authors of those books), alleged "transformational" leadership qualities, and other psychological and personal traits. The same is true for most executive education courses on the topic. But as a great organizational scholar, James March, once put it, "Leadership involves plumbing as well as poetry."[1] His point was that whatever else they do or say, effective leaders help busy people in their firms to deal behaviorally with the practical problems they face and thus increase their contributions and productivity.

This is especially true when it comes to the lifeblood of a for-profit company: the acquisition and retention of customers. Yet, many senior leaders are out of touch with the changes discussed in this book and the implications for their firms' sales

The causes of this shift are understandable. But the result is that the C-suite in many companies is increasingly siloed among functional specialists. Ironically, people in senior roles in many organizations are now more like discipline-based academics at universities rather than been-there-done-that practitioners of the art of profit maximization. Further, more senior executives than ever have made it to the top without prolonged customer-contact experience throughout their careers.

These changes affect a core task of executives: formulating and implementing a market-relevant strategy. To stay in business, any business must be about customer value and efficiently tailoring sales and other activities to serve target customers better or differently than others. But surveys indicate that in most firms, less than 50 percent of employees say they understand their firm's strategy, and that percentage *decreases* the closer you get to the customer in responses from sales and service employees.[4]

Consider the following research with over seven hundred respondents—senior executives, middle managers, and sales reps from companies of all sizes in industries ranging from consumer goods and manufacturing to telecom, wholesaling, and travel/hospitality. An assessment asked questions about strategies and core elements of sales efforts at those companies: their target customers, the sales tasks generated by those customers' buying journeys, the type of salespeople best suited to perform those tasks, how the firm organizes its go-to-market efforts, and the cross-functional interactions required to sell and deliver value to customers. Not surprisingly, executives feel that they have a high level of understanding of their companies' strategic priorities, while those in sales—who aren't typically in the planning meetings with the people crafting strategy—say they do not. But note the gap in responses about whether or not these companies' sales processes align with business objectives (see figure 11-1).

FIGURE 11-1

How well do companies' sales processes align with their business objectives?

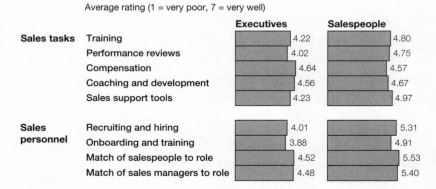

Average rating (1 = very poor, 7 = very well)

		Executives	Salespeople
Sales tasks	Training	4.22	4.80
	Performance reviews	4.02	4.75
	Compensation	4.64	4.57
	Coaching and development	4.56	4.67
	Sales support tools	4.23	4.97
Sales personnel	Recruiting and hiring	4.01	5.31
	Onboarding and training	3.88	4.91
	Match of salespeople to role	4.52	5.53
	Match of sales managers to role	4.48	5.40

Source: Frank Cespedes and Christopher Wallace, "Executives and Salespeople Are Misaligned—and the Effects Are Costly," HBR.org, January 2017.

Senior leaders see deficiencies in most areas related to sales tasks and sales personnel: training, performance reviews, coaching, sales support tools, recruitment of salespeople, onboarding, and the fit of sales reps and sales managers with their roles. Aside from that, Mrs. Lincoln, how do you like your company's sales force? The only category in which executives rate their sales practices more positively than salespeople do is compensation, perhaps because executives determine pay policies.

A representative story emerges from these results. Senior leaders have a better relative understanding of their company's direction than sales personnel but are concerned that they don't have the right sales processes and people. For their part, salespeople may be confident in their abilities to execute, but have little understanding of the company's strategic direction and its implications for their behaviors. Also, the groups are far apart on basic elements such as recruiting, hiring, training, and role alignment. You can see why "I'm from corporate and I'm here to help you" is a perennial punch line in many organizations.

When leaders want to make changes, this misalignment sets up a costly and frustrating cycle. The sales force is unclear or mistaken about performance expectations, and companies fail to get the most out of the billions they spend annually on sales training and sales enablement tools. Hiring the right people becomes a problem as changing buying processes reshape selling tasks. If information isn't flowing between senior executives and frontline customer-contact people, then taking any or all of these steps is likely to lead to the competency traps discussed in chapter 3: established routines keep the firm, and its leadership team, from gaining insight and experience with processes more relevant to changing market conditions. Neither group can keep up with the capabilities they should be developing.

Orthogonal Requirements

In many firms, sales is still treated as a mysterious black box—essential for meeting quarterly targets, but hermetically sealed off from other functions as a tactical tool that's rarely part of strategy formulation. Moreover, many sales leaders like it that way. It's a dialogue that never happens, and *that's* how companies get disrupted.

To close this gap and improve productivity, companies must treat causes, not symptoms. This is often difficult with sales because multiple groups across functions must invest in new approaches while still meeting their ongoing functional and financial obligations weekly, monthly, and quarterly. Theorists refer to this situation as a problem in organizational ambidexterity—a firm's ability to efficiently manage today's business and activities while adapting to changing demand by putting in place processes that move beyond status quo

FIGURE 11-2

Orthogonal requirements

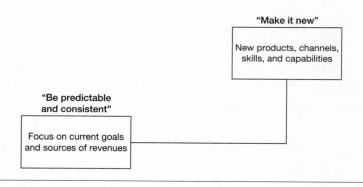

products and performance.[5] I describe this perennial challenge as involving "orthogonal requirements."[6] (In geometry, orthogonal lines meet at right angles; see figure 11-2.)

Be Predictable and Consistent

Because forecasting, capacity planning, operations, cash-flow estimates, and hiring patterns throughout the firm are typically contingent on revenue targets, the sales organization is under constant pressure to "make the numbers." This is increasingly true as software and other technologies become a bigger part of products, service, and the internet of things: fixed-cost investments must often be made way in advance of the introduction of products and generation of revenues. Hence, the drumbeat and desire in the past decade for "predictable revenue," because predictability and consistency in sales are valued by other functions in the firm as well as investors.

Make It New

At the same time, a firm needs to generate new sources of revenue through new products, channels, applications, markets, or segments. This is increasingly true as shorter product life cycles and more information available to buyers become bigger aspects of competition. Hence, sales must constantly develop new skills and capabilities—while maintaining current sources of revenue.

Less grandiosely and with street-smart sarcasm, sales managers often refer to these dual requirements as the "monkey theory of management."[7] Their metaphor is that, in making its way through the competitive jungle, the smart monkey never lets go of one branch (an established means of generating sales) until its other hand is fastened to the next branch because, if that monkey swings and misses, there's a predator out there who just found lunch. The problem is that this view of change is a prescription for inertia, not adaptation and innovation. In fact, monkeys often do let go of one branch before grabbing the next. The smart monkey, and a well-run company, can calibrate the required leap.

Leadership can make a difference here when senior leaders understand how sales initiatives impact enterprise value and their ability to manage orthogonal requirements in changing markets. In any company, profitable growth and enterprise value require the ability to invest in projects that earn more than their cost of capital, reduce the assets devoted to activities that earn less than their cost of capital, and (when possible) reduce the cost of capital itself. For better or for worse, a firm's selling activities always affect these drivers of enterprise value:

- In most firms, projects and asset deployment are driven by revenue-seeking activities with customers. The customer-selection dynamics inherent in a sales model, as explained in chapter 5, directly impact which activities the firm (knowingly or unknowingly) invests in.

- Reducing the assets devoted to underperforming activities requires understanding changing buying behavior and the customer conversion analytics discussed in chapter 6.

- Financing needs are set in large part by the cash on hand versus the working capital needed to conduct and grow the business. The selling cycle is usually the biggest driver of cash out and cash in. That's why close rates, an efficient sales model, and the sales incentives discussed in chapter 7 are strategic issues, not only sales management tasks.

Closing the Gap

So what can you do to close the gap? Start by complementing vision and purpose with good organizational plumbing in areas like priorities, people, and process, including pricing and performance management processes.

Priorities

It's tough for people to implement what they don't understand. Communicating priorities to the front line is highly correlated with business performance.[8] Yet, companies are bad at communicating their strategies to their employees, and executives often resist making their strategic priorities explicit. The most common reason is fear that this information will get to competitors. This fear is unwarranted. The strategies of successful firms are usually well publicized in articles, consulting studies, and often by those firms themselves. How many books, blogs, and case studies get written about Amazon, Apple, Google, IKEA, and others? For decades, Toyota allowed outsiders to study its factories on-site, but as a study of Toyota's production system concluded, "Observers confuse the tools and practices they see on their plant visits with the system itself."[9] As a leader, you have bigger things to worry about than competitors knowing your firm's priorities if your own people don't know them.

Strategic priorities are about the choices a company makes as it competes in a market. Some choices are explicit and put in a plan. But many are implicit in the daily decisions about resource allocation. For example, any budget—big or small, smart or stupid—involves choices about who and what gets more or less of available resources. Any sales model makes implicit choices: money, time, and attention spent pursuing and servicing account A are resources not available for accounts B, C, and so on. The inevitability and impact of opportunity costs are most real in sales and, as I argued in chapter 1, it's not the responsibility of the customer to tell you when you are barking up the wrong tree. It's your responsibility to make and communicate priorities to the sales force.

Not communicating priorities also incurs other costs, organizationally, culturally, and strategically. A vague or unarticulated set of choices cannot be tested and contested as market conditions change. People talk in abstractions ("innovate!"), while daily call patterns enact the sunk-cost fallacy: throwing good money after bad. If priorities remain implicit in the intuition of even a gifted or charismatic leader, then at best, alignment is only as strong as that leader's reach and, more often, as weak as the weakest link in the organization.

Without clarity about priorities, people—especially salespeople with quotas—only pick up random cues about strategy, and alignment is then hit and miss. Over time, the company becomes a "global mediocrity": good at many things, but not especially good at any particular things. And the essence of competitive advantage is being very good at things your target customers value and that others find hard to imitate.

People

As I explained in chapter 2, hiring in sales is, in the aggregate, as or more expensive than most capex decisions in companies, yet rarely gets the same attention and analysis from senior leaders. As I indicated in chapter 3, companies spend more per capita on sales training than they spend in other functions, yet the ROI of most current sales training is disappointing. Sales tasks have changed, and one impact is that sales hiring is taking longer, is more expensive, and productivity ramp-up times have lengthened. Each hire is a bigger sunk cost for a longer time. Yet, how often in strategic planning, capital budgeting, or board discussions does the senior executive group examine how your firm—and the people who are responsible for sales hiring and training—deals with these crucial talent-management activities?

Globally, new technologies are transforming the nature of work, and sales is no exception. The labor-market research firm Burning Glass Technologies and the consulting firm BCG examined job market trends during the period 2015–2018 in over 95 million online job postings in the United States.[10] They categorized as "flagship jobs" those with postings of 10,000 to 1 million per year. These jobs represented the bulk of the US labor market in 2018. In this category, "sales reps" experienced double-digit growth, as did "customer service representatives," many of whom are de facto salespeople in their daily tasks and/or the source of sales reps in many firms. Similarly, among the skills most in demand—that is, with the highest annual growth rates during the period of this study—are "general sales practices" (9 percent average annual growth), "general sales" (8 percent), and "basic customer service" (11 percent)—cumulatively the highest-ranked category of desired skills, by far, in job postings. The C-suite must address these labor-market changes, or else talk about talent management and "the future of work" is just talk and can lead to bad resource allocations—for your company and for society.

Senior leaders establish the foundational conditions for talent recruitment and development in their organizations through business reviews. It's crucial that sales talent stay up to date, and as explained in earlier chapters, there are few educational priors for most sales positions in contrast to hiring new engineers, programmers, accountants, or financial analysts. Few schools teach sales at all, and—again in contrast to engineering or coding or GAAP principles—the nature of effective selling is highly context-dependent. Most learning in sales is, by necessity as well as by default, on-the-job learning. As I show in chapter 10, selling now also means working with channel partners in order to deal with multichannel buying journeys, but those skills are rarely taught in most sales training programs.

Companies must have relevant and disciplined hiring approaches linked to strategy (not a generic selling methodology) and focused training initiatives where it counts so salespeople can adapt their skills as markets change. All serious research underscores these abiding fundamentals and debunks glib prescriptions about talent acquisition. Firms need to rethink hiring processes and how they allocate people to roles. Sales talent comes in all shapes and sizes. Diversity discussions, for example, would typically benefit from more attention to the hidden talent available to firms when they clarify sales tasks and sales models. In chapters 4 and 5, I explain practical ways to do this. The involvement of leaders increases accountability and capability in sales talent management *and* the relevance of your strategy.

Process

Alignment is a set of processes, not a one-shot deal or teamwork speech at a meeting. At a minimum, it requires ongoing customer information for strategy development and then, in execution, relevant sales performance management processes.

Consider pricing, which, as I've emphasized, builds or destroys value faster than almost any other business action. Actual price realization, however, means linking price, value, and selling behaviors. Does your sales compensation plan provide incentives for the behaviors required to extract that value, as I explained in chapter 7? Does your firm have the information and process required to link price with customer value as in the Zolam example in chapter 8? How often do senior leaders actually test price and discuss what the test results mean for framing and selling value, as I explained in chapter 9?

My experience on boards and in work with leadership teams is that branding discussions are fun and quarterly financial results are tracked closely. But the information required to examine and improve a key driver of brand positioning and bottom-line outcomes—how the sales force frames and delivers the value proposition, including price—is often lacking. Or even worse, the incentive system and other sales metrics emphasize volume, while senior executives believe their strategy is about premium value in a given segment. If a leadership team can't make these crucial connections between strategy and sales, it can end up pressing for better execution when the firm really needs a more market-relevant strategy or changing strategic direction when it should be focusing on these selling basics.

In most businesses, much of the relevant information for these connections occurs at the account level. That's where performance management processes in sales are relevant. When busy sales managers do sloppy or quickie reviews, they perpetuate a culture of underperformance and inhibit a vital flow of organizational information. As I explained in chapter 7, moreover, context matters in diagnosing and evaluating sales performance. No data speaks for itself. Interpreting data and extracting the "so what, now what" implications are what managers must do.

Executives seeking effective strategy execution can't afford to leave this process to chance. Their oversight is as important here as it is in the capital budgeting process. Leadership groups that do not stay engaged with these sales processes will inevitably share the fate of companies where "customer focus" is a perennial slogan but not organizational reality.

Shining Light on the Links: A Leadership Diagnostic

Organizational change starts at the top. But I am not suggesting, like many leadership gurus, that executives must somehow become renaissance women and men, knowing everything about everything. CFOs and CIOs, for instance, don't need to know how to manage a sales force. But they should know the key customer-acquisition tasks inherent in their firm's business strategy and the right sales questions to consider in planning, budgeting, and resource allocations. Answering the questions in table 11-1 can spur useful dialogue among senior leaders and help better align a company's sales efforts and investments with its business goals.

Consider a large home energy provider in a mature market where product commoditization and deregulation were driving down revenue and profit. To spur growth, the company adopted a strategy of diversifying its product and service offering. This meant selling value-added services and transforming a sales force conditioned to sell on price. After the kind of dialogue instigated by this sort of diagnostic, the leadership team did the following.

TABLE 11-1

A leadership diagnostic

In our company, how well do we . . .

Articulate our strategy in ways that our customer contact people understand?	1 2 3 4 5 6 7
Specify in our strategy or planning discussions the markets and segments where we do and don't play?	1 2 3 4 5 6 7
Understand across functions how our go-to-market activities affect drivers of enterprise value?	1 2 3 4 5 6 7
Make clear the implications of our business priorities for selling objectives, behaviors, and metrics?	1 2 3 4 5 6 7
Understand what our target customers do (and do not) value: in product? in service? in support?	1 2 3 4 5 6 7
Continuously update our understanding of customer value by segment?	1 2 3 4 5 6 7
Discuss and manage our total value proposition: internally? with the right people at customers?	1 2 3 4 5 6 7
Reflect and manage the relevant components of customer value in our product, marketing, and pricing activities?	1 2 3 4 5 6 7
Focus our go-to-market training on the high-impact tasks?	1 2 3 4 5 6 7
Put the right people in the right jobs with the right metrics?	1 2 3 4 5 6 7
Design and improve core account management and account support processes?	1 2 3 4 5 6 7
Utilize technology and/or channel partners to improve capacity, market access, or close rates?	1 2 3 4 5 6 7
Manage the strategy ⟶ sales performance management cycle on an ongoing basis?	1 2 3 4 5 6 7

Priorities: The Leadership Team Clarified and Linked the Strategic Priorities to Behaviors

Beginning with conversations with frontline sales managers, they asked, "Are our salespeople having conversations that help customers see the value of these services?" In the cases where reps weren't, the team identified the selling behaviors that needed to be changed and then, working with managers, established a new sales model and clarified the relevant sales tasks.

People: The Team Changed Its Approach to Training and Sales Management

The leadership group initiated an intensive effort that spread the learning over a series of weeks, allowing the incumbent salespeople to apply behaviors gradually rather than trying to learn the entire process at once. The team heeded one of the lessons emphasized in chapter 3: the importance of deliberate practice in training for behavioral change. Simultaneously, sales managers went through sessions on coaching skills so they could focus performance management conversations on the selling behaviors inherent in the strategy. A longer-term change involved criteria for choosing sales managers: more emphasis on the ability to manage people in line with the strategy, and less emphasis on historical performance as a salesperson.

Process: The Team Revamped Compensation and Evaluation Criteria as Well as Hiring Efforts

Sales commissions were adjusted to reflect the importance of the value-added services, and incentives were added to reward call patterns and other leading-indicator behaviors required to execute the strategy. Further, adherence to the sales process was added to the salesperson's evaluation scorecard used in performance reviews and incorporated into onboarding for new hires.

Sales performance and competitive positioning improved significantly for this company when its leadership group articulated the firm's strategy and analyzed the gap between the current sales model and the sales behaviors required to meet new business objectives. Its approach involved priorities, people, and process, and the sequence in which it addressed those areas drove alignment. The lesson is that effective leaders can make sales what it should always be: a core agent of strategy.

Social Impact

This book has focused on for-profit companies. But improving sales productivity has implications for society, not only shareholders. Remember that in the United States, for example, the number of salespeople listed by the Bureau of Labor Statistics is more than 10 percent of the country's labor force and has *increased* during the twenty-first century. Further, BLS data undercounts the reality because, in a service economy, business developers are often not placed in a sales category for labor-department reporting purposes. One estimate two economists made some years ago found that "sweet talk"—the practice of persuasion in the US economy—accounts for fully a quarter of total labor income.[11] Author Daniel Pink has popularized the notion that "we're all in sales."[12] I don't go this far. There's a difference between lawyering, arguing, or wooing, and what I mean by selling. But even if we restrict ourselves to designated "sales" jobs, the amount US companies alone spend annually on sales compensation, travel, entertainment and back-office expenses for sales tools is more than the size of most industries.

Hiring and training salespeople directly affects the lives of millions of people, and their productivity in turn affects a core driver of economic growth and opportunity for millions more. The slowdown in growth and productivity in the United States and many other economies is well documented. Through most of the twentieth century, the average growth rate of the US economy was about 2 percent annually, despite world wars, a great depression, globalization, and higher and lower tax rates. But for the past two decades, the average growth rate of per capita GDP has been about 1 percent—half of what many previous generations of Americans experienced. The same is true in France, Germany, Japan, the United Kingdom, and other economies. Productivity of people—human capital—is a major driver of economic growth, and that has also declined in the twenty-first century in the United States and other industrialized countries.[13]

What we don't know with certainty, however, are the root causes of this decline. Some cite a failure of innovation or the allocation of creative ingenuity to what these critics see as trivial pursuits like tweeting or selfies versus "breakthroughs" like electricity, air conditioning, and so on. Others blame global trade or government regulations, view it as a measurement problem, or simply cite "secular stagnation"—often a fancy way of saying, "God's will." Empirical analyses find little evidence for these causes. Instead, as economist Dietrich Vollrath explains, the biggest causes seem to be demographics (lower birth rates) and the shift in economic activity from manufacturing into services.[14] In the United States, manufacturing declined from about 23 percent of GDP in 1970 to 12.5 percent in 2015, while the share of expenditures on services climbed to 70 percent, with the remainder spent on durable goods (e.g., cars, dishwashers) and nondurable goods (e.g., food, clothes). Professional services alone doubled as a share of GDP during this period.

Productivity in services tends to be lower than in goods-producing industries, due to what the economist William Baumol famously labeled the "cost disease."[15] In producing goods, labor is a contingent part of the process; you can increase productivity by doing more with less labor—which is what happened in agriculture and manufacturing in the past century. In most services, however, the human component *is* the product or a core (not contingent) part of the deliverable. It's harder to get a better outcome by doing more with less. Baumol's examples were health care, teaching, and the performing arts. There are only twenty-four hours in the day for a doctor to meet patients or a teacher to teach students, and a concerto played faster or with fewer musicians is not better music. In services, as Vollrath notes, "you are almost always purchasing people's time and attention as opposed to any tangible good . . . As our spending shifted toward services, we were shifting toward lower productivity growth as well (and) the shift into services could account for almost all of the drop in productivity growth that is behind the growth slowdown."[16]

Following Baumol's analysis, Vollrath and others see this as an inevitable consequence of higher living standards, success in making material goods less expensive, and the shift in buying to more services. The diagnosis is persuasive, but I see this social conclusion as Panglossian. Looking at economic history in the United States, Europe, and the developing world, the economist Benjamin Friedman documented the moral consequences of economic growth—meaning a rising standard of living for the clear majority of citizens—for tolerance of diversity, social mobility, commitment to fairness, opportunity for advancement, social progress, and democratic values. As Friedman emphasizes, "The value of a rising standard of living lies not just in the concrete improvements it brings to how individuals live but in how it shapes the social, political, and ultimately the moral character of a people . . . and it is in significant part the *growth* rather than just the level of people's living standards that matters for this purpose."[17]

As so often in his remarkable career, Peter Drucker was prescient about this issue. Thirty years ago, he argued that "The most pressing social challenge developed countries face will be to raise the productivity of service work. Unless this challenge is met, the developed world will face increasing social tensions, increasing polarization, increasing radicalization, possibly even class war."[18] Drucker made important distinctions that executives and public policy makers dealing with economic change and its social tensions would do well to understand. He pointed out that "In making and moving things, the task is always taken for granted. In knowledge and service work, however, the first questions in increasing productivity—and working smarter—have to be, What is the task? What are we trying to accomplish? Why do it at all?" Drucker used sales as an example, noting (thirty years ago!) that salespeople "now spend so much time serving computers (and) filling out reports rather than calling on customers . . . This is not job enrichment; it is job impoverishment. It destroys productivity."

Whether tools help or harm productivity depends on what people do with them. Research shows large, persistent productivity differences across businesses even within narrowly defined industries, and it's estimated that about 25 percent of cross-country and within-country productivity gaps can be attributed to management practices.[19] Especially in service activities, bosses vary greatly in their impact. Replacing a manager in the lower tenth percentile with one in the ninetieth percentile increases a team's output by the same amount as adding a worker to a nine-member team would, while reducing turnover, and the leverage from better bosses persists for some time after the service person leaves that boss.[20]

Management matters qualitatively and quantitatively, even in the places cited by Baumol as inevitable victims of the cost disease. Management practices increase or decrease productivity in emergency departments, radiology, and other areas of health care.[21] Controlling for characteristics of the market and employees, the same is true in retail banking.[22] Even in education: from 2007 to 2017, the average annual cost of a degree at a four-year public university rose from about $15,000 to more than $19,000, but Purdue University has kept its tuition and fees at $9,992 since 2013, while also reducing the price of food services and books, increasing enrollment and faculty (and faculty pay), and *lowering* the student-teacher ratio to thirteen to one compared to a Big Ten average of more than fifteen to one.[23] The productivity improvements are in large part attributable to how Purdue, under Mitch Daniels's leadership, organized and managed services ranging from residence halls to payroll and textbooks. About 70 percent of college students take out loans to finance their education, and the $1.5 trillion in US student debt affects job choices, marriage plans, decisions to have children, personal stress, and the economy. Meanwhile, at Purdue, about 60 percent of undergraduates leave school without any debt at all. *That's* social impact.

We do cure many diseases, and we can improve productivity in service activities without lowering quality of outcomes. Sales is probably a good place to start in your company. About 8.5 percent of the US workforce is in the manufacturing sectors, while millions more work in sales. Yet 66 percent of industrial R&D spending is on manufacturing. How much impact would a relatively modest reallocation of money, attention, and ingenuity add to services productivity? If you're a senior executive, consider:

- In chapters 2 and 3, I indicated how and why ramp-up time in sales has increased in the past decade and the failure of most hiring and training processes to keep pace. What's the value in your business of devoting more attention and resources to the crucial first six months of a salesperson's time in your company? What's the economic gain from decreasing time to productivity in your sales team by one month, two months, three months, or more? What's the value to the salesperson, quantitatively and qualitatively?

- In chapters 5–7, I explained how different sales models mean different choices in customer selection, incentives, and relevant analytics. Smart use of AI and other tools requires the ongoing interpretation and application of data to these activities. Drucker was right: the first questions in increasing service productivity are not, can we get more data, but what's the task, what are we trying to accomplish, why do it this way at all? There's a big gap between how senior executives and frontline salespeople frame and answer those questions. What's the value in your business of closing that gap?

- I have emphasized how buying is changing and the manifold impact on people, processes, pricing, partners, and productivity of sales efforts. Don't look for a set of universal propositions. Improvements here are more like engineering know-how: error-tested recipes for specific circumstances and purposes. Selling software is different than selling capital equipment; selling in the United States is different than selling in China, Latin America, or the Middle East. It's now common to experiment with "minimum viable products," because experiments, guided by insight, yield actionable, market-tested information sooner. The same applies to sales and marketing. In business, an innovation is a better product + strategy + go-to-market plan linked to strategy. It's rare to get the go-to-market plan right from day one. Experiments here help executives know when a new product or strategy requires a behavior change: by your sales team, by channel partners, and perhaps in the behavior and dialogue of the leadership group itself.

In 2019, with much publicity, the Business Roundtable (the CEOs of more than 180 companies that, at the time, had a market capitalization exceeding $13 trillion) "committed" to "lead their companies to the benefit of all stakeholders": employees, customers, suppliers, and communities, not only shareholders.[24] A 2020 Davos Manifesto announced an "industrial revolution": "the purpose of a company is to engage all its stakeholders in shared and sustained value creation."[25] Well, as the saying has it, people don't care what you know unless they know you care. Acknowledge the reality of externalities, and leave aside the contradictions, ambiguities (who's a stakeholder? who's not?), and silence about trade-offs embedded in these stakeholder manifestos.[26] Instead, first look homeward, CEO. Selling in your firm is not only a core profit-maximizing activity, for which you need not apologize (that added value is invested elsewhere in the economy) and for which you are paid a lot to develop. It's also a social issue that affects growth, living standards, opportunities, and the lives of millions of people. It is, in fact, a core social responsibility of management in economic life.

I hope this book helps managers better understand that responsibility and how to fulfill it.

NOTES

Chapter 1

1. Quoted in Chris Zook and James Allen, *The Founder's Mentality* (Boston: Harvard Business Review Press, 2016), 54. See also Marshall Fisher, Santiago Gallino, and Sergui Netessine, "Retailers Are Squandering Their Most Potent Weapons," *Harvard Business Review*, January–February 2019, 72–79.

2. An influential early description of the AIDA formula was Harold C. Cash and W. J. E. Crissy, "Ways of Looking at Selling," in *Managerial Marketing: Perspectives and Viewpoints*, 2nd ed., ed. William Lazer and Eugene Kelley (Homewood, IL: Richard D. Irwin, Inc., 1962): 554–559.

3. Many studies now indicate differences between current buying processes and linear AIDA representations of buying. See, for example, the "State of the Connected Customer" report at salesforce.com/research; Marisa Kopec and Jennifer Ross, "Demystifying B-to-B Buying," Sirius Decisions Research Report, 2015; Nicolas Maechler, Kevin Neher, and Robert Park, "From Touchpoints to Journeys: Seeing the World as Customers Do," McKinsey & Company, March 2016. The framework of explore, evaluate, engage, and experience is based on Frank V. Cespedes and Tiffani Bova, "What Salespeople Need to Know About the New B2B Landscape," HBR.org, August 5, 2015, https://hbr.org/2015/08/what-salespeople-need-to-know-about-the-new-b2b-landscape.

4. J.D. Power study as cited in Adrienne Roberts, "Car Buyers Get New Routes," *Wall Street Journal*, December 31, 2018, B1.

5. See "The Evolving Sales Process," DrivingSales Research Report, 2015; and Frank V. Cespedes and Jared Hamilton, "Selling to Consumers Who Do Their Homework Online," HBR.org, March 16, 2016, https://hbr.org/2016/03/selling-to-customers-who-do-their-homework-online. The study included in-home interviews and dealership shop-alongs; webcam interviews with customers at the online stage of the shopping process; and phone interviews conducted with customers in dealers with follow-up discussion. The quantitative research included factor analysis to identify key drivers of dealer and brand selection and rejection, and conjoint analysis to understand what dealership characteristics and behaviors are most important and valued. References in this chapter to car shopping are to this study unless otherwise noted.

6. Cespedes and Bova, "What Salespeople Need to Know About the New B2B Landscape." The study involved 503 companies; all respondents held management positions in lines of business, marketing, or IT and were personally involved in choosing suppliers. The survey asked these respondents to focus on the type of purchase with which they were most familiar.

7. "State of the Connected Customer" and "State of Sales Report" at salesforce.com/research. See also Frank V. Cespedes and Tiffani Bova, "The Changing Craft of Selling," *Top Sales Magazine*, May 2018, 16–19.

8. See the BLS website for sales employment: https://www.bls.gov/oes /current/oes410000.htm.

9. US Census Bureau, "E-Commerce Statistics (E-Stats)," http://www .census.gov/programs-surveys/e-stats.html. In Q2 2020—during the most stringent lockdown conditions in the US as of this writing—ecommerce sales as a percentage of total retail sales were 16.5 percent, a gain of only 5 percent versus 2019 in presumably optimal conditions for online buying.

10. Sunil Gupta, *Driving Digital Strategy* (Boston: Harvard Business Review Press, 2018), Chapter 9.

11. David R. Bell, *Location Is (Still) Everything: The Surprising Influence of the Real World on How We Search, Shop, and Sell in the Virtual One* (New York: New Harvest, 2014).

12. S. Kapner and K. Safdar, "Menu for Delivering Online Goods Grows," *Wall Street Journal*, November 19, 2018, B3.

13. Carol Ryan, "A Consumer Slump Threatens European Online Retailers," *Wall Street Journal*, December 21, 2018, B12.

14. Leigh Kamping-Carder, "A Retail Disrupter's Outlook," *Wall Street Journal*, December 1–2, 2018, B6.

15. Edison Research, 2019 Social Habit Report, https://www .convinceandconvert.com/social-media-research/social-media-usage-statistics.

16. See Daniel Colin James, "This Is How Google Collapsed," Forward Tick, April 24, 2017, https://medium.com/forwardtick/how-google-collapsed -b6ffa82198ee.

17. See "Unit Economics Aren't What They Used To Be," at https:// tomtungunz.com/cac-increase/.

Chapter 2

1. See *CSO Insights: 2018 Sales Talent Study* (Miller Heiman, 2018), 6.

2. The Glassdoor estimate for SDRs as cited in Harrison Horan, "The Paper-Thin Reason Your Company Is Missing Sales Talent," *Forbes*, October 21, 2016, https://www.forbes.com/sites/gradsoflife/2016/09/29/the -paper-thin-reason-your-company-is-missing-sales-talent/#696e1b701f26; the enterprise sales rep estimate is from the study "The World's 100 Largest Sales Forces," SBI, Spring 2016, 82.

3. *CSO Insights: 2018 Sales Talent Study*, 6.

4. *CSO Insights: 2018 Sales Talent Study*, 9.

5. Ernest O'Boyle Jr. and Herman Agunis, "The Best and the Rest: Revisiting the Norm of Normality of Individual Performance," *Personal Psychology* 65 (2012): 79–119, which examined studies of more than 600,000 people in various fields and found power performance curves across performance measures and time frames.

6. Boris Groysberg, *Chasing Stars: The Myth of Talent and the Portability of Performance* (Princeton, NJ: Princeton University Press, 2010).

7. Frank V. Cespedes, *Aligning Strategy and Sales* (Boston: Harvard Business Review Press, 2014).

8. This line of research is voluminous and goes back for decades in reaching the same results about interviews. See, as a sample from each of the past four decades, the following: John E. Hunter and R. F. Hunter, "Validity and Utility of Alternative Predictors of Job Performance," *Psychological Bulletin* 96 (1984): 72–98; F. L. Schmidt and J. E. Hunter, "The Validity and Utility of Selection Methods in Personnel Psychology: Practical and Theoretical Implications of 85 Years of Research Findings," *Psychological Bulletin* 124 (1998): 262–274; S. Highhouse, "Stubborn Reliance on Intuition and Subjectivity in Employee Selection," *Industrial and Organizational Psychology* (September 2008): 333–342; Jason Dana, Robyn Dawes, and Nathaniel Peterson, "Belief in the Unstructured Interview: The Persistence of an Illusion," *Judgment and Decision Making* 8, no. 5 (September 2013): 512–520.

9. For an excellent review of the research about first impressions, see Alexander Todorov, *Face Value: The Irresistible Influence of First Impressions* (Princeton, NJ: Princeton University Press, 2018).

10. Michael Lewis, *The Undoing Project* (New York: W.W. Norton & Company, 2017), 40.

11. Daniel Kahneman, *Thinking Fast and Slow* (New York: Farrar, Straus and Giroux, 2011), 225.

12. For a history and critique of personality tests, see Merve Emre, *The Personality Brokers: The Strange History of Myers-Briggs and the Birth of Personality Testing* (New York: Doubleday, 2018).

13. See Cespedes, *Aligning Strategy and Sales*, chapter 6, for more on the research between personality and selling effectiveness and the implications for assessing sales skills.

14. The lists come from, in order: Joseph Curtis, "The 5 Things All Great Salespeople Do," HBR.org, December 18, 2018, https://hbr.org/2018/12/the-5-things-all-great-salespeople-do; Marc Odenweller, "4 Signs a Sales Manager Can Recognize an 'A' Player in an Interview," https://salesbenchmarkindex.com/insights/4-signs-a-sales-manager-can-recognise-in-an-interview-2/; Jim Cathcart, "10 Vital Sales Traits," *Top Sales Magazine*, September 2018, 28–29.

15. Peter Cappelli, "Your Approach to Hiring Is All Wrong," *Harvard Business Review*, May–June 2019.

16. Iris Bohnet, *What Works: Gender Equality by Design* (Cambridge, MA: Harvard University Press, 2016), 107.

17. Frank V. Cespedes, "InsideSales.com (A)," Case 817-018 (Boston: Harvard Business School, 2016).

18. Russell Groves, Kun Lueck, and Stefano Redaelli, "Commercial Excellence: Your Path to Growth," McKinsey & Company, October 2018.

19. Joseph Fuller, et al., *Dismissed by Degrees: How Degree Inflation is Undermining U.S. Competitiveness and Hurting America's Middle Class*, Accenture, Grads of Life, and Harvard Business School, 2017; Ellen Ruppel Shell, *The Job: Work and Its Future in a Time of Radical Change* (New York: Currency, 2018) estimates that as much as 40% of college graduates work at jobs that do not require a college degree.

20. Don A. Moore, "How to Improve the Accuracy and Reduce the Cost of Personnel Selection," *California Management Review* 60 (2017): 8–17.

21. Laszlo Bock, *Work Rules! Insights from Inside Google* (New York: Hachette Book Group, 2015).

22. Stephen T. Ziliak and Deirdre N. McCloskey, *The Cult of Statistical Significance* (Ann Arbor: University of Michigan Press, 2011), discuss the limitations and misuse of correlations in areas ranging from economics and psychometrics to clinical trials. Their book should be required reading for big-data enthusiasts, but unfortunately is not. For a hilarious but sobering look at silly but statistically significant correlation studies, see Tyler Vigen, *Spurious Correlations* (New York: Hachette Books, 2015) and do check out his wonderful website: http://www.tylervigen.com/.

23. Katherine B. Coffman, Christine L. Exley, and Muriel Niederle, "When Gender Discrimination Is Not About Gender," working paper, Harvard Business School, Boston, May 2018. More generally, see the examples and discussion in Jonathan Uanian, "Unmasking A.I.'s Bias Problem," *Fortune*, July 2018, https://fortune.com/longform/ai-bias-problem/.

24. Moore, "How to Improve the Accuracy and Reduce the Cost of Personnel Selection," 16.

25. Alana Samuels, "Why Amazon Pays Some of Its Workers to Quit," *Atlantic*, February 14, 2018, https://www.theatlantic.com/business/archive/2018/02/amazon-offer-pay-quit/553202/.

26. Svetlana Andrianova, Dana Maor, and Bill Schaninger, "Winning with Your Talent Management Strategy," McKinsey & Company, August 2018.

Chapter 3

1. Peter Coy, "Companies Give Worker Training Another Try," *Bloomberg Businessweek*, October 29, 2018, 36–37.

2. Jimmy Touchstone, *The Sales Training Dilemma*, Sales Performance International, March 2019.

3. Frank V. Cespedes, *Concurrent Marketing: Integrating Product, Sales, and Service* (Boston: Harvard Business School Press, 1995), 79–82. I borrowed the term from two great theorists of organizations: Barbara Levitt and James G. March, "Organizational Learning," *Annual Review of Sociology* 14 (1988): 319–340.

4. Frank V. Cespedes and Alex Gooden, "Andrew Sullivan and Faraway Ltd.," Case 9-813-104 (Boston: Harvard Business School, 2012).

5. B. Weitz, "Effectiveness in Sales Interactions: A Contingency Framework," *Journal of Marketing* 45 (1981): 85–105; T. Leigh and A. Rethans, "A Script-Theoretic Analysis of Industrial Purchasing Behavior," *Journal of Marketing* 48 (1984): 22–32; B. Weitz, H. Sujan, and M. Sujan, "Knowledge, Motivation, and Adaptive Behavior," *Journal of Marketing* 50 (1986): 174–191.

6. R. Marks, D. W. Voorhees, and G. Badovick, "A Psychometric Evaluation of the ADAPTS Scale: A Critique and Recommendations," *Journal of Personal Selling and Sales Management* 16 (1996): 53–65; L. Robinson Jr. et al., "Toward a Shortened Measure of Adaptive Selling," *Journal of Personal Selling and Sales Management* 22 (2002): 111–119; J. J. Withey and E. Panitz, "Face-to-Face Selling: Making It More Effective," *Industrial Marketing Management* 24 (1995): 239; J. Park and B. B. Holloway, "Adaptive Selling Behavior Revisited: An Empirical Examination of Learning Orientation, Sales Performance, and Job Satisfaction," *Journal of Personal Selling and Sales Management* 23 (2003): 239–251; R. L. Spiro and W. D. Perreaul Jr., "Influence Use by Industrial Salesmen: Influence-Strategy Mixes and Situational Determinants," *Journal of Business* 52 (1979): 435; R. Brennan and P. W. Turnbull, "Adaptive Behavior in Buyer-Supplier Relationships," *Industrial Marketing Management* 28 (1999): 481–495.

7. See S. Ambrose et al., *How Learning Works: Seven Research-Based Principles for Smart Teaching* (San Francisco: Jossey-Bass, 2010), and P. Brown, H. Roediger, and M. McDaniel, *Make It Stick: The Science of Successful Learning* (Cambridge, MA: Harvard University Press, 2014). I am grateful to my colleague Tom Eisenmann for introducing me to this stream of learning theory and for his working paper on its implications for management development, from which I draw in this section of the chapter.

8. Andy Paul, *The Sales House* newsletter, March 4, 2019.

9. See K. Anders Ericsson, "The Influence of Experience and Deliberate Practice on the Development of Superior Expert Performance," in *The Cambridge Handbook of Expertise and Expert Performance*, ed. K. Anders Ericsson et al. (New York: Cambridge University Press, 2006), 683–703; and K. Anders Ericsson, Ralf Th. Krampe, and Clemens Tesch-Romer, "The Role of Deliberate Practice in Acquisition of Expert Performance," *Psychological Review* 100, no. 3 (July 1993): 363–406. For an engaging review of the research about deliberate practice and performance feedback, see Geoffrey Colvin, *Talent Is Overrated* (New York: Portfolio Books, 2008).

10. For the research supporting the assertions in this paragraph about practice and adult learning, see Donald A. Schon, *Educating the Reflective Practitioner* (San Francisco: Jossey-Bass, 1987); John Whitmore, *Coaching for Performance: Growing People, Performance, and Purpose* (Boston: Nicholas Brealey, 2002); and "Unlocking the DNA of the Adaptable

Workforce," Global Human Capital Study 2008, IBM, 2008. For the importance of practice in sales training in particular, see Neil Rackham's still-pertinent discussion in *SPIN Selling* (New York: McGraw-Hill, 1988), chapter 8.

11. A useful discussion of the origins and conduct of an AAR is in Gordon R. Sullivan and Michael V. Harper, *Hope Is Not a Method* (New York: Random House, 1996), chapter 11, and Marilyn Darling, Charles Parry, and Joseph Moore, "Learning in the Thick of It," *Harvard Business Review*, July 2005. For the relevance and use of after-action reviews in win/loss analyses, see Frank V. Cespedes, *Aligning Strategy and Sales: The Choices, Systems, and Behaviors That Drive Effective Selling* (Boston: Harvard Business Review Press, 2014), 148–151.

12. Brown, Roediger, and McDaniel, *Make It Stick.*

13. Thomas Steenburgh and Alexander Crisses, "ScriptLogic: Point, Click, Done!" Case 9-508-114 (Boston: Harvard Business School, 2008; rev. 2010).

14. Frank V. Cespedes, "InsideSales.com (A)," Case 9-817-018 (Boston: Harvard Business School, 2017), 6.

15. David P. Godes, "Hale and Dorr (A)," Case 9-505-005 (Boston: Harvard Business School, 2005).

16. H. Igor Ansoff, *Corporate Strategy: An Analytic Approach to Business Policy for Growth and Expansion* (New York: McGraw-Hill, 1965).

17. This framework is adapted from Frank V. Cespedes, "Customer Visits for Entrepreneurs," Case 9-812-098 (Boston: Harvard Business School, 2011; rev. 2012). See also Edward F. McQuarrie, *Customer Visits: Building a Better Market Focus* (Thousand Oaks, CA: Sage Publications, 1993), which remains a comprehensive and useful guide to planning and conducting customer visits.

18. Cindy Alvarez, "10 Things I've Learned," *The Experience is the Product* blog, September 8, 2011, http://www.cindyalvarez.com/roundups/10 -things-ive-learned.

19. *Sales Mastery Workbook*, Sandler Systems, Inc., chapter 3. See also the case and video, Frank V. Cespedes and David Mattson, "Performance Improvement Consulting and Hi-R-Me: Making Sales Calls," Case 9-819-043 (Boston: Harvard Business School, 2018) for an example and additional commentary on up-front contracts.

20. For an overview of the research, see Frank V. Cespedes and David Hoffeld, "To Increase Sales, Get Customers to Commit a Little at a Time," HBR.org, July 20, 2016. For more detail about the research and excellent advice about how to reflect incremental commitments in selling activities, see David Hoffeld, *The Science of Selling* (New York: Penguin Random House, 2016), chapter 8.

21. This example draws on information in Frank V. Cespedes and David Mattson, "How a Fast-Growing Startup Built Its Sales Team for Long-Term Success," HBR.org, December 4, 2017, https://hbr.org/2017/12/how-a-fast -growing-startup-built-its-sales-team-for-long-term-success.

Chapter 4

1. Sabrin Chowdhury, Bill Schaninger, and Elizabeth Hioe, "Harnessing the Power of Performance Management," McKinsey & Company, 2018; and *Re-Engineering Performance Management*, Gallup, Inc., 2017.

2. Marcus Buckingham and Ashley Goodall, "The Feedback Fallacy," *Harvard Business Review*, March–April 2019.

3. Bryan Hancock and Bill Schaninger, "Why We All Need Performance Ratings on a Regular Basis," McKinsey & Company, April 8, 2019, https://www.mckinsey.com/business-functions/organization/our-insights.

4. Peter Cappelli, "The Common Myths About Performance Reviews, Debunked," HBR.org, July 26, 2016, https://hbr.org/2016/07/the-common-myths-about-performance-reviews-debunked.

5. Frank V. Cespedes, *Aligning Strategy and Sales* (Boston: Harvard Business Review Press, 2014), 43–49.

6. For data about the growing prevalence and responsibilities of sales operations groups, see CSO Insights, "2018 Sales Operations Optimization Study," Miller Heiman Group, 2018.

7. See Boris Ewenstein, Bryan Hancock, and Asmus Komm, "Ahead of the Curve: The Future of Performance Management," *McKinsey Quarterly*, May 2016.

8. Kasey Panetta, "5 Trends Emerge in the Gartner Hype Cycle for Emerging Technologies, 2018," Gartner, August 16, 2018, https://www.gartner.com/smarterwithgartner/5-trends-emerge-in-gartner-hype-cycle-for-emerging-technologies-2018.

9. Daniela Hernandez, "Computers Can Now Bluff Like a Poker Champ. Better, Actually," *Wall Street Journal*, July 11, 2019, B1.

10. Peter F. Drucker, "The Manager and the Moron," *McKinsey Quarterly*, December 1967.

11. Srikant M. Datar and Caitlin N. Bowler, "The Oakland Athletics: Strategy and Metrics for a Budget," Case 118-010 (Boston: Harvard Business School, August 1, 2018).

12. Jack Zenger and Joseph Folkman, "People Who Think They're Great Coaches Often Aren't," HBR.org, June 23, 2016, https://hbr.org/2016/06/people-who-think-theyre-great-coaches-often-arent.

13. Dave Mattson, "The Future of Sales in 2019 (Part Two), " *Sandler* blog, https://www.sandler.com/blog/goal-setting-habits-of-leaders-to-implement.

14. Julia Milner and Trenton Milner, "Most Managers Don't Know How to Coach People. But They Can Learn," HBR.org, August 14, 2018, https://hbr.org/2018/08/most-managers-dont-know-how-to-coach-people-but-they-can-learn.

15. Mark Roberge, "ZenRecruit: Sales Coaching and Performance Reviews," Case 817-041 (Boston: Harvard Business School, revised February 16, 2017). I am grateful to Mark for developing the case study and for his insights about interpreting the performance data in the case.

16. See research by HubSpot and the table labeled "Most salespeople look to their peers to improve," https://blog.hubspot.com/sales/sales-managers-leading-or-coaching?utm_campaign=Sales.

17. *Best Practices in Sales Coaching Across the Workforce*, survey, Richardson and Training Industry, Inc., 2016.

Chapter 5

1. Tripp Mickle, "Apple's New iPhone Seeks Broader Appeal," *Wall Street Journal*, April 16, 2020, https://www.wsj.com/articles/apple-unveils-low-priced-iphone-in-bid-to-capture-emerging-markets-11586965159; Christopher Mims, "The iPhone Isn't the Cash Cow It Once Was. Apple Isn't Worried," *Wall Street Journal*, June 20, 2020, https://www.wsj.com/articles/the-iphone-isnt-the-cash-cow-it-once-was-apple-isnt-worried-11592625642.

2. mThink, "Affiliate Marketing Industry to Grow to $6.8 Billion over Next Five Years," Blue Book, February 4, 2016, http://mthink.com/affiliate-marketing-industry-grow-6-8-billion-next-five-years/, accessed March 2017.

3. Frank V. Cespedes, "Clef Company: Turnover," Case 814-100 (Boston: Harvard Business School, 2014).

4. Frank V. Cespedes and Amy Handlin, "Promontory," Case 917-535 (Boston: Harvard Business School, 2017).

5. For an overview of the study, see Nina Trentmann and Ezequiel Minaya, "CFOs Face a Tough Task: Freeing Cash Trapped on Their Balance Sheets," *Wall Street Journal*, November 29, 2018, B1.

6. For more detail about scope, strategy, and sales behaviors, see Frank V. Cespedes, *Aligning Strategy and Sales* (Boston: Harvard Business Review Press, 2014), 70–77.

7. Elie Ofek and Matthew Preble, "TaKaDu," Case 514-011 (Boston: Harvard Business School, 2013, rev. 2014).

8. Scott Kirsner, "Toast Finds Its Bread-and-Butter Business," *Boston Globe*, September 21, 2018.

9. Graham Kenny, "Are You Ready to Change Your Target Customer?," HBR.org, March 28, 2019, https://hbr.org/2019/03/are-you-ready-to-change-your-target-customer.

10. Geoffrey A. Moore, *Crossing the Chasm: Marketing and Selling Disruptive Products to Mainstream Customers*, 3rd ed. (New York: HarperCollins, 2014).

11. I have adapted these examples from Jamie P. Monat, "Industrial Sales Lead Conversion Modeling," *Marketing Intelligence and Planning* 29, no. 2 (2011): 178–194, which also provides a useful lead-modeling framework.

12. This example is also discussed in Frank V. Cespedes and Steve Thompson, "Don't Turn Your Sales Team Loose Without a Strategy," HBR.org, December 15, 2015, https://hbr.org/2015/12/dont-turn-your-sales-team-loose-without-a-strategy.

13. Frank V. Cespedes and Amram Migdal, "Oversight Systems," Case 9-817-015 (Boston: Harvard Business School, 2016).

14. See the research by Steve W. Martin, "Buyer Persona Research Findings That Will Improve Sales Success," Discoverorg.com and SteveWMartin.com.

15. For relevant and different buyer journey frameworks, see, for example, Adele Revella, *Buyer Personas: How to Gain Insight into Your Customer's Expectations* (New York: Wiley, 2015) and her blogs at www .buyerpersona.com; the sample worksheets at www.gadarian.com or www .mereo.com; or Nicole Leong, "Mapping Your Content to the Buyer's Journey" at www.bluechipcommunication.com.au/blog/mapping-your-content-to-the -buyers-journey.

16. Sirius Decisions, https://www.siriusdecisions.com/Blog/2013/May /Summit-2013-Highlights-Inciting-a-BtoB-Content-Revolution; and American Marketing Association, *Proceedings of the Customer Message Management Forums* (2010): "80 to 90% of marketing collateral is considered useless by sales."

17. Table 5-1 is adapted from data in David Court et al., "The Consumer Decision Journey," *McKinsey Quarterly*, no. 3 (2009).

18. Thales S. Teixeira, *Unlocking the Customer Value Chain* (New York: Currency Books, 2019) documents this process across a range of examples.

Chapter 6

1. "Big Data: The Next Frontier for Innovation, Competition, and Productivity," McKinsey Global Institute Report, May 2011.

2. Nassim M. Taleb, "Beware the Big Errors of 'Big Data,'" *Wired*, February 8, 2013, http://www.wired.com/2013/02/big-data-means-big -errors-people.

3. Information and data about Showpad from Frank V. Cespedes, "Showpad," Case 9-817-006 (Boston: Harvard Business School, 2016, rev. 2017).

4. See, for example, Matthew Dixon, Simon Frewer, and Andrew Kent, "Are Your Reps Spending Too Much Time in Front of Customers?," HBR .org, February 8, 2011, where the estimate is that, on average, only 26% of sales force time is spent in front of customers.

5. Prabhakant Sinha and Andris A. Zoltners, "Sales-Force Decision Models: Insights from 25 Years of Implementation," *Interfaces* 31, no. 3 (May–June 2001): S8–S44.

6. Sanaz Namdar and Ryan Fuller, "A Look into Microsoft's Data-Driven Approach to Improving Sales," HBR.org, December 17, 2018, https://hbr.org /2018/12/a-look-into-microsofts-data-driven-approach-to-improving-sales.

7. David Collis and Ashley Hartman, "Edward Jones: Implementing the Solutions Approach," Case 9-718-478 (Boston: Harvard Business School, 2018).

8. For an excellent discussion of baseline lift, see Paul W. Farris et al., "Marketing Return on Investment: Seeking Clarity for Concept and Measurement," Marketing Science Institute, Report No. 14-108.

9. Information about Pandora comes from Tiffani Bova and Frank V. Cespedes, "The Changing Craft of Selling," *Top Sales Magazine*, May 2018, 16–19.

10. Spencer Anderson, "New Trends in Technology Enabling the Inside Sales Function," Sales Benchmark Index, October 1, 2018, https://salesbenchmarkindex.com/insights/new-trends-in-technology-enabling-the-inside-sales-function.

11. Ken Krogue, "Top Inside Sales Challenges: New Research," *Forbes*, August 5, 2018, https://www.forbes.com/sites/kenkrogue/2015/08/05/top-inside-sales-challenges-in-2015-new-research-#3cObc90744c7.

12. Gaurav Sabnis et al., "The Sales Lead Black Hole: On Sales Reps' Follow-Up of Marketing Leads," *Journal of Marketing* 77 (January 2013): 52–67.

13. This data comes from a study of customer-content interactions on DocSend's platform, which allows organizations to upload and share documents with prospects. For more detail, see Frank V. Cespedes and Russ Heddleston, "4 Ways to Improve Your Content Marketing," HBR.org, April 19, 2018, https://hbr.org/2018/04/4-ways-to-improve-your-content-marketing.

14. Frank V. Cespedes and Matthew G. Preble, "DoubleDutch," Case 9-815-044 (Boston: Harvard Business School, 2014; rev. 2016).

15. Nick Mehta, "Five Organizational Models of Customer Success," www.evernote.com/Home.action#n=92. Mehta discusses a fifth model, "Partnership CS," but I find it indistinguishable from his "Integrated CS" model.

16. Adrian Swinscoe, "Customer Success Needs to be the Responsibility of the Entire Organization: Interview with Fred Shilmover," Apple Podcasts, http://customerthink.com/customer-success-needs-to-be-the-responsibility-of-the-entire-organisation-interview-with-fred-shilmover.

Chapter 7

1. Frank V. Cespedes, *Aligning Strategy and Sales* (Boston: Harvard Business Review Press, 2014), 171–182.

2. Richard M. Titmuss, *The Gift Relationship* (Crows Nest, Australia: Allen and Unwin, 1970).

3. See the following articles for good reviews of the relevant psychology and economics literatures, respectively, about the effects of monetary and non-monetary incentives: Edward L. Deci, Richard Koestner, and Richard M. Ryan, "A Meta-Analytic Review of Experiments Examining the Effects of Extrinsic Rewards on Intrinsic Motivation," *Psychological Bulletin* 125 (1999): 627–637; Uri Gneezy, Stephen Meier, and Pedro Rey-Biel,

"When and Why Incentives (Don't) Work to Modify Behavior," *Journal of Economic Perspectives* 25 (2011): 191–210.

4. Jason Sandvik et al., "The Power (of) Lunch and the Role of Incentives for Fostering Productive Interactions," working paper, Harvard Business School, Boston, August 2018.

5. K. Joseph and M. U. Kalwani, "The Role of Bonus Pay in Salesforce Compensation Plans," *Industrial Marketing Management* 27 (1998): 147–159.

6. "The World's 100 Largest Sales Forces," SBI, Spring 2016, 16.

7. Andris Zoltners, Prabhakant Sinha, and Sally Lorimer, "Breaking the Sales Force Incentive Addiction: A Balanced Approach to Sales Force Effectiveness," *Journal of Personal Selling and Sales Management* 32 (2012): 171–186.

8. Stephen Hall, Dan Lovallo, and Reinier Musters, "How to Put Your Money Where Your Strategy Is," *McKinsey Quarterly*, March 2012.

9. For a good review of common principles affecting pay level and pay mix, see Pankaj M. Madhani, "Sales Compensation Strategy: An Optimal Design of Pay Level and Pay Mix," *Compensation and Benefits Review* 47 (2015): 107–120.

10. Mark Roberge, "The Right Way to Use Compensation," *Harvard Business Review*, April 2015.

11. "Opening Up About Comp Isn't Easy—Here's How to Get More Transparent," October 30, 2018, https://firstround.com/review/opening-up -about-comp-isnt-easy-heres-how-to-get-more-transparent.

12. Jordi Blanes i Vidal and Mareike Nossol, "Tournaments Without Prizes: Evidence from Personnel Records," *Management Science* 58 (2012): 94–113.

13. Zoe B. Cullen and Ricardo Perez-Truglia, "The Motivating (and Demotivating) Effects of Learning Others' Salaries," HBR.org, October 25, 2018. For the research itself, see Zoe Cullen and Ricardo Perez-Truglia, "How Much Does Your Boss Make? The Effects of Salary Comparisons," working paper 24841, National Bureau of Economic Research, August 2018, with a data appendix available at http://www.nber.org/data-appendix /w24841. Other research supports similar conclusions about the differential impact of pay comparisons in sales: see, for example, T. J. Arnold et al., "The Role of Equity and Work Environment in the Formation of Salesperson Distributive Fairness Judgments," *Journal of Personal Selling and Sales Management* 29 (2009): 61–80.

14. "Opening Up About Comp Isn't Easy."

15. Madhu Viswanathan et al., "Is Cash King for Sales Compensation Plans? Evidence from a Large-Scale Field Intervention," *Journal of Marketing Research* 55 (June 2018): 368–381.

16. See Joel Brockner, "Making Sense of Procedural Fairness," *Academy of Management Review* 27 (2002): 58–76; and W. Chan Kim and Renee Mauborgne, "Fair Process: Managing in the Knowledge Economy," *Harvard Business Review*, January 2003, 127–137.

17. S. N. Ramaswami and J. Singh, "Antecedents and Consequences of Merit Pay Fairness for Industrial Salespeople," *Journal of Marketing* 67 (2003): 46–66. More generally, for an excellent review of the studies about fairness and peer effects in sales compensation, see Dominique Rouzies and Vincent Onyemah, "Sales Force Compensation: Trends and Research Opportunities," *Foundations and Trends in Marketing* 11, no. 3 (2018): 143–214.

18. See Dominique Rouzies et al., "Determinants of Pay Levels and Structures in Sales Organizations," *Journal of Marketing* 73 (November 2009): 92–104.

19. Raghu Bommaraju and Sebastian Hohenberg, "Self-Selected Sales Incentives: Evidence of Their Effectiveness, Persistence, Durability, and Underlying Mechanisms," *Journal of Marketing* 82 (September 2018): 106–124.

20. Proskauer-International HR Best Practices, www.proskauer.com.

21. Information about Elmenus.com and Bigbelly comes from Frank V. Cespedes, "Sales Compensation Vignettes," Case 816-092 (Boston: Harvard Business School, 2016).

22. Bryan Hancock, Elizabeth Hioe, and Bill Schaninger, "The Fairness Factor in Performance Management," *McKinsey Quarterly*, April 2018.

Chapter 8

1. Warren Buffett's comments before the Financial Crisis Inquiry Commission (FCIC), May 26, 2010.

2. See the research and research reviews in Indrajit Sinha and Rajeev Batra, "The Effect of Consumer Price Consciousness on Private Label Purchase," *International Journal of Research in Marketing* 16 (1999): 237–251; and Lisa E. Bolton, Luk Warlop, and Joseph W. Alba, "Consumer Perceptions of Price (Un)Fairness," *Journal of Consumer Research* 29 (2003): 474–491. The now-standard explanation for these views is known as the principle of dual entitlement: price fairness perceptions are governed by a belief that firms are entitled to a reference profit and customers are entitled to a reference price, with the referents typically set by legacy prices, competitor prices, and perceived cost of goods sold in that market or product category: see Daniel Kahneman, Jack L. Knetsch, and Richard H. Thaler, "Fairness and the Assumptions of Economics," *Journal of Business* 59 (1986): S285–S300.

3. Anita Elberse, *Blockbusters: Hit-Making, Risk-Taking, and the Big Business of Entertainment* (New York: Henry Holt, 2013), 173.

4. The results of the survey as reported in "It's Price Before Product. Period," http://firstround.com/review/its-price-before-product-period/?utm_campaign=new_article&utm_medium=email&utm_source=newsletter.

5. M. E. Raynor and M. Ahmed, "Three Rules for Making a Company Truly Great," HBR.org, April 11, 2013, https://hbr.org/2013/04/three-rules-for-making-a-company-truly-great.

6. Doug J. Chung, Ho Kim, and Reo Song, "The Comprehensive Effects of a Digital Paywall Sales Strategy," working paper, Harvard Business School, Boston, 2019.

7. These are 2018 prices as reported in Heather Haddon and Annie Gasparro, "Food Makers Are Raising Prices by Using a Pinch of Innovation," *Wall Street Journal*, December 20, 2018, B1–B2.

8. Prices for the ink products as cited in Daniel Taub, "Sincerely: Indulgent Inks Will Lend Your Handwritten Notes a Signature Sparkle," *Bloomberg Businessweek*, October 29, 2018, 74.

9. Justin Fox, "Money Managers Aren't Dead Yet," *Bloomberg Businessweek*, August 13, 2018, 27–29.

10. Here and in subsequent sections of this chapter, I have adapted concepts and some examples from Frank V. Cespedes, Benson P. Shapiro, and Elliot B. Ross, "Pricing, Profits, and Customer Value," Case 811-016 (Boston: Harvard Business School, 2010; rev. August 26, 2011).

11. Ted Williams and John Underwood, *The Science of Hitting* (New York: Simon & Schuster, 1971), 36–37.

12. See Christopher Mims, "Why Amazon Prices Fluctuate So Wildly," *Wall Street Journal*, March 27, 2017, B1.

13. Tripp Mickle, Yoko Kubota, and Takashi Mochizuki, "Apple Overhauls Its iPhone Sales Strategy," *Wall Street Journal*, September 20, 2018, B1.

14. A seminal discussion of how pricing differences promote buyer and seller efficiencies is in Robert Frank, "When Are Price Differentials Discriminatory?," *Journal of Policy Analysis and Management* (Winter 1983): 238–255.

15. See, for instance, the data and surveys cited in Andreas Hinterhuber, "Value Quantification: Processes and Best Practices to Document and Quantify Value in B2B," in *Value First Then Price*, ed. Andreas Hinterhuber and Todd C. Snelgrove (Abingdon, UK: Routledge, 2017), 61–74.

16. See chapter 5 of *The Wealth of Nations* for Adam Smith's distinction between "money price" and "real price."

17. See Donald Ngwe and Thales Teixeira, "Improving Online Retail Margins by Increasing Search Frictions," working paper, Harvard Business School, Boston, July 2018.

18. Roger L. Martin, "Pricing Needs to Reflect Who People Want to Be, Not Just What They Want," HBR.org, January 25, 2019.

19. C. Palmeri, "Wal-Mart Is Up for This Downturn," *Business Week*, November 10, 2008, 34.

20. Herb Sorenson, *Inside the Mind of the Shopper: The Science of Retailing* (Upper Saddle River, NJ: FT Press, 2009).

21. For an analysis of Costco's economics, see Thales A. Teixeira, *Unlocking the Customer Value Chain* (New York: Currency Books, 2019), 41–42.

22. Robert Barro and Paul Romer, "Ski-Lift Pricing, with Applications to Labor and Other Markets," *American Economic Review*, December 1987, 875–890; and Andreas Hinterhuber, Evandro Pollomo, and Mark Shafer,

"Elevating the Cost of Doing Nothing: An Interview with Mark Shafer," *Journal of Revenue and Pricing Management* 17 (2018): 3–10.

23. Michael D. Smith and Rahul Telang, "Netflix and the Economics of Bundling," HBR.org, February 25, 2019, https://hbr.org/2019/02/netflix-and -the-economics-of-bundling, and, more generally, their excellent book about the changing nature of the entertainment industry, *Streaming, Sharing, Stealing: Big Data and the Future of Entertainment* (Cambridge, MA: MIT Press, 2016).

Chapter 9

1. For good analyses and discussions of freemium pricing in the context of SaaS models, see the blogs and white papers published by Open View Partners, for example, "The Ultimate SaaS Pricing Guide for Seed Stage Companies," http://offers.openviewpartners.com/seed-stage-saas-pricing-guide.

2. Jennifer Maloney and Vipal Monga, "Corona Brewer's Big Bet on Pot Gets Messy," *Wall Street Journal*, July 3, 2019, B1.

3. I am grateful to Michael Eckhardt, a director at The Chasm Institute, for suggesting the comparisons in table 9-1 and the distinction between "first provers" of a value proposition versus "first movers."

4. See the discussions of early adopters in the work of Geoffrey Moore, in Eric von Hippel, *Democratizing Innovation* (Cambridge, MA: MIT Press, 2005), and in Amar Bhide, *The Venturesome Economy* (Princeton, NJ: Princeton University Press, 2008).

5. Frank V. Cespedes, Julia Kelley, and Amram Migdal, "Pricing Patient-Ping," Case 818-017 (Boston: Harvard Business School, 2017).

6. Diana Pearl, "75% of Estee Lauder's Digital Marketing Budget Is Going to Influencers," *AdWeek*, https://www.adweek.com/brand-marketing /75-of-estee-lauders-marketing-budget-is-going-to-influencers/.

7. For a more detailed discussion of OpenTable's pivot and the implications for platform businesses, see David Evans and Richard Schmalensee, *Matchmakers: The New Economics of Multisided Platforms* (Boston: Harvard Business Review Press, 2016), chapter 1.

8. For a good nontechnical review of the relevant psychology research and practical implications for selling, see David Hoffeld, *The Science of Selling* (New York: Random House, 2016).

9. Donald Ngwe, "Fake Discounts Drive Real Revenues in Retail," working paper, Harvard Business School, Boston, 2018.

10. Daniel Kahneman, *Thinking Fast and Slow* (New York: Farrar, Straus, and Giroux, 2011), 178.

11. In this section about framing value, I have used research and examples from Frank V. Cespedes and Tracy DeCicco, "Why 'Tell Them Something They Don't Know' Is Bad Advice in B2B Sales," HBR.org, August 19, 2019.

12. Chris Orlob, "The Sobering Truth: Why You Can't Sell to C-Suite Executives," *The Revenue Intelligence* blog, February 12, 2019, https://www.gong.io/search/The+Sobering+Truth.

13. See Matthew Feinberg and Robb Willer, "From Gulf to Bridge: When Do Moral Arguments Facilitate Political Influence," *Personality and Social Psychology Bulletin* 41, no. 12 (2015).

14. See, for instance, the following string of pricing studies over the past four decades: Gerald Tellis, "The Price Elasticity of Selective Demand: A Meta-Analysis of Econometric Models of Sales," *Journal of Marketing Research* 25 (November 1988): 331–341; Michael Marn and Robert Rosiello, "Managing Price, Gaining Profit," *Harvard Business Review*, September–October 1992, 84–94; Walter L. Baker, Michael V. Mann, and Craig C. Zawada, "Building a Better Pricing Infrastructure," *McKinsey Quarterly*, August 2010; Ron Kermisch and David Burns, "A Survey of 1,700 Companies Reveals Common B2B Pricing Mistakes," HBR.org, June 7, 2018, https://hbr.org/2018/06/a-survey-of-1700-companies-reveals-common-b2b-pricing-mistakes; and the impact of a 2% price increase on profits of Global 500 companies in "Global 500: The World's Largest Corporation," *Fortune*, July 22, 2013, F-1–22, where the estimated increase on profits ranges from 5 to 200%.

15. Kyle Poyar, "The Unspoken Impact of Pricing Changes," https://labs.openviewpartners.com/the-unspoken-impact-of-pricing-changes/?utm_campaign=General%Newsletter&utm.

16. Ravi Sethuraman and Gerald Tellis, "Analysis of the Tradeoff between Advertising and Price Discounting," *Journal of Marketing Research* 28 (May 1991): 168.

17. David Ogilvy, *Confessions of an Advertising Man* (London: Southbank Publishing, 2004; originally published, 1963).

18. The core studies are nicely reviewed and explained in Kahneman, *Thinking Fast and Slow,* and by Richard Thaler, *Quasi-Rational Economics* (New York: Russell Sage, 1994).

19. Hermann Simon, *Confessions of the Pricing Man* (New York: Springer, 2015), 110–111; and Lester G. Tesler, "The Demand for Branded Goods as Estimated from Consumer Panel Data," *Review of Economic Statistics* 3 (1962): 300–324.

20. All information about Basecamp and its pricing tests are from Frank Cespedes and Robb Fitzsimmons, "Basecamp: Pricing," Case 817-067 (Boston: Harvard Business School, 2016; revised April 4, 2017).

21. Wilson McCrory et al., "How to Unlock Growth in the Largest Accounts," *McKinsey on Marketing and Sales*, September 2016.

22. Seth Stephens-Davidowitz, *Everybody Lies: Big Data, New Data, and What the Internet Can Tell Us About Who We Really Are* (New York: HarperCollins, 2017). The specific quote is on page 156, but it is the premise and repeated theme throughout the book's analyses of Google data.

Chapter 10

1. Blake Droesch, "What Ecommerce Sellers Need to Watch for When Expanding to Marketplaces," *eMarketer*, September 12, 2019.

2. Frank V. Cespedes, *Aligning Strategy and Sales* (Boston: Harvard Business Review Press, 2014), Chapter 7.

3. Holly Briedis et al., "Ready to 'Where': Getting Sharp on Apparel Omnichannel Excellence," *McKinsey Quarterly*, August 2019.

4. Frank V. Cespedes, Olivia Hull, and Amram Migdal, "Formlabs: Selling a New 3D Printer," Case 817-001 (Boston: Harvard Business School, 2016; rev. 2017).

5. In this section of the chapter, I have drawn on frameworks first discussed in Frank V. Cespedes, "Control vs. Resources in Channel Design," *Industrial Marketing Management* 17, no. 3 (1988): 215–227. This article further analyzes the implications and managerial issues inherent in this trade-off.

6. Robert B. Cialdini, *Influence: The Psychology of Persuasion*, rev. ed. (New York: HarperBusiness, 2007), 18. For an application of Cialdini's rule of reciprocation to internal cross-functional relations that affect sales effectiveness, see Frank V. Cespedes, *Aligning Strategy and Sales* (Boston: Harvard Business Review Press, 2014), 249–255.

7. Frank V. Cespedes and Amram Migdal, "Oversight Systems," Case 9-817-015 (Boston: Harvard Business School, 2016; rev. 2017), 8–9.

8. Bud Hyler, president of Logical Marketing, in personal communication to the author.

9. Jay McBain, "What I See Coming for the Channel in 2019," Forrester Research, January 16, 2019, https://go.forrester.com/blogs/what-i-see-coming-for-the-channel-in-2019/.

10. Frank V. Cespedes and Tiffani Bova, "The Changing Craft of Selling," *Top Sales Magazine*, May 2018, 18.

11. See Ryan Brier, "The Sales Role Multinationals Need in Emerging Markets," HBR.org, October 31, 2016, https://hbr.org/2016/10/the-sales-role-multinationals-need-in-emerging-markets.

12. E. Raymond Corey, Frank V. Cespedes, and V. Kasturi Rangan, *Going to Market: Distribution Systems for Industrial Products* (Boston: Harvard Business School Press, 1989), 281.

13. V. Kasturi Rangan with Marie Bell, *Transforming Your Go-to-Market Strategy: The Three Disciplines of Channel Management* (Boston: Harvard Business Press, 2006), 97–99.

14. For studies indicating the often beneficial effects of channel conflict, see A. Menon, S. G. Bharadwaj, and R. Howell, "The Quality and Effectiveness of Marketing Strategy: Effects of Functional and Dysfunctional Conflict in Intraorganizational Relationships," *Journal of the Academy of Marketing Science* 24, no. 4 (1996): 229–313; G. M. Rose et al., "Manufacturer Perceptions of the Consequences of Task and Emotional Conflict within Domestic

Channels of Distribution," *Journal of Business Research* 60, no. 4 (2007): 296–304; K. H. Chang and D. F. Gotcher, "Conflict-Coordination Learning in Marketing Channel Relationships: The Distributor View," *Industrial Marketing Management* 39, no. 2 (2010): 287–297; and D. Claro, D. Vojnovskis, and C. Ramos, "When Channel Conflict Positively Affects Performance: Evidence from ICT Supplier Reseller Relationships," *Journal of Business and Industrial Marketing* 33, no. 2 (2018): 228–239.

15. For multiple examples of this dynamic, see Lawrence Ingrassia, *Billion Dollar Brand Club* (New York: Holt, 2020).

16. Daniel Fisher, "Dell's Next Games," *Forbes*, June 10, 2002, 104.

17. For data on the prevalence of gray markets in various product categories, see Kersia Antia, Mark Bergen, and Shantanu Dutta, "Competing With Gray Markets," *Sloan Management Review* 40, no. 1 (Fall 2004). For an analysis of gray markets, see Frank V. Cespedes, E. Raymond Corey, and V. Kasturi Rangan, "Gray Markets: Causes and Cures," *Harvard Business Review*, July–August 1988.

Chapter 11

1. Quoted in M. Augier, "James March on Education, Leadership, and Don Quixote: Introduction and Interview," *Academy of Management Learning and Education* 3 (2004): 173.

2. Julie Wulf, "The Flattened Firm: Not as Advertised," *California Management Review* 55, no. 1 (2012): 5–23. For the study's sample and methods, see Raghuram G. Rajan and Julie Wulf, "The Flattening Firm: Evidence from Panel Data on the Changing Nature of Corporate Hierarchies," *Review of Economics and Statistics* 88, no. 4 (2006); and Maria Guadalupe, Hongyi Li, and Julie Wulf, "Who Lives in the C-Suite? Organizational Structure and the Division of Labor in Top Management," working paper, Harvard Business School, Boston, March 2013.

3. Jason Karalan, *The Chief Financial Officer* (New York: Public Affairs Books, 2014), 9.

4. Data from Effectory surveys of employees in companies across industries, a database of about 300,000 responses from companies worldwide. See Chris Zook and James Allen, *Repeatability* (Boston: Harvard Business Review Press, 2012), 44.

5. Core works in the large literature about this topic include: Robert Duncan, "The Ambidextrous Organization: Designing Dual Structures for Innovation," in *The Management of Organization*, ed. R. H. Killman, L. R. Pondy, and D. Steven (New York: North Holland, 1976): 167–188; James G. March, "Exploration and Exploitation in Organizational Learning," *Organization Science* 2 (1991): 71–87; and Michael L. Tushman and Charles A. O'Reilly III, *Winning Through Innovation: A Practical Guide to Leading Organizational Change and Renewal* (Boston: Harvard Business School Press, 1997, 2002).

6. See Frank V. Cespedes, *Concurrent Marketing: Integrating Product, Sales, and Service* (Boston: Harvard Business School Press, 1995), 91–95.

7. For more on the "monkey challenge" and its relevance to market changes and required sales capabilities, see Frank V. Cespedes, *Aligning Strategy and Sales* (Boston: Harvard Business Review Press, 2014), 255–258.

8. For research documenting the performance link between communication and execution, see, for example, Mark Morgan, Raymond E. Levitt, and William Malek, *Executing Your Strategy* (Boston: Harvard Business School Press, 2007); Donald Sull and Kathleen M. Eisenhardt, "Simple Rules for a Complex World," *Harvard Business Review*, September 2012; and Zook and Allen, *Repeatability*.

9. Steven Spear and H. Kent Bowen, "Decoding the DNA of the Toyota Production System," *Harvard Business Review*, September–October 1999.

10. Rainer Stark et al., *What's Trending in Jobs and Skills*, BCG and Burning Glass Technologies, September 2019.

11. Arjo Klamer and Deirdre Nansen McCloskey, "One Quarter of GDP Is Persuasion," *American Economic Review* 85 (May 1995): 191–195.

12. Daniel H. Pink, *To Sell Is Human* (New York: Riverhead Books, 2012).

13. *OECD Compendium of Productivity Indicators 2019* (Paris: OECD Publishing), https://doi.org/10.1787/b2774f97-en; Jason Furman, "Should We Be Reassured If Automation in the Future Looks Like Automation in the Past?" in *The Economics of Artificial Intelligence*, ed. Ajay Agrawal, Joshua S. Gans, and Avi Goldfarb (Chicago: University of Chicago Press, 2019), found that 36 of 37 advanced economies had slower productivity growth in 2000–2016 compared to 1996–2006 and, across these economies, growth slowed from a 2.7% average rate to 1%.

14. Dietrich Vollrath, *Fully Grown: Why a Stagnant Economy Is a Sign of Success* (Chicago: University of Chicago Press, 2020).

15. William J. Baumol and William G. Bowen, "On the Performing Arts: The Anatomy of Their Economic Problems," *American Economic Review* 55 (1965): 495–502; and William J. Baumol, *The Cost Disease: Why Computers Get Cheaper but Healthcare Doesn't* (New Haven, CT: Yale University Press, 2012).

16. Vollrath, *Fully Grown*, 79 and 89.

17. Benjamin M. Friedman, *The Moral Consequences of Economic Growth* (New York: Random House, 2005), 4, 11.

18. Peter F. Drucker, "The New Productivity Challenge," *Harvard Business Review*, November–December 1991.

19. Cindy Cunningham et al., "Dispersion in Dispersion: Measuring Establishment-Level Differences in Productivity," working paper 18-25R Center for Economic Studies, US Census Bureau, Washington, DC, September 2019; Nicholas Bloom et al., "The New Empirical Economics of Management," working paper 20102, National Bureau of Economic Research, Cambridge, MA, May 2014, http://www.nber.org/papers/w20102.

20. Edward Lazear, Kathryn L. Shaw, and Christopher T. Stanton, "The Value of Bosses," *Journal of Labor Economics* 33, no. 4 (October 2015): 823–861.

21. See the studies by David Chan, especially "The Efficiency of Slacking Off: Evidence from the Emergency Department," *Econometrica* 86, no. 3 (May 2018): 997–1030.

22. Ann Bartel, "Human Resource Management and Performance in the Service Sector: The Case of Bank Branches," working paper 7467, National Bureau of Economic Research, Cambridge, MA, January 2000, http://www.nber.org/papers/w7467.

23. Andrew Ferguson, "Tight with a Dollar," *Atlantic*, April 2020, 13–16.

24. Business Roundtable, *Statement on the Purpose of a Corporation*, August 19, 2019, https://opportunity.businessroundtable.org/wp-content/uploads/2019/BRT-Statement-on-the-Purpose-of-a-Corporation-with-Signatures.pdf.

25. Davos Manifesto 2020: The Universal Purpose of a Company in the Fourth Industrial Revolution, December 2, 2019, https://www.weforum.org/agenda/2019/12/davos-manifesto-2020-the-universal-purpose-of-a-company-in-the-fourth-industrial-revolution/.

26. For an excellent discussion of stakeholderism, including how it is in practice usually counterproductive to its stated aims, see the critique by law professors Lucian A. Bebchuk and Roberto Tallarita, "The Illusory Promise of Stakeholder Governance," March 2020, https://ssrn.com/abstract=3544978.

INDEX

ACKNOWLEDGMENTS

I've had the help of many people in researching, articulating, and testing the ideas and recommendations in this book.

At Harvard Business School, I benefited from conversations, teaching, and work on articles or course development with Lynda Applegate, Doug Chung, Tom Eisenmann, Joe Fuller, Boris Groysberg, Sunil Gupta, Linda Hill, Bill Kerr, Josh Lerner, Das Narayandas, Elie Ofek, Kash Rangan, Mark Roberge, Lou Shipley, Christopher Stanton, Thales Teixeira (now head of Decoupling.co), and Mitchell Weiss.

Beyond academia, many executives helped with topics discussed in the book, including Tiffani Bova of Salesforce, David Boyce of XANT, Douglas Cole of LinkedIn, Tracy DeCicco of HCL, Michael Eckhardt of The Chasm Institute, Jonathan Farrington of *Top Sales* magazine, Jay Galeota of Inheris Biopharma Inc., Paul Gudonis of Myomo, Jared Hamilton of Driving Sales, Russ Heddleston of DocSend, David Hoffeld of Hoffeld Group, Neil Hoyne of Google, Bud Hyler of Logical Marketing, Jonathan Isaacson of Gemline, Samuel Lam of Linkage Asia, Yuchun Lee and Mark Magnacca of Allego, Tom Magnuson of Magnuson Hotels, Robert Marsh of Level Eleven, David Mattson of Sandler Training, Steve Maughan of Cozmix, Andy Paul of The Sales House, Amir Peleg of TaKaDu, Hermann Simon of Simon-Kucher, Marc Simon of HALO Branded Solutions, Steve Thompson of PureForge, Jacco van der Kooij of Winning By Design, Diana Finley and Christopher Wallace of InnerView, Dan Weinfurter of Mentor Group, and Michael Wong of EPAM Systems.

I received feedback and examples from attendees of executive programs at Harvard, especially the Aligning Strategy & Sales and Owner-President Management (OPM) programs, and events sponsored by Young Presidents' Organization (YPO), Women's Presidents' Organization (WPO), and Entrepreneurs' Organization (EO) where I presented this research. A special thanks to those who allowed me to do more than preach to their organizations, including Husodo Angkosubroto and Bobby Galvez of Gunung Sewu, Seth Berkowitz of Edmunds.com, Kol Birke of Commonwealth Financial Network, Jerry Chen of H&T Realty, Mitch Derrick and Ray Clayton of Derrick Corporation, Marcel Fournier of Castle Harlan, Przemyslaw Gacek of Grupa Pracuj, Mike Lawrence of Tensar, Karoly Nagy of Promelek, Shaun Sheffield of Austral, Jon Szobody of Tensar, and Oscar Torres of Dassault Systèmes.

In turn, that work often led to case studies cited in this book. I thank Amir Allam of Elmenus.com, Pieterjan Bouten and Louis Jonckheere of Showpad, Jay Desai of PatientPing, Jason Fried of Basecamp, Ken Krogue of Inside Sales.com, Jack Kutner of Bigbelly, Patrick Taylor of Oversight Systems, and Luke Winston of Formlabs. My gratitude as well to those who helped to develop the case studies: Mariana Call, Robb Fitzsimmons, Alex Gooden, Olivia Hull, Julia Kelley, Amram Migdal, Maria Fernanda Miguel, Matthew Preble, and Laura Urdapilleta. At Harvard's Baker Library—a jewel in the crown—Jennifer Beauregard, Leslie Burmeister, Kathleen Ryan, Rhys Sevier, and Inku Subedi provided data, articles, and reports cited throughout the book.

Benson P. Shapiro has long influenced how I view sales practices, and work with Ben and with Elliot Ross of The MFL Group is the basis for chapter 8 on pricing. Jon Younger read the manuscript and, as in the past, provided excellent advice: *muchas gracias*. Gabriella Knox and Marc Poirot helped to keep track of multiple revisions.

At Harvard Business Review Press, my sincere thank you to Kevin Evers, who is a great editor, and to Jennifer Waring and Jane Gebhart for their work on the manuscript. For helping to market and disseminate the ideas in the book, my gratitude to Lindsey Dietrich, Julie Devoll, Erika Heilman, Felicia Sinusas, Sally Ashworth, Alexandra Kephart, and Jon Shipley.

My wife, Bonnie Costello, and our daughters, Elizabeth and Helen and their spouses, enrich a world that never stops changing, while our grandson, Marcus, now begins to make his changes—*vive la différence.*

—Boston, September 2020

ABOUT THE AUTHOR

Frank V. Cespedes is the MBA Class of 1973 Senior Lecturer of Business Administration at Harvard Business School. He has run a business, served on boards for startups and corporations, and consulted to many companies. He is the author of articles in *Harvard Business Review*, the *Wall Street Journal*, *California Management Review*, *Organization Science*, and other publications as well as six books including *Aligning Strategy and Sales* (Harvard Business Review Press, 2014), which was cited as "the best sales book of the year" (*strategy+business*), "a must read" (Gartner), and "perhaps the best sales book ever" (*Forbes*).